HENRY JAMES
and the
NATURALIST MOVEMENT

HENRY JAMES

and the

NATURALIST
MOVEMENT

by

LYALL H. POWERS

MICHIGAN STATE UNIVERSITY PRESS

Copyright © 1971
Michigan State University Press
Standard Book Number: 87013-156-7
Library of Congress Catalog Card Number: 70-121687
MANUFACTURED IN THE UNITED STATES OF AMERICA

★
 ★
★
 ★
 ★

Excerpts from *The Princess Casamassima* are reprinted by permission of Charles
Scribner's Sons from Volumes V and VI, THE NOVELS AND TALES OF HENRY
JAMES. Copyright 1908 Charles Scribner's Sons; renewal copyright 1936 Henry
James.

Excerpts from *The Tragic Muse* are reprinted by permission of Charles Scribner's Sons
from Volumes VII and VIII, THE NOVELS AND TALES OF HENRY JAMES. Copyright 1908 Charles Scribner's Sons; renewal copyright 1936 Henry James.

For Jean

Acknowledgements

I am pleased to acknowledge my initial indebtedness to Professor Leon Edel for valuable counsel during the early stages of my study of Henry James. I am particularly grateful to Marchesa Nannina Fossi-Rucellai, Count Bernardo Rucellai, and Count Gian-Guilio Rucellai for graciously allowing me to consult James's letters to their mother, Edith, Contessa Rucellai, and to their grandmother, Mrs. Katherine de Kay Bronson, in the family archives of the Palazzo Rucellai in Florence; and for permitting me to quote from that correspondence. My thanks are due to Professor Mario Praz for his cordial assistance during my research in Italy.

I am indebted to the keeper of the Bretherton Collection in the library of the University of Leeds for allowing me access to the James-Gosse correspondence and granting me permission to quote from it. And I am pleased to express my thanks to Mr. and Mrs. H. Montgomery Hyde for the generous hospitality they extended to me at Lamb House, Rye.

I must acknowledge the kindness of the Oxford University Press for permission to quote from *The Notebooks of Henry James;* and of Random House for permission to quote from *The Bostonians.* And I am grateful for the generosity and trust of the Horace H. Rackham foundation of the University of Michigan in giving me two research grants which enabled me to carry this study of Henry James to its completion.

Finally, I would add a very special word of thanks to my wife for her patience and encouragement while I was at work on this book.

Contents

- What was going on in James' World?
- Who was influencing him?

While it may be debatable that life began for Henry James at forty, it is certainly true that at that age he saw his career take a definitely new turn. He had by that time written one unmistakable masterpiece, had seen one of his novelettes enjoy the success of a best-seller, and had tasted the bitterness of disappointment as one of his earliest and dearest ambitions—to write for the theater—was frustrated at the last moment. The dramatization of his best-selling *Daisy Miller* just failed to reach the stage. Anyone familiar with James's early fiction up to the publication of *The Portrait of a Lady* (1880-1881) will notice in the fiction that followed a marked change both in subject matter and, more arresting, in narrative technique. The difference is especially noticeable in the major fiction—*The Bostonians, The Princess Casamassima,* and *The Tragic Muse.* These are by no means the "international novels" typically associated with James; attention is here drawn much more to the lower classes of society—away from polite drawing rooms and into the streets; the style of description and the nature of the dominant motifs are quite different from what is to be found in *The American,* in *The Europeans,* even in *Washington Square.* The changes in James's art of fiction can most satisfactorily be accounted for by referring to the influence exerted upon him by the group of realist and naturalist writers to whom he was introduced in 1875: Gustave Flaubert, Edmond de Goncourt, Ivan Turgenev, Emile Zola, Alphonse Daudet, and Guy de Maupassant. James called the group "the grandsons of Balzac."[1]

I speak of the influence of the group rather than of the several individual members of the group, for what chiefly matters is not specific novel-to-novel relationship or even writer-to-writer relationship. To be sure, a strong case can be made for the direct influence of Daudet's *L'Evangéliste* on *The Bostonians* or of Turgenev's *Virgin Soil* on *The Princess Casamassima.* Much more important than those instances, however, is the broader general influence of the aesthetic principles and the professional attitude to the art of fiction which the group as a whole shared among themselves.

The fact of that influence will appear clearly enough; but to posit that fact is to raise several questions about it. Why should this influ-

1

ence in particular have exerted itself on James? What factors of
James's early life (both the experience of family and immediate environment as well as the experience of the general atmosphere of the
times) would account for his attraction to that group, what would
have prepared him to be receptive to their ideas and sympathetic
with their professional attitude? To answer these questions the first
chapter presents a brief survey of James's family and the cultural
milieu, the background against which he must be seen. The second
chapter traces the development of the young James as a man of
letters, noting his principal preoccupations in literature, his critical
taste, and his artistic achievement; it illustrates the tendency which
his earliest experience had fostered.

Then, too, it might be asked what congeries of events made a
particular moment in the early 1880's propitious for James to respond
to that influence which he had been introduced to almost a decade
earlier: why just at that moment should the influence have made
overt appearance in James's writing? The first section of the third
chapter addresses itself to this question, paying close attention to
particular events in James's family life, to the point he had reached
in his artistic career, and to other related events involving friends and
colleagues. An arresting convergence of apparently discrete occur-
rences is shown to account for the distinctly new turn in James's life
and career, emphasized as that new turn is by the beginning of his
extended expatriation. Finally I raise the question of whether that
influence continued to exert itself through to the end of his career.
It seems evident enough that it persisted until James turned in 1890
to his experiment with writing for the theater; but it might be interesting to determine whether it carried on into the fiction of his major
phase. The concluding chapter will indicate what evidence of continued influence is discernible to the end of James's career.

No one, certainly, would ever confuse one of James's novels with
a novel by Zola or even with one by Daudet. When I speak of James's
"Naturalist Period" I do not mean to suggest that during the 1880's
he was doing in English exactly what Zola and Daudet and the others
were doing in French: of course one looks in vain for a Jamesian *Nana!*
I like to think of James's work of the period in question as evidence
of his attempt to apply with some strictness the aesthetic principles
of the Flaubert group, and to adapt to his own taste and capacities
the literary mode and manner of those writers. It is in that sense,
then, that I would be understood when I refer to James's "Naturalist

experiment." The third, fourth, and fifth chapters offer an extensive examination of, respectively, his three major novels of this period— *The Bostonians* (1886), *The Princess Casamassima* (1886), and *The Tragic Muse* (1890). Each of those chapters consults some of James's contemporary minor fiction as well as pertinent critical essays. And my concern always is to indicate how the influence of the grandsons of Balzac manifests itself and how James has used it to achieve his own artistic ends.

CHAPTER I

The Cultural Background

IT WAS ALMOST inevitable that Henry James should have come to be known as the "international novelist." He seems to have been born facing East, and from the beginning his life was tinged with an international, cosmopolitan air. He always maintained that his earliest memory was of the Place Vendôme in Paris: himself in baby clothes, held on someone's knee, opposite his parents, and waggling his feet, he had "crossed the Rue Castiglione and taken in, for all my time, the admirable aspect of the Place and the Colonne Vendôme."[1] By the time he reached his majority James had spent about a quarter of his life in Europe, in part as a result of his father's ideas about educating the boys. In 1849, James Sr. explained to his friend Emerson that he wanted to take them to Europe to absorb French and German and to get a better "sensuous education" than they could in America.[2] So it was not merely as a tourist that James travelled abroad; he got to know his Europe and its culture as a resident and as a young student. He attended four schools in Switzerland, including what is now the University of Geneva, a Fourierist school in Paris, and the Collège Impériale in Boulogne, where a classmate was the young Coquelin, destined to become one of the great French actors; he had a Scots tutor in London and a French one in France, and in Bonn he studied at the Pension of a Dr. Humpert.

The rich cultural atmosphere was maintained as well in the James household in America, and it had a definite cosmopolitan tinge. A list of James Sr.'s friends and acquaintances who visited his home would include the names of Greeley, Dana, Ripley, Emerson, Margaret Fuller, Channing, Bronson Alcott, Thoreau, Carlyle, and Thackeray. It must have been a stimulating home for young William and Henry, particularly so since while still in their early teens they were encouraged to participate in the discussions that arose in the family parlor or around the dinner table.[3]

The teen-age Henry enjoyed a reputation as a devourer of libraries. The voracious youth numbered in his own library the works of George Eliot and George Sand, Browning, Sainte-Beuve and Taine, Goethe, Gautier, and Balzac. He also read periodicals—notably the *Revue des Duex Mondes*, the *Cornhill Magazine*, and *Once A Week*. In his twenties he met Dickens, who was on a reading tour of America. While his formal education ended with a year in the Harvard Law School, 1862-63, his "sensuous education" in cosmopolitan culture continued as it had begun.

One of the great moments of his earlier years was a fifteen-month sojourn (February 1869-May 1870) in England, Switzerland, and Italy. The glory of the whole trip was his first experience of Rome, through the streets of which he went "reeling and moaning" (as he wrote to William) "in a fever of enjoyment."[4] But England held some rare moments for him also. He went with Grace Norton to visit George Eliot at North Bank; he dined with Ruskin at Denmark Hill and with Charles Darwin at Down; he spent an evening with William Morris and even caught a glimpse of D. G. Rossetti. This extended visit, which carried him into his twenty-seventh year, brought James's youth to a close. His meeting with George Eliot had held particular meaning for him because his admiration for her was shared with his beloved cousin Minny Temple (perhaps the one great love of his life). He and Minny had planned, before he set out on the trip, that they would meet in Italy; but he never saw her again, as she died a few months after he left. He was deeply touched by her death and noted, years later, that for both him and William it marked "the end of our youth."[5]

James had by this time already begun on the career that was to raise his name into, and ultimately beyond, the ranks of those whom he had so thrillingly met in his early years. The striking feature of those early years is the stimulating intellectual and cultural atmosphere, with its strong cosmopolitan flavor, which fostered his growth. It was an exciting time in which to be growing up—and exciting not only for one interested in the realm of art and letters, like the young Henry James, for there was the more broadly interesting development in scientific thought. It was really nothing less than a new Age of Enlightenment.

The general cultural movement that began to manifest itself in Europe during the first half of the nineteenth century can best be described by the French term *le scientisme.* It was an age of expanding scientific activity, an age which produced the nebular hypothesis of the astronomer Laplace, the *transformisme* of Lamarck which anticipated the theories of Darwin, and of course Darwin himself. The advance of science awakened immense and indeed extravagant hopes in the power of scientists to measure all of life and reduce it to regular laws. Science offered an appealing resource to those whom revealed religion was increasingly failing to satisfy. The Positivist philosophy of Auguste Comte attempted specifically to fill the void left by forms of belief no longer acceptable. Scientists generally proposed to themselves the task of freeing humanity of its illusions, of breaking its deceiving idols.[6] Faith found a happier object in the prowess of human reason: the mysterious forces which rule the world and shape our ends were being discovered, stripped of their mystery, by human reason. Not only was the realm of the known being expanded, it was felt that ultimately (and before very long!) all would be known and, hence, brought under man's control. Science would not only predict the future accurately, it would determine it. Fate would no longer be inscrutable!

The impact of *scientisme* on literature, and especially on the literature of those writers with whom we shall be principally concerned, may be suggested by an early essay of Emile Zola's. In 1861 he was at work on an essay called "On Science and Civilization in their Relation with Poetry." There he pleads for the incorporation of scientific discovery in the realm of literature. At present, he complains, poets subscribe to antique fables and generally give a false interpretation of life. "Let us turn ourselves into scientists . . . let us be new Lucretiuses," he urges his fellows, for the new knowledge can make them great.[7] The new knowledge which those writers were to adapt from science was chiefly the experimental method. In a sense, of course, much of the scientific revolution owed its impulse to the liberating influence of empiricism, to experimental research— close and objective observation, careful recording of observed phenomena, strict adherence to fact, and reliance on demonstrable data.

Quite obviously, writers intent on giving a faithful representation of life as it actually is (or appears to be) would see a real benefit in the use of an experimental method themselves: they would observe closely, record details faithfully, and rely on the discovered data resolutely. And they would thus, perhaps, find it possible to create a more accurate and convincing picture of real life. The problem with this scheme, of course, turned out to be the fact that human beings in their customary milieu, the complex world of social intercourse, present a much more difficult object to manage than inorganic phenomena or even other animal life. The troublesome quantity in the human being was his mind, his soul, his psyche. The mere observation of external features could hardly lead one to *that,* man's essential being. Or could it?

The answer to that crucial question was supplied by Hippolyte Taine. A follower of Lamarck, Spencer, and Darwin, Hippolyte Taine was one of those figures who seem to bridge the gap between science and literature. In the Introduction to his famous *Histoire de la littérature anglaise* he frames his answer to the crucial question: that as one observes the external features of man, one inevitably seeks beneath that visible exterior the invisible man; the words he utters, the gestures he makes, the attitudes he assumes, his very clothes are all expressive of the invisible essence that lies beneath—his soul.

There is an internal man hidden beneath the external man, and the latter only manifests the former. You look at his house, his furniture, his clothing. . . . You listen to his conversation and note the inflections of his voice. . . . All these externalities are merely avenues which converge at a central point; you must be involved in reaching that central point, for there is the true man.[8]

Presumably, then, one can reach the essential man. Taine shared the faith of Auguste Comte that one can indeed discover the laws which govern human behavior and that once they have been discovered and ordered we shall be able not only to predict but to control that behavior. Vice and virture, Taine affirms, are simply products in the sense that vitriol and sugar are products: "in the moral sciences as in the physical sciences . . . the material is the same and is similarly composed of forces, tendencies, and qualities, and it may be said that in both cases the end result is produced according to the same rules."[9]

On the basis of that belief lies Taine's method as a scientific literary historian. He accounts for the various literary phenomena by positing the determining influence of *"les trois forces primordiales"—la race, le milieu, le moment.* Taine in fact pretends to have discovered certain general rules which account for the nature of the several writers and of the works they produce—scientific rules. And there is of course a marked parallel between this element of Taine's critical work and the studies of Charles Darwin, as seen in his *Origin of Species.*

Taine's role in spreading the influence of *scientisme* to America was of considerable importance. During the years immediately following the Civil War the impact of European scientific thought and development quickly made itself felt. John Fiske and Edward Livingstone Youmans were among the first to spread the new ideas on this side of the Atlantic. Darwin, Spencer, and the theory of evolution were the topic of widespread earnest debate, for they struck at the heart of revealed religion—or certainly seemed to. Involved in the debate were men like Asa Gray, Le Conte, Draper, and Louis Agassiz; and even the James brothers were touched by the controversy—William quite intimately. He had entered the Lawrence Scientific School at Harvard in 1861, and came immediately under the influence of Agassiz, whom he was to accompany on a scientific expedition to Brazil in 1865. Both William and Henry contributed, furthermore, to the popularizing of Taine's work in America. John Fiske wrote his introduction to the American edition of Taine's *Philosophy of History* (1868), and during the next decade a substantial body of reviews and commentaries devoted to Taine appeared.

Henry James's first notice of the Darwinian man of letters was published in the *Nation* on May 7, 1868. In reviewing the English translation of *Italy: Rome and Naples,* he speaks of Taine as the most powerful writer of the day. He chooses two characteristics for special praise: 1) Taine's having a method or guiding theory; and 2) his vigilance of observation. This review established the theme that is to dominate James's subsequent remarks on Taine (another half-dozen pieces published in the *Nation,* the *Atlantic Monthly,* and the *New York Tribune,* during the next eight years)—

M. Taine, in effect, studies man as a plant or as a machine. You obtain an intimate knowledge of the plant by a study of the soil and climate in which it grows, and of the machine by taking it apart and inspecting its component pieces. M. Taine applies this process to the human

mind, to history, art, and literature, with the most fruitful results. The
question remains . . . as to whether his famous theory of *la race, le
milieu, le moment* is an adequate explanation of the various complications of any human organism. . . . But . . . the theory makes
incomparable observers. . . .[10]

He comments again and again on the importance of Taine as a scientific observer—on his constant demand for facts, on his methodical
manner, on the positive and definite statement of his carefully noted
impressions.

It is quite understandable that while still in his early twenties James
should have been directly caught up in the surge of the new scientific
renaissance generally and in the cult of Hippolyte Taine particularly.
His own artistic taste was from earliest times receptive to the kind
of literature that was encouraged by *scientisme.* For the literary
climate that fostered that taste matched nicely the new scientific
climate; they were reciprocally genial.

In the American literary scene which fostered James's taste in
letters, three figures stand out: Nathaniel Hawthorne, Oliver Wendell
Holmes, and William Dean Howells. Hawthorne was the greatest and
most persistent of the American literary influences on him—his "real
progenitor," as F. O. Matthiessen called him.[11] Aside from certain
ideas and moral attitudes of Hawthorne's that affected him profoundly, there was a particular feature of his progenitor's art which
he professedly admired early and late; it was the ability to express
the essence of the New England atmosphere and to demonstrate the
effects of that ambient air upon his fictional creatures. James explained in his critical biography that Hawthorne "testifies to the
sentiments of the society in which he flourished almost as pertinently
(proportions observed) as Balzac and some of his descendants—Mm
Flaubert and Zola—testify to the manners and morals of the French
people."[12] Certainly he was finally to charge Hawthorne with insufficient realism, but it is important that he coupled him with Balzac,
Flaubert, and Zola as a writer with certain realist facets.

The name of Oliver Wendell Holmes might well be added to that
group. His influence on James was obviously nowhere near so great
as Hawthorne's, yet it is of peculiar significance. Holmes' position was
like Taine's in that it spanned the two realms of science and literature. If we remember him as the author of "The Autocrat of the
Breakfast Table", we also recall that he was a medical man, a scientist, and the author of several important scientific papers. Holmes had

been something of a pioneer in the field of medicine. He had studied
in Paris under the great Pierre Charles Alexandre Louis at a time
when the new experimental techniques were making the study of
medicine a truly respectable science. Not only did Holmes help to
introduce the new techniques—scientific methods of work and habits of accurate, systematic observation[13]—to America; he adapted the
methods of science to literature as well. He wrote a series of three
"scientific" novels—*Elsie Venner* (1861), *The Guardian Angel*
(1867), and *A Mortal Antipathy* (1885). James knew him in both his
roles, as part of his Harvard associations and in connection with the
early days of the *Atlantic.* And for our immediate purposes it is
important to notice that he remembered him in later years not only
as the author of the "Autocrat" but also as the author of "scientific"
novels.[14] Holmes' "Second Preface" to *Elsie Venner* explains what he
was attempting in the novel:

The real aim of the story was to test the doctrine of 'original sin' and
human responsibility for the disordered volition coming under that
technical denomination. Was Elsie Venner poisoned by the venom of
a crotalus before she was born, morally responsible for the 'volitional'
aberrations, which translated into acts became what is known as sin,
and, it may be, what is punished as crime? If, on presentation of the
evidence, she becomes by the verdict of the human conscience a
proper object of divine pity and not of divine wrath, as a subject of
moral poisoning, wherein lies the difference between her position at
the bar of judgment, human or divine, and that of the unfortunate
victim who received a moral poison from a remote ancestor before
he drew his first breath?[15]

In thus setting out a scientific and moral experiment in fiction, considering the determining influence of heredity, Holmes was in a
sense anticipating Emile Zola's theory of *le roman expérimental.*
James's experience of Holmes' scientific fiction doubtless helped prepare him to be receptive to the ideas of Zola as he would encounter
them in Paris: ideas concerning naturalism and the experimental
novel.

Finally, James's association with William Dean Howells, the father
of American Realism, would have contributed further to the training
of his taste for literary realism and naturalism. Their association began early: Howells was not the first to publish him but, as Leon Edel
says, "the first editor to take him seriously as a writer of fiction and
to see that he had a future."[16] Thus James was pleased to remember

him in his gratulatory letter for Howells' seventy-fifth anniversary.[17] The friendship of the two men ripened quickly and endured throughout their long lives. James was clearly aware of his friend's limitations as a writer, but was able to cherish his virtues—the strong "feeling of life," the sense of the "impression at first hand," the evidence of "observation, of patient and definite notation."[18] Howells managed very well to capture the look of things, even if it was not always "the look that conveyed their meaning"; and he did recognizably render the aspects of American life, even if preponderantly (not to say exclusively) its "smiling aspects."

All three of these writers contributed significantly to the literary atmosphere in which James's taste was developing, an atmosphere that fostered increasingly his interest in scientific and realistic (and ultimately, indeed, naturalistic) literature. His responses to Hawthorne and Howells have two marked similarities of particular significance for his subsequent development. He admired the sense of life conveyed in the writings of both men, yet found their realism ultimately insufficient—ultimately a partial and wilfully truncated expression. Second, he liked the unmistakably American flavor, the sense of the American scene, that the writings of both men had; but he felt there was an important connection between the quality of the purely American and the quality of the insufficiently real. The fault, James was increasingly to believe, lay not in the two writers themselves but in the thinness of American life upon which they were obliged to draw. It was not, of course, that American life was unreal, but rather that it lacked meaningful social expression of itself: one could see how it *looked,* but the looks conveyed no significant sense. At worst Hawthorne descended into allegory to achieve meaningful expression, and Howells contented himself with merely the realistic reproduction of the smiling surface. At best ... but unfortunately one was less than best.

Yet they had whetted his appetite with their offerings, sharpened it for more satisfactory fare of the kind he was coming more and more to desire. The satisfaction (never really complete for the exacting appetite of Henry James) finally was to come from the group of French writers he called collectively "the grandsons of Balzac." But it came also, at first, from European writers of his own tongue, and principally from George Eliot.

His admiration for Eliot began early, and it was all the dearer to him in that he shared it with his cousin Minny Temple. He found in

George Eliot many interesting and attractive features: she was something of a cosmopolite, an intellectual imbued with the spirit of the age; the companion and at last the wife of George Henry Lewes, friend of men like Huxley and Spencer, and most certainly a follower of Auguste Comte. She shared Lewes' enthusiasm for Comte as the harbinger of a new era, a man of the new science who offered a thoroughly homogeneous and methodical system to explain men, society, and the world. Such a woman, turning her talents to literature, could not but produce the kind of fiction James desired— scientific realism, or perhaps naturalism.

George Eliot explained her aims as a novelist in the familiar chapter 17, Book II, of *Adam Bede*. She says there that her effort is directed to avoiding the arbitrary and remaining strictly faithful to life as it has mirrored itself in her mind—as faithful "as if I were in the witness box narrating my experience on oath." She confesses that her "mirror" may be defective, but the she can rely on nothing else. That confession has a striking affinity with Zola's recognition (yet to come) that the novelist will present life "vue à travers un tempéra- ment"—as reflected, so to speak, in *his* mirror. Another interesting note is the simile of the witness box that Eliot uses, for it anticipates the avowal of Guy de Maupassant, in his preface to *Pierre et Jean,* to present "la vérité, rien que la vérité, toute la vérité." The passage in *Adam Bede* also echoes Comte in its humanitarian flavor, in its demand that the simple people be accepted as they are and presented in one's fiction just as they are. It concludes with the challenging demand that a writer simply tell the truth: "Falsehood is so easy, truth so difficult." Challenging, because it flings down the gauntlet at once to those creators of rosy-hued "romantic" stories in which all is smiling and sweet—and false (Zola was to call it "la littérature imbécile"); and also to those finicky critics of honest art who would object to the degraded and degrading subject matter (as they saw it) of the realistic writers. She addresses to the latter the direct plea, which is repeated in many essays of her contemporaries and followers, "do not impose on us any aesthetic rules" that will limit the area of our choice of subject.

The best of Eliot realizes the aims thus set forth. Her characters impress us as being faithfully drawn, the peculiarities of rustic speech are convincingly captured, and details of dress are accurately recorded. Further, Eliot gives generous attention to the countryside, to the dwellings of her characters, and to the shops and tools of their particular trades. Like Balzac, she knew that the setting—the milieu —is important in completing and defining the characters themselves, that it is a formative and determining influence. And her work is marked by her own brand of determinism—a profoundly moral brand, which is to be as clearly seen functioning in *Middlemarch* as in any other of her works. Her intention was, she said, to trace the influence of ordinary causes—not the extraordinary—and in certain directions which do not simply follow the beaten path. In view, then, of her ideas and intentions regarding the art of fiction, and of her accomplishment in her work, it is quite understandable that Ferdinand Brunetière should have written, in 1881, that "George Eliot raised the flag of naturalism in England a good twenty-five years ago."[19]

James was impressed with Eliot's literary achievement, although critical, as he was in every case, with her shortcomings. James always regretted the failure of absolute perfection in those he most admired, as though the very excellence of their work made their weaknesses all the more regrettable. He devoted several essays to her work as the best of English realists. He was also interested in similar work of the other leading English novelists of the day—especially Dickens, Thackeray, and Trollope; and they with Eliot may be said to represent the main stream of nascent realism in English fiction. At their back, of course, we discern the imposing figure of Sir Walter Scott, the best of whose historical romances represent the *realization* of various moments of history. That realization results from attention to detail of costume, dwelling, and speech—a solidity of specification which, James felt, made us see those characters from the past in their very habits as they actually lived. And all of these writers contributed to the development of James's taste for realistic fiction. The essays in which he examines their work fully testify to his interest and education, as we shall see.

But he had not yet really found the meat to satisfy his taste. It was a short and "indicated" step to turn from the English realists to their cousins across the channel. As Scott is discernible in the background behind Eliot and the others, so is his presence felt behind the colossus of French fiction, Honoré de Balzac. George Eliot and her colleagues who wrote for the *Westminster Review* during the fifties referred constantly to the work of Balzac as a touchstone for gauging excellence in prose fiction. They held up as a standard of perfection Balzac's "rugged truthfulness," his use of vast inventories of detail to

complete the realization of his characters and to account for their
future action. They recognized, further, that his presentation of life
was largely uncommented—it was fashioned to express only itself
and its implicit lesson.[20]

The cross-channel associations were close, as I say; and in any case,
James was no stranger to Balzac's work. In 1860, his friend John La
Farge, the American painter, had introduced him to Balzac's novels
at Newport. And the great Frenchman occupies a place at the side
of Hawthorne as the other principal master of Henry James. His
appreciation of Balzac and his sense of deep indebtedness to him
persisted to the very end. In 1902, he wrote an introduction to an
English translation of *Les Duex Jeunes Mariées* in which he speaks of
Balzac as being "signally alone" in his craft—"the first and foremost
member."[21] Most impressive is the lengthy tribute, "The Lesson of
Balzac," which was one of two lectures James used on his lecture tour
of the United States in 1904. He refers to him as "the greatest master," "the father of us all"; and of his indebtedness to him James says:
"I speak of him, and can only speak, as a man of his own craft, an
emulous fellow-worker, who has learned from him more of the lessons
of the engaging mystery of fiction than from anyone else, and who
is conscious of so large a debt to repay that it has had positively to
be discharged in installments; as if one could never have at once all
the necessary cash in hand."[22] Here, then, was the impressive and
satisfying fact; in James's eyes at least, the large and attractive figure
of Honoré de Balzac dominated the European literary scene. His
increasing knowledge of Balzac's fiction was a very significant item
in James's maturing taste.

In Balzac he found a most accomplished novelist who quite inten-
tionally wrote "scientific" fiction. Balzac claimed, in the 1842 Forward to his *Oeuvres Complètes,* to have done in literature what
Buffon had done in zoology. The idea for his *Comédie Humaine* came
to him as a result of comparing the human and the animal kingdom.
Rehearsing briefly the argument between Cuvier and Geoffroy Saint-
Hilaire, he concludes that there is but one animal—"The Creator
used only a single model for all organic beings." The differences of
external form which we observe among these beings, Balzac explains, result from the different environments in which they are
obliged to live. Then—

I saw that, in this connection, society resembled nature. Does not society make of man, according to the environment in which he acts out his life, as many different men as there are varieties in zoology? ... If Buffon created a magnificent work in trying to represent all of zoology in a single book, was there not a similar work to be done on society?[23]

Now Balzac does recognize that working with the human animal is a more complicated affair than the zoologist has to face; but his tone is optimistic. The reason for that optimism is most instructive in that it places Balzac squarely in the camp of Darwinism—before the fact, of course. While Buffon has noted that the life of animals is extremely simple, "man, according to a law yet to be discovered, tends to reflect his manners, his thought and his life in all that he appropriates to his needs."[24] To understand man in his essential self, Balzac tells us, look at his total environment: successful artistic representation demands that the artist catch the meaning hidden beneath the myriad items with which man surrounds himself.

Thus Balzac's answer to the problem confronting the writer of scientific literature was essentially the same as Taine's. And in his fiction he illustrates his principles impressively: typically, he gives a fully detailed description of the person and costume of his character and then provides an elaborate description of his environment. The solid specification of the milieu in which the character is set serves to define and explain him and, as we see in retrospect, to account largely for his behavior. Explanations by the author himself are superfluous: the setting expresses what we need to know.[25]

At Balzac's death in 1850, his mantle fell upon the shoulders of Gustave Flaubert, who began his famous *Madame Bovary* the following year. Flaubert would become the center of a group of writers, near contemporaries of Henry James, who were fiercely devoted to the art of fiction. The group was comprised of men whose literary taste had developed along the same lines as James's, and who together would tend to codify the principles upon which their literary theory and practice could be based. It now seems inevitable that James should have been drawn to that group as to the most sympathetic figures in the realm of prose fiction.

There are three features of Flaubert's career that concern us in the present context. First, his dedication to the realistic depiction of life. His brand of realism differs from Balzac's chiefly in its use of descriptive detail. Whereas Balzac always offered the full catalogue, Flaubert was highly selective and chose to present only the few most telling details to suggest the whole piece. But he believed in the value of first-hand experience, of the necessity of familiarity with one's data. He would devour a score of medical books to be sure that his presentation of Charles Bovary's disastrous operation on Hippolyte's club foot would be authentic. Like Balzac, he aimed at a choice and arrangement of detail that would express the "interior man" (in Taine's phrase). Like Balzac also, he would make the arrangement of his material as self-sufficient as possible so as to remove any need for the author's explanatory intrusion in his story. "Soyons exposants et non discutants," he would urge his colleagues—let us show rather than tell our stories.

The second feature, then, is Flaubert's scrupulous attention to style: his preoccupation with the choice of the most appropriate word for the occasion, with planning the rolling cadences of his paragraphs even before their verbal content was actually composed, with testing the aural effect of his sentences—roaring them out at the top of his lungs—to assure himself of their excellence as prose. In addition to that, of course, there is his attention to the architecture of his whole story, his concern with its organic wholeness—

... what I should like to write, is a book ... dependent on nothing external, which would be held together by the strength of its style .... a book which would have almost no subject, or at least in which the subject would be almost invisible, if such a thing is possible. ... the closer expression comes to thought, the closer language comes to coinciding and merging with it, the finer the result. I believe that the future of Art lies in this direction.[26]

Flaubert concluded that statement of principle, which he wrote to Louise Colet during the composition of *Madame Bovary*, with a truly prophetic utterance: "From the standpoint of pure Art one might almost establish the axiom that there is no such thing as subject, style in itself being an absolute manner of seeing things." And *Madame Bovary* well exemplifies the stylistic concerns of its creator: the careful setting of Emma's career within the framework of Charles' life, the counterpoint arrangement of the agriculture fair and Rudolph's overtures to the willing Emma, the use of repetition to develop expressive motifs, the striking symbolic significance of the blind beggar. Here indeed was realism raised to the highest art.

Finally, Flaubert's position as the somewhat unwilling *chef d'école,* his central position among the new votaries of realism, gave his word especial authority. He was indeed the master and theorist as well as the host of the weekly meetings of the group. Those meetings were to be extremely important for the future of prose fiction: it is not too much to claim that virtually all the currents of "modern fiction" flowed from this common source, the *cercle Flaubert.*

But to discuss the Flaubert group is to move from James's background squarely into what is to be the foreground of this study. Nevertheless, it is useful at this point to consider briefly the composition of that group and the ways in which, collectively and individually, the members reflect the atmosphere of the times—the times which had molded the aesthetic attitudes of Henry James. We can also get some sense of the momentum in which the group was caught and the directions in which it might be carried.

The Flaubert group was actually a development or off-shoot from an earlier group which had met for literary dinners at the famous Magny restaurant in Paris. Begun in 1862, largely through the efforts of the Goncourt brothers, these bimonthly meetings included Edmond and Jules de Goncourt, Flaubert, Théophile Gautier, the critics Ernest Renan, Sainte-Beuve, and Taine, and the Russian expatriate Ivan Turgenev. (The Académie Goncourt traces its beginnings to the Magny dinners.) After the death of Jules de Goncourt in 1870, the smaller group, consisting of Flaubert, Edmond de Goncourt, Turgenev, and two younger men, Emile Zola and Alphonse Daudet, used to meet regularly at Flaubert's Paris home for literary discussion. Before long, a young protégé of Flaubert's, Guy de Maupassant, joined the circle.

In 1865, the Goncourts had indicated their affiliation with the current of the times by offering to the public *Germinie Lacerteux,* the Preface to which announced it to be a "roman vrai." The Preface offers a summary view of the current situation of the novel, and in doing so sounds two notes of particular importance: "the Novel has taken upon itself the studies and duties of science," and, second, since it has become "the moral History of the present time . . . let it have that religion which the last century called . . . Humanity."[27] This second note is an echo of Comte's interest in social solidarity—an indication of the spreading concern about "the people." And it reminds us that Karl Marx had already published his *Communist Manifesto* and would shortly publish *Das Kapital.* This new interest in the common folk had begun to appear in much realistic fiction. Charles

Dickens had exposed various social ills in his novels; George Eliot would plead for honest attention to the ordinary people; and, somewhat ironically, the masterpiece of bourgeois-baiting Flaubert in France brought sharply into focus the possibility of using an ordinary, mediocre member of the people as a viable hero of fiction. Ivan Turgenev's stories of the Russian peasants further developed interest in the ordinary hero, and indeed the Naturalist group as a whole shared the attitudes expressed in the Preface to *Germinie Lacerteux.*

This novel may almost be said to mark the beginning of the battle for Naturalism in fiction: it is a scientific study and to some extent an "experimental novel." Its publication gave Zola the occasion for his first important public utterance. His review makes two significant claims for the novel. First, that it has all the powerful appeal of a physiological or a phychological problem—indeed, of a scientific experiment in which an object possessing certain characteristics (i.e. Germinie) is placed in a situation where it is subjected to certain selected forces, the effect of the interaction is carefully noted and faithfully reported by the experimenter, the novelist. Zola's brief rehearsal of this case underlines the arresting similarity between it and the case of Emma Bovary, and therefore also suggests the "experimental" quality of Flaubert's novel.[28] "Imagine a creature full of passion and tenderness . . . capable of ultimate shame and ultimate devotion [etc.] . . . . Place this strong but trembling woman in a gross environment which will wound all her delicacy, which will appeal to her common clay, and which will gradually kill her soul by smothering it under the ardors of the body and the excitement of the senses."[29] His concluding observation is that there are two contradictory beings in Germinie, and that the victory in the strife between them will be determined solely by the influence of her environment.

Zola's second claim for *Germinie* is its right to the moral freedom it has tacitly claimed to present the realistic truth as frankly as it has. He equates morality with truth—or realism—and stoutly defends the Goncourts against critical attack on the grounds of immorality. There is in principal, he claims, no limit to be placed on the study of truth; and he affirms that the only thing "wrong" with *Germinie* is its courage in speaking the truth aloud: "Le crime est donc d'avoir dit tout haut ce que beaucoup d'autres pensent tout bas." He has here made his defense a prophetic counter-charge of hypocrisy on the part of the carping critics. This plea for artistic freedom we have heard before (in George Eliot for example), and will hear again.

Leave the artist alone, will be the cry: let him write as seems best to him. "Par grâce, laissez-le écrire comme bon lui semble," Zola exclaims. And in this there is the implicit understanding that the artist will give us the truth *as it appears to him;* he will present a corner of life "vue à travers un tempérament." But he must be left free to relate honestly and frankly what he sees "through his peculiar temperament," or what is reflected in his own mirror—to employ Eliot's appropriate metaphor.

While it seems correct to say that Zola's review of *Germinie* is the beginning of his battle for Naturalism in literature, he does not call the Goncourts' novel an example of Naturalism. His first official use of the term "le naturalisme" appears in his preface to the second edition of his own *Thérèse Raquin* (1868). Nevertheless, Professor Hemmings reminds us, "there are earlier instances of his use of the word from which we can see how Zola came to remove it out of its original context, a purely biological one, and gave it a literary connotation."[30] The conception, if not the term, was apparently clearly in his mind in the middle sixties.

Zola bases his literary professions and demands on a firm scientific background. In addition to the influence of Auguste Comte and Hippolyte Taine, Zola responded to the impact of scientists like Letourneau (his *Physiologie des passions,* 1868, was a comparatively primitive study of the laws of heredity), Prosper Lucas (*Traité philosophique et physiologique de l'hérédité naturelle,* 1847-50),[31] and Dr. Claude Bernard, whose *Introduction à l'étude de la médecine expérimentale* (1865) became the actual source of Zola's theory of the novel as contained in his *Roman expérimental,* first published in 1880.[32] He begins, like Balzac, maintaining the legitimacy of adapting the scientific method to literature. Assuming, like his predecessors in science, the fundamental unity of natural phenomena, he argues that there is a chain of scientific studies in which chemistry is linked to physiology, physiology to anthropology and thence to sociology, and so to the end of the chain where we find the experimental novel. The aim of the experimental method and indeed of all science, Zola claims, is the same for the organic as for the inorganic: that aim is to find the relations which connect any phenomenon whatsoever to its immediate cause, or in other words to determine the conditions necessary for the appearance of that phenomenon. After developing this line of argument he finally concludes: "All these considerations are strictly applicable to the experimental novel." He mentions the important influence of heredity and environment in determining the intellectual and sensual nature of man, and indicates that it is the task of the novelist to show how those forces work in given instances on a chosen subject. The novelist's task is thus a king of "Scientific" experiment:

And that is what constitutes the experimental novel: to grasp the mechanism of phenomena in man, to show the working of intellectual and sensuous manifestations as physiology explains them to us, under the influence of heredity and surrounding circumstance, then to show man living in the social milieu which he himself has produced, which he alters daily, and in the heart of which he in turn experiences a continual transformation.[33]

The experimental novelist, Zola adds, will draw no conclusions about social amelioration; he simply undertakes his experiment and demonstrates the results—simply discovers the determinism in social phenomena. It is left to the legislators to control these phenomena, developing the good and suppressing the bad. The scientific writer remains objective and impartial but *engagé:* he is concerned only with discovering the truth, with demonstrating how life really is. The novelist is then free of all narrowly moral concerns; yet he is in the broadest sense entirely moral, as his goal is *truth.*

Lurking in the shadows just behind this frank statement is, of course, the whole vexed question of morality in literature—the question which Zola directly addressed in his review of *Germinie Lacerteux.* The particular opponent Zola has in mind in debating this question is the purveyor of what he calls "la littérature imbécile"— romantic literature. He sets up an interesting pair of equations with the term "ideal," which he uses interchangeably with, on the one hand, "the unknown" and, on the other, "romantic." The aim of science, obviously, is to overcome the unknown, to reduce ignorance: "All that we do not know, all that still eludes us, is the ideal, and the goal of our effort is daily to reduce the ideal, to overcome the unknown with truth."[34] The works of the romantic writer are not scientifically based but imaginative, fanciful, divorced from reality. They nourish superstition and perpetuate ignorance as they refuse to expose the truth of life. They are dishonest and hence harmful, and they produce misguided wretches like Emma Bovary. So runs Zola's argument:

Our French girls, whose training and education are deplorable... are the product of this idiot literature [la littérature imbécile] in which a young maiden is deemed the more noble the closer she is to being a well wound up mechanical doll. Oh, educate our girls, fashion them for us and for the life they will have to lead, put them in touch as quickly as possible with the realities of existence; that will be an excellent task.[35]

This attitude is typical of the Naturalists and goes a long way toward explaining the predominance of "unpleasantness" in their writings. The romantic writers either overlook the seamy side of life or gloss it over with sugary sentimentality; so in righteous opposition to this nefarious tendency the Naturalist will insist on displaying all those "non-smiling" aspects of life which the *littérature imbécile* modestly blinks at—misery, poverty, squalor, depravity, viciousness and a frank treatment of love in its various aspects. The Naturalist reaction is, if something of an over-compensation, at least understandable. Yet how completely frank dare literature be? Where is the line to be drawn? Does it not, after all, run the risk of becoming obscene? "For me there are no obscene works," Zola predictably replies; "there are only poorly conceived and poorly executed ones." He claims not to understand what is meant by a "moral writer"; for him the question is exclusively whether the writer is talented—and if he is, all may be permitted him. "A page well written has its own morality, which is in its beauty, in the intensity of its life and accent .... For me there are no obscene works. . . ."[36]

If the experimental method was the salvation of science, so was it in Zola's eyes the saving of literature. And just as the scientist must be free of moral legislators, so must the scientific novelist. To be engaged in the discovery of truth, in the overcoming of ignorance, is to be moral enough and to spare. Zola's watchword, then, was something like "Trust Science, see all, nor be afraid!"

Zola's aesthetic is based on the foregoing principles. His initial advice to the writer consists in telling him that if he wants to paint life he had better look at it hard and render exactly the impression it makes on him. Observe it and note it like the careful scientist, and be honest in recording what you see. Factual detail is required, and in thick and solidly satisfying abundance—so Zola advised. And notice that the impression of life derives not only from its appearance, but also from its sound and smell and taste, from its bustle and activity as well. He allowed, of course, for individual differences, for the nature of the particular observer on whom life showered its impressions, demanding only that the scientific method obtain.

With all this emphasis on fact, on the recording and reporting of data, Zola found himself in the somewhat strange position of having to admit that imagination did, after all, have a role to play in the writing of fiction. But it was a small role, and it had certainly to be founded on accurate factual observation. The novelist has imaginatively to invent his plan, the little nub of drama that becomes the plot or story of his novel, Zola agrees.[37] But he is cautious in this allowance, and he is careful to distinguish between the creative imagination of the Naturalist, who depends on fact, and the "unbridled fancy" (let us say) of the writer who overturns all that we commonly know of actual life. Zola conceives even of a kind of poetic naturalism, in which the imagination carried a good bit beyond mere cold fact; and that is acceptable so long as it remains, as he finds the Goncourts' *Frères Zemganno* does, a work of analysis and a work of logic. Yet the safest line is to eschew the poetic and hew to the scientific.

For himself and his own work, Zola affirmed, "I am . . . a positivist, an evolutionist, a materialist; my system is heredity. . . . My work . . . will be in conformity with this science. I am going to picture the physiological man. This is my formula; and best of all it will be a new art, a new literature, which will be my own literature, my own art."[38] Even a brief summary view of Zola's production—and especially, of course, the *Rougon-Macquart* series—shows that he followed his avowed method fairly closely. The milieu in which the action of a given novel is set is always most fully described in exhaustive detail. The effect of the force of that milieu depends regularly upon the nature of the character on which it acts; that is, the element of heredity is of equal importance in determining the outcome of a particular "experiment." To show the determining effect of heredity properly, Zola had to trace his characters through several generations, and this he was able to do by his plan of developing the various branches and generations of the teeming Rougon-Macquart families. Thus we have, for instance, our view of little Anna Coupeau at a tender age manifesting a definite character in *L'Assommoir*—kissing the little boys, falling asleep in their embrace, and generally behaving during her mother's goose feast like a miniature *poule de luxe*. When she steps before us again on the stage of Paris to make that gay city pant in anticipation and chant her name—Nana!—we recognize and understand the *fille* whom Gervaise Macquart and Coupeau have produced.

Also Zola's devotion to copious documentation, to taking exhaustive notes of the sights and sounds of the milieu he was to employ, served to provide him with a factually real basis for his "experiments" in fiction. And his determination not to point a moral, indeed to meddle as little as possible, in conducting those experiments, contibuted greatly to the achievement of the air of reality and lifelikeness in his work at its best. The scientific basis of his method is in good part responsible for Zola's advancing the development of the art of the real in fiction.

Another aspect of Zola's practice that is worth our attention is his confining himself, in some of his novels, to the point of view of the principal character alone—keeping him central and consistently in the reader's eye. This practice heightens the dramatic element of the novel by deemphasizing the role of the controlling author. In *L'Assommoir,* possible the greatest of the *Rougon-Macquart* series, he focuses constantly on Gervaise Coupeau. We are thus intimately concerned with her and involved in *her* story; Zola furthers this concern by referring all the action of the novel to this one center. Gervaise's children, Etienne and Afina, benefit similarly from their central roles in the two later novels in which they predominate. Zola in fact advances this technique a step further in works like *Germinal*, where the central character is on the verge of becoming an eye for the reader: our attention there is constantly on Etienne, and his is fixed on the scene in which he is placed. To a great extent we see only what he sees, and as he sees it. It is not difficult to perceive the direction in which this particular development was moving.

With this device of focusing on the central character Zola sometimes employed another which tended further to mask his role as omniscient author. Ideally, of course, he ought to be quite absent, and the novel left to express itself; yet he sometimes cannot avoid commenting on the action and the characters, though at his best he does so by directing those comments to us in the idiom of the character before us: he thus can create the illusion that the comments are those of the character alone. Consider this passage from *L'Assommoir,* which is left in the original so that it retains its full flavor:

A cette époque, elle aurait encore vécu très heureuse, sans Coupeau, qui tournait mal, décidément. Un jour, elle revenait justement de la forge, lorsqu'elle crut reconnaître Coupeau dans l'Assommoir du père Colombe, en train de se payer des tournées de vitriol, avec Mes-Bottes, Bibi-la-Grillade et Bec-Salé, dit Bois-Sans-Soif. Elle passa vite pour ne pas avoir l'air de les moucharder. Mais elle se retourna: c'était bien Coupeau qui se jetait son petit verre de schnick dans le gosier d'un geste familier déjà. Il mentait donc, il en était à l'eau-de-vie maintenant! Elle rentra désespérée; toute son épouvante de l'eau-de-vie la reprenait. Le vin, elle le pardonnait, parce que le vin nourrit l'ouvrier, les alcools au contraire, étaient des saletés, des poisons qui ôtaient à l'ouvrier le goût du pain. Ah! le gouvernement aurait bien dû empêcher la fabrication de ces cochonneries.

The first sentence or so is Zola's narration; but before we get to the end of the second sentence the burden has been taken up by Gervaise's idiom—"des tournées de vitriol" and the sobriquets of Coupeau's drinking companions smack of her own speech. The third sentence, ending as it does with the colloquial "l'air de les moucharder," again seems to be Gervaise's speech—as though she were commenting on her own actions, or as though Zola had expressed her thoughts for us as she would herself. The same effect is achieved similarly in the next two sentences—the "verre de schnick dans le gosier" and the turn of phrase of the sentence following are unmistakably Gervaise's idiom. Then we perhaps feel Zola's intrusion with "Elle rentra désespérée. . . ." but the thought in the subsequent sentence is certainly Gervaise's and is couched in phraseology that might well be hers. The last sentence of the passage—"Ah! . . . ces cochonneries."—is certainly redolent of Gervaise herself. The whole passage is strongly charged with the flavor of Gervaise's idiom and manages to convey the impression that it is she and she alone who has been tacitly narrating her own experience to our reading ears.

It is an interesting commentary on Zola's skill in this technique that the novel was criticized because "the author spoke like his characters"! Henri Barbusse observed that "the novelist had been up to then only a supplementary objective character, a sort of director of the book, stage manager, stationed not on the boards but in the audience, who jotted down as marginal notes to the action his psychological comments, his precious interpretation, and read out his conclusions."[39] With his strident claims for Naturalism and his publicity-seeking as champion of the Naturalist cause, Zola nevertheless was capable of some technical subtlety.

Zola is of course the large central fact of Naturalism. But to either side of him, or perhaps between him and Flaubert, were two other members of the group—Alphonse Daudet and Ivan Turgenev. Daudet came to embrace what he did of Naturalism only gradually and rather late in his career. He much less conscientiously sought out documental data for his work, but was more a passive spectator of life. He was also blessed with a larger sympathy and a livelier sense of humor than his colleagues, and so casts a less lugubrious light on his fiction than is to be found in the more typical Naturalist offering. Zola himself observed the difference and coupled Daudet with the Goncourts in calling him a "poetic" Naturalist. And Pierre Martino agrees that Daudet belongs in the Naturalist camp for all his poetry: he finds *Les Rois en exil* and *Numa Roumestan* "bourrés de documents exacts et d'histoires vraies," and notes the clearly Naturalist intention of both *Sappho* and *L'Evangéliste*.[40] Daudet's work in a couple of important instances exerted significant influence on Henry James, and he was to become one of James's closest friends among the French. And a strong argument can be made for the case that Daudet's peculiar brand of poetic Naturalism was the most appealing brand in James's opinion.[41]

Ivan Turgenev was also a close friend to James for a time before his death in 1883, and had been James's means of introduction to the Flaubert group. He was like James in several superficial ways—an expatriate and a cosmopolite who nevertheless retained a strong love of his homeland; and he also shared several artistic qualities with the young American. He too exerted considerable influence on James in certain specific instances.[42] Turgenev was much concerned with the autonomy of art, interested in the Art for Art's Sake school of thought, and a stern defender of artistic freedom from moral legislation for the writer. His scenes of Russian life, done with no apparent didactic intention—quite in accord with the shared principles of the Flaubert group—were taken up eagerly by social reformers; they seem, thus, to offer an excellent realization of the ideals set forth in Zola's "Roman expérimental." Yet it may be most true to say that Turgenev was a step ahead of the group of writers who surrounded Flaubert, that his work was already on the road which Naturalism was bound to take. He would have agreed with his young confrère Maupassant that the real aim of literature should be, not realism, but *illusionnisme*. Indeed, Turgenev declared that he was not a naturalist but rather a *surnaturaliste*.[43]

Guy de Maupassant rounds out the group as it concerns us. He was the youngest member, a protégé of Flaubert's; and in some important respects he is closer to Flaubert than to any of the others. He shared their general theories regarding literature—the primary importance of creating a faithful representation of life, the illusion of reality, or, as he put it, of truth,—"la vérité, rien que la vérité, toute la vérité."[44] He had learned under Flaubert's tutelage the value of keen observation and notation of details, and to appreciate the importance of first-hand experience of the material to be used in his fiction. And he also recognized the virtue of keeping out of his stories, of making them capable of standing independent, on their own feet. The typical Maupassant story, then, is firmly structured, a triumph of compactness and economy of means which create a solidness and hardness of surface, a tight perfection that seems to rely on no external support: it strikes the reader with all the dramatic immediacy of the direct perception of life.

In part Maupassant's style depends on the lesson of Flaubert—the careful selection of significant detail, rather than the abundance of Balzac and Zola. It is the realization of his belief that art should not attempt to compete with life on its own terms: since it cannot hope to provide a true reproduction of actuality, it must create the *illusion* of reality. The artist must attend to the *vraisemblable* rather than to the *vrai* (the distinction is Aristotle's); that—

to give the complete illusion of the true according to the ordinary logic of facts, not merely to transcribe them in their actual pêle-mêle sequence. . . . I conclude that the talented Realists ought rather to call themselves Illusionists.[45]

Nevertheless he unmistakably belongs at the side of Zola. If he is not primarily interested in demonstrating the effect of the forces of heredity and environment on the human being, his short fiction does offer an excellent example of the "scientific" method: his objectivity, his use of observed detail, and his refusal to point a moral, all these emphasize Maupassant's relation to the author of the *Rougon-Macquart* series. And like Zola and the others, Maupassant is sternly opposed both to the basic dishonesty of the "littérature imbécile" and to the interference of moral legislators masquerading as critics. The frankness of his own fiction and the unambiguous comments in his critical writing clearly attest to his position as the youngest grandson of Balzac.

This is the essential complement of the group Henry James met in Paris—those writers who had the most to offer his literary taste. James had been sharpening his aesthetic sense, confirming his own taste, during those years in his practice as a fledgling literary critic. The development of his artistic attitude is recorded in these early critical pieces, and they too indicate the tendency of his development— clearly in the direction of the Flaubert circle.

CHAPTER II

Principles and Expectations

Henry James's important decision to quit his native shores in 1875 and establish residence in Paris now appears to have been quite in accord with the natural course of events. His youthful experience of Europe had convinced him that the world of culture was to be found there, that American soil afforded too little nourishment to support any artist but the greatest genius—and he felt he was not that. But he was an artist, or at least determined to be nothing else. That would seem reason enough, then, to account for his flight from America in October of his thirty-third year. His immediate choice of Paris as his goal was certainly an obvious one: it was the capital of the world of Western culture. More than that, however, Paris was the site of the remarkable literary triumph of Honoré de Balzac, whom James admired virtually beyond all others in the practice of fiction. It was inevitable, therefore, that James should have been drawn to that group of writers in Paris whom he recognized as Balzac's literary descendants—the new votaries of realism, the grandsons of Balzac.

James's taste for realistic literature had been shaped by certain trends of the times; his early performances in literary criticism record the progress of that developing taste. Much of his criticism during the first fifteen years of his productive life was based on principles—usually only implicit and still in a formative stage—that would put him quite in sympathy with the theory and practice of the young French school. Throughout James's early reviews the name of Balzac constantly recurs—as it recurred in the pages of Lewes' *Westminster*

Review a decade earlier—as a standard measure of excellence in prose fiction.

James's first critical performance, a review of Nassau Senior's "Essays in Fiction," does not discuss Balzac, yet it is concerned with a common interest of his and James's—Sir Walter Scott. James heartily approved of Scott's *Waverly* because it avoided the didactic: it was "self-forgetful," a term he would use interchangeably with "irresponsible" to describe those works which had no axe to grind, which were there just to amuse in an apparently artless and unselfconscious way. *Waverly* undertook, James wrote, "to prove nothing but facts." That is all. But *that* is a great deal: to be factual is to be real, it is to give us life itself. In a review some three months later the same note is sustained, and the name of Balzac is added. James indicates the weakness of the unconvincing descriptive passages in the forgotten novel *Azarian* by comparing them with passages in Balzac's work. Balzac's description convinces because "it was scientifically done. . . . He aimed at local colour; that is, at giving the facts of things."[1] The adverb "scientifically" echoes in our ear, recalling the tenor of Balzac's Preface of 1842, for example; and it suggests that the influence represented by Hippolyte Taine had begun its work. It almost coincides with Zola's approval of the Goncourts' scientific achievement in *Germinie Lacerteux*.

Another aspect of Balzac's technique that James finds attractive is the functional nature of his descriptions; they are integrated parts of the organic whole which the novel must be. James's way of putting it suggests that the descriptive passages are also "self-forgetful"—"these things [setting, dress, furniture, etc.] are all described *only in so far as they bear upon the action*, and not in the least for themselves." And finally his comment on characterization recalls the words of both Balzac and Taine on the relation between the "exterior" man and the "interior" man—the relation between the visible facts and the invisible soul. "What do we care," James asks, "of the beauty of a man or woman in comparison with their humanity?"

In a novel we crave the spectacle of that of which we may feel that we *know* it. The only lasting fictions are those which have spoken to the reader's heart, not to his eye; those which have introduced him to an atmosphere in which it was credible that human beings might exist, and to human beings with whom he might be tempted to claim kinship.

Passages like this clearly imply that while the writer must certainly capture the look of things, he has to make sure that it is the look which conveys their meaning. In other words, James insists on an active artistic imagination. He attributes certain failures in George Eliot's work to a deficiency of imagination, and his review of *Azarian* further claims that for the fiction writer "there is no grander instrument than a potent imagination"; to that affirmation he adds, as if to clarify his meaning, "there is no more pernicious dependence than an unbridled fancy." Now James never clearly defined the distinction between the terms "imagination" and "fancy"; in some instances he uses them interchangeably, more often he uses "fancy" pejoratively, but usually adds a qualifying adjective to the term which makes his intention clear. In a discussion of Dickens, in 1865, he strongly objects to the fantastic element in some of Dickens' fiction; he finds virtually every character in *Our Mutual Friend* "a mere bundle of eccentricities animated by no principle of nature whatsoever." But he would accept the fantastic when it is the result of a "lively and vigorous" creative fancy: he defends some of Dickens' fantastic creations—Newman Noggs, Pecksniff, Micawber—as merely exaggerated statements of types that really exist. It would seem that a lively and vigorous fancy works, like the imagination, from a firm basis of fact: the acceptably fantastic is a development of the real material of actual life, whereas the "unbridled" fantastic is a complete departure from that material—it is merely cerebral. "Seldom had we read a book [*Our Mutual Friend*] so intensely written, so little seen, known, or felt."[2]

These examples of James's earliest critical performance indicate some three or four guiding principles which persist and develop in his criticism of the whole decade. Fiction must avoid the didactic, it must not be selfconsciously intent on any function other than the entertaining representation of actual life—it must be self-forgetful. Second it must approach its proper business scientifically, notebook in hand, and attend to its proper data—the facts of real life. But, third, it must not merely add the facts one to one as though for their own sake: those facts—description of setting, development of character, narration of action—must all be functioning items contributing to the organic structure of the story as a whole. Therefore, finally, the facts must be chosen, arranged, and presented with the aid of the true artistic imagination—or of a lively and vigorous fancy. These are the principles implicit in those representative critical pieces of James's first two years of publication; and they are the principles which were to find sympathetic echo in the critical theory and realization in much of the practice of the Flaubert circle.

As the first decade of James's career drew to a close he turned his critical attention to some of the members of that circle. The first important piece was a thirty-page article, in the *North American Review* for April, 1874, which is full of admiration and praise for Turgenev's fiction. James finds it effective because it is firmly based on fact: as Scott "undertakes to prove nothing but facts" and as Balzac "aims at giving the facts of things," so Turgenev has created tales that are "a magazine of small facts . . . taken, as the phrase is, *sur le vif.*" Significantly, his fiction is the result not merely of accurate observation and factual reporting: James is quick to add that Turgenev's artistic imagination is always lending a hand, guiding and modulating his touch, and making the artist worthy of the observer. He also defends "The Memoirs of a Sportsman" (*A Sportsman's Sketches*) against the charge of didacticism—of being a polemical document under the guise of a novel. The French translator of the novel had compared it to *Uncle Tom's Cabin*: the one pleading against serfdom in Russia as the other had against slavery in the United States. James counters with the observation that there is no indication of any episode's making the direct appeal, that any sense of moral concern is a result of the total impact of the novel as a whole—in the cumulative testimony of a multitude of fine touches. The book points no moral, it merely renders actual life. "It offers a capital example of moral meaning giving a sense to form and form giving relief to moral meaning."[3]

In his insistence on organic wholeness James takes a further step: he explains that a particular virtue of Turgenev's fiction is its "dramatic" quality. And he intends the term to be taken literally—"like a play on the stage." His point is that not only should the novel's action (and its meaning) be fully *expressed,* but also that it should be independent of external aid—especially of the controlling and explanatory hand of the author. James aptly illustrates this quality of dramatic self-sufficiency in Turgenev's fiction with a passage chosen from *A Nest of Noblemen:*

When Lavretsky reads in the *chronique* of a French newspaper that his wife is dead, there is no description of his feeling, no portrayal of his mental attitude. The living, moving narrative has so effectively

put us in the way of feeling with him that we can be depended upon.
He had been reading in bed before going to sleep, had taken up the
paper and discovered the momentous paragraph. He "threw himself
into his clothes," the author simply says, "went into the garden, and
walked up and down till morning in the same alley." We close the
book for a moment and pause, with a sense of personal excitement.[4]

The Turgenev essay was followed by two essays which neatly group
themselves with it to illustrate James's position as critic at the moment of his decision to leave America and take up life in Paris. They
were an essay on Balzac, published in December 1875, and another
on Charles de Bernard and Gustave Flaubert, published in February
1876. The earlier is a full-blown piece of admiration of Balzac's tremendous genius as a "realistic romancer." James draws an instructive
analogy between the *Comédie Humaine* and Comte's "Positive
Philosophy," and notes Balzac's great ability to represent in factual
detail the French civilization of his day. He compares Balzac and
Turgenev as masters of definite representation, and again emphasized the invaluable role of the imagination that makes their characters spring into being. The most noteworthy item in the essay makes
explicit and beautifully illustrates James's appreciation of Balzac's
functional description of setting; the passage chosen, from *Le Père
Goriot,* exemplifies his attention to organic unity and to the importance of *milieu* in characterization. Incidentally, James's comments
are an arresting anticipation of Erich Auerbach's treatment of the
same passage (the description of the Maison Vauquer) in his *Mimesis,*
even to the extent of quoting Balzac's words on Madame Vauquer:
"her whole person, in short, is an explanation of the boarding-house,
as the boarding-house is an implication of her person."

The later essay discusses both Charles de Bernard and Flaubert. In
the part devoted to Flaubert James explains the relationship among
the French writers—that Flaubert is of the school of Balzac, and the
Goncourt brothers and Zola are of the school of Flaubert. But
primarily the essay deals with *Madame Bovary*, which he calls the
last word in realism; and of course he has generous praise for Flaubert's objective relating of facts, his refusal to point a moral, his
ability to make the novel self-sufficient. A note of special emphasis is
his direct dealing with the moral question as it touches the art of
fiction. He agrees that *Bovary* is the reverse of what is usually considered family reading, yet he suggests that it might serve well as a
Sunday School tract. Twenty years earlier the book had enjoyed its

succès de scandale. As James discusses this aspect, we find him making a somewhat unfamiliar use of the term "moral." He is not principally concerned with a code of ethics, but rather with the serious and honest confrontation of life as it really is. To take actual life seriously, James seems to say, is to be moral. That must be the chief concern of the artist. We can get at this sense of the term by looking at a passage in that part of the essay devoted to Bernard, whose failure James attributes to the fact that "he had no morality."

By this we of course do not mean that he did not choose to write didactic tales ... We mean that he had no moral emotion, no preferences, no instincts—no moral imagination, in a word. His morality was altogether traditional, and, such as it was, it seems to have held him in a very loose grasp. It was not the current social notion of right and wrong, of honour and dishonour, that he represented, but something even less consistent. What we find in him is not the average morality, but a morality decidedly below the average. He does not care, he does not feel, and yet his indifference is not philosophic. ... He belongs to the intellectual family—and very large it is in France—of the amusing author of 'Gil Blas.' All its members know how to write, and how, up to a point, to observe; but their observation has no reflex action, as it were, and they remain as dry as they are brilliant.[5]

This lengthy observation on Bernard's weakness deserves close attention, for it prepares us to understand much of James's subsequent comments on literature and morality. The moral question is of course very important for the realists, determined as they were to look at life without evading the unpleasant, the sordid, the depraved. In the passage quoted, James is concerned not with some moral system—understood in the traditional sense of the term—but with a serious involvement with life, with the attitude that life matters. His objection to Bernard is that he merely notes the look of things, but the look has no significance: it does not dilate the reader's imagination and it provokes no serious thought about life as it actually is. His point is simply that to achieve that dilation and that provocation is to be a moral artist. Read against the background of this passage, his succinct comment about *Bovary* seems rich in meaning: "Every out-and-out realist who provokes serious meditation may claim that he is a moralist; for that, after all, is the most that the moralist can do for us."[6]

With the peculiar emphasis and development found in these three essays, we have a good picture of James's basic aesthetic at the middle of the seventies, the moment when he decided to leave home for Paris. The essay on Turgenev, furthermore, served as the means of gaining him entry to the literary group of Flaubert's. Henry's father had thought the essay somewhat harsh—it objected to Turgenev's pessimism—so he took it upon himself as an admirer of Turgenev to write him a cordial letter as compensation for the son's strictures, and to extend a warm invitation for a visit to the James home in Massachusetts. Henry also sent a copy of his essay to Turgenev. This correspondence established a new and firm enough personal link between James and Paris: it was Turgenev who met the young American expatriate and introduced him to Flaubert and his circle.

Here was the great moment, the autumn of 1875. We can easily imagine what James's emotions must have been at the prospect of being introduced to the shrine, indeed to the very foot of the altar (as he thought of it) at which the "new votaries of realism" were celebrating the cult of Balzac. His initial conversations with Turgenev must have confirmed his feeling that there was much in common between himself and the European realists. It is important to bear in mind the high expectations that must have been alive in James at the moment of his introduction to the sacred circle, for the reaction which followed his initial associations with the realists can be understood only in the light of those expectations and of the situation as it obtained in Paris. James must certainly have been expecting a great deal; yet he remained in Paris only a very few months.

There is still the suspicion in some quarters that his meeting with the Flaubert group was on the whole a sad and fruitless one, and the usual explanation is that James left in disgust with them, having learned little but a rather prudish distaste for their wares. There is, to be sure, some evidence of such a reaction; for example, he wrote to Howells saying, "I don't like their wares, and they don't like any others." Also, he sent a copy of one of Zola's novels to Perry, describing it as "simply hideous."[7] But this by no means tells the whole story. To begin with, what James originally felt to be a chill welcome must have been due at least partially to his own failure to make an impression on the group. It is a somewhat damning comment on their insularity, however, that they could not respond to what was surely James's best gambit: he recommended to them the writings of George Eliot. Their reply was, in effect, a fishy stare and a "Who's he?" There is a peculiar irony in their lack of interest in the unfamiliar name, for George Eliot was really laboring in the same artistic vineyard. But in all fairness to the Flaubert group, it must be remembered that she was virtually unknown in France at that time.

The specific failure, as James felt it, of the group to live up to his expectations was actually just the most salient aspect of the general failure of Paris. His letters record that larger failure. To Howells he wrote the complaint that "of pure Parisianism I see absolutely nothing"; and to his brother William, "I have got nothing important out of Paris. . . . A good deal of Boulevard and third-rate Americanism: few retributive relations otherwise."[8] What had happened was that the city had kept her real self hidden and merely turned her tourist side to him. A note of loneliness and homesickness creeps into the letters of his first months: "If I had a single good friend in London I would go thither."[9] In short, the grapes of Paris had refused to yield themselves to the grasp of this eager and lonely figure—and consequently had proven themselves sour! James left France early in the new year.

Yet when he looked back on that experience after an interval of almost six years it appeared in quite a different light. At the beginning of his second Notebook, under the date November 25, 1881, he affirms that his time in Paris, 1875-76, was by no means misspent; he lists a few of the acquaintances he had made—Turgenev, Zola, Goncourt, and Daudet—and remembers with particular fondness a wonderful afternoon when he had had Flaubert all to himself. What, during the six-year interval, could have happened to cause this apparent about-face?

Perhaps it was simply a matter of maturing. James's critical performances during the intervening years exhibit a definite tendency, a strengthening of his commitment to realism in fiction. Far from indicating a repulsion from the kind of thing produced by Flaubert and company, his remarks show him approaching ever closer to their very position. Two aspects of his criticism catch the eye: a de-emphasizing of the role of the imagination in favor of accurate factual presentation, and a struggle finally to come to terms with the moral problem he had wrestled with earlier. The problem was both more urgent and more vexed, as he was faced with the increasing frankness of, say, Zola's fiction and at the same time with his own growing awareness of the very real artistic accomplishment that went along with that frankness. In fact, his reactions to Zola alone during the interim years

afford quite an accurate indication of James's development in the
direction of the realist-naturalist aesthetic position. More and more,
indeed, one is led to expect that James will ultimately burst out with
the bald confession that he is himself "quite the naturalist"!

At the end of 1876, James published an essay on Eliot's *Daniel
Deronda* in which he discusses the functions of observation and
invention in the creation of fictional characters. Neither function
alone suffices, although one of the two may preponderate. His significant point here is that those of her characters which owe more to
invention than to observation, are simply brilliant failures. Here "invention" seems to be equivalent to "unbridled fancy"; but the essay
so emphasizes the necessity of *observation*, reliance on factual data,
as to suggest that the alternatives he is concerned with are not so
much "imagination" versus "fancy" as they are "the real" versus "the
made up." If this seems to be a nice distinction, it is nevertheless an
important one. That the distinction, however nice, is quite real, is
clearly indicated by his strictures on Hawthorne's fiction. In the
critical biography of 1879, James finds that his earliest master failed
in not being a realist—or at least "not to my mind enough of one."
The condemnation of this failure in Hawthorne is couched in terms
the significance of which is immediately relevant. The weakness of
The Scarlet Letter, James says, derives from "a want of reality, and
an abuse of the fanciful element"; in *The Blithedale Romance* "we
get too much out of reality, and cease to feel beneath our feet the firm
ground of an appeal to our vision of the world—our observation." His
general condemnation is aimed at "something light and thin—something belonging to the imagination alone—which indicates a man but
little disposed to multiply his relations, his points of contact with
society."[10] Four years later his essay on Alphonse Daudet favors the
Frenchman as "much more an observer than an inventor";[11] he adds
that the invented part of his tales is vague and ineffective and romantic.

Now it is true that these passages might well be laid beside the
earlier passages on "imagination" and "fancy" as merely an extension of James's attempts at defining the term "artistic imagination."
But it is imperative to notice the distinction rather than the similarity
—that he has shifted his emphasis to insist on the primary importance
of observation for the artist in fiction. In his comments on Hawthorne
he clearly opposes to "observation" both "the fanciful" and "imagination alone"; the distinction that most interested him at that partic-

ular moment of his career is surely inescapably clear.

With this new whole-hearted commitment, in theory, to "the real," James found himself once again face to face with the old moral question—and more immediately, as I say, than ever before. Confirmed in the idea that life as it is commonly observed must be the material of fiction, and fully sympathetic with the demands of the writers he most admired—demands for freedom to depict whatever of life they chose to observe—James found the "moral problem" more pressing than heretofore. But he was in a sense already committed: he had rather surprisingly preferred Lockhart's *Adam Blair* to *The Scarlet Letter* as being "more grossly human and vulgarly natural"; he praised Lockhart's heroine for her "credible, visible, palpable property, a vulgar roundness and relief." He had to decide, then, how grossly human and vulgarly rounded he could stand the characters of fiction to be. Where could he draw the line—or expect a fellow artist to draw it? His decision was complicated by the saucy presence of Zola's fiction. James had thought at the outset that Zola was the chief offender in failing to make the distinction between "earthiness" and "dirtiness"; yet it is difficult to say just how he would have defined the two terms himself.

His initial response to Zola, in an essay of 1876, ranks him as "the most thoroughgoing" of the realist group but expresses little sympathy: "Unfortunately, the real for him, means exclusively the unclean, and he utters his crudities with an air of bravado, which makes him doubly intolerable."[12] By the beginning of 1877, he can recommend Zola's latest novel to Howells—if his stomach can stand it. But the appearance of *L'Assommoir* later that year made an indelible and favorable impression on James, so that while he must still regret the grossness he can recommend it as "a literary performance; you must be tolerably clever to appreciate it."[13] And so it went, until by the end of the decade James would exclaim, in an enthusiastic letter to Perry, that there is just nobody like Zola![14] Yet even in that letter the dubious distinction between earthiness and dirtiness raises its dusky head. "Zola's naturalism is ugly & dirty, but he seems to me to be *doing something*—which surely (in the imaginative line) no one in England or the U.S. is,—& no one else here."

The note of reluctance, certainly, is still discernible: James is still uncomfortable with the ugliness and especially with the dirtiness. He must have recognized, however, that the line between dirtiness and earthiness was a fine, if not an invisible one. It would therefore have occurred to him that it was preferable, after all, to risk having both than to risk having neither—that if one had to accept the ugly and dirty from an artist attempting to achieve a "vulgar roundness and relief" in his representation, he had better settle for that than risk having a spineless novel written with clean hands and a poor heart. So he praised the achievement and kept quiet about the dirt: he did not want to lose the baby with the bath water.

When, in 1881, Zola established himself and literary Naturalism as a *fait accompli* with the triple publication of *Nana, Le Roman expéri-mental,* and *Les Soirées de Médan,* James took generous account of the impressive fact. His review of *Nana,* naughty sequel to the impos-ing *L'Assommoir,* apparently exhibits a somewhat ambivalent atti-tude; for while he acknowledges Zola's accomplishment he takes him to task for the "monstrous uncleanness" of the novel. The reason for his objection, however, is that not his moral sense but his aesthetic sense has been offended:

The figure of the brutal *fille,* without a conscience or a soul, with nothing but devouring appetites and impudences, has become the stalest of the stock properties of French fiction, and M. Zola's treat-ment has here imparted to her no touch of superior verity. He is welcome to draw as many figures of the same type as he finds neces-sary, if he will only make them human; this is as good a way of making a contribution to our knowledge of ourselves as another. It is not his choice of subject that has shocked us; it is the melancholy dryness of his execution, which gives us all the bad taste of a disagreeable dish and none of the nourishment.[15]

Now it is easy to see behind this sort of comment the same man who objected to Charles de Bernard for having no morality. It is likewise apparent that here James is again talking about his own sense of *the moral.* The very terms in the two passages are the same. He might well have coupled Zola with Bernard as another member of the family of Le Sage: "their observation has no reflex action, as it were, and they remain as dry [nota] as they are brilliant."[16] Or he might have said, taking up his phrase on Flaubert in the same essay, that *Nana* does not "provoke serious meditation." The difference is, of course, that with Zola the "dish" is typically a much stronger concoction than that brewed by either Bernard or Flaubert; but we feel a willingness in James to gulp it bravely down, dirt and all, provided only that it prove nourishing. He explained to Perry that

Zola had both faults and merits, but as the latter are "rare, valuable, extremely solid," it seems unimportant to discuss the faults. To resume the metaphor, James will accept the dirty bath water for the sake of not losing the baby. That metaphor seems particularly apt when we consider James's further comment in the letter to Perry: "You say that literature is going down in the U.S.A. I agree with you —the stuff that is sent me seems to me to be written by eunuchs and sempstresses."[17] Eunuchs indeed! No bath water, but no baby either.

So James made his slightly qualified peace with Zola and his Naturalistic fiction. Within a couple of years' time he will be able to give a favorable nod even to the ugliness and dirtiness that had bothered him. In his essay on Daudet in 1883, he remarks that Zola's sense of the ugly, the unclean, is at times very valuable in his fiction. This marks a definite advance. But the essay has other indications of James's steadily increasing approval of Naturalism and the Naturalist and Realist writers; it shows a perfectly unqualified acceptance of what he found to be the most appealing brand of Naturalism—the "poetic" Naturalism of Alphonse Daudet.[18]

The series of James's responses to Daudet's fiction exhibits (as we might expect) a development of attitude that distinctly parallels the development of his attitude to Zola's. It also illustrates the particular attraction for James of the poetic quality in Daudet's Naturalism. His first published notice was a very unfavorable review of *Fromont Jeune et Risler aîné* in 1875. He begins by identifying Daudet as a realist and observing that his aspiration indicates that "the appetite for this sort of thing in France has not yet begun to fail. We think it a pity...." The pity is, to be sure, largely a moral pity (conventionally speaking) that the nasty stuff some Frenchmen were producing continued to enjoy a vogue. The novel in question narrates the career of Sidonie Chèbe, "a young woman of depraved and licentious instincts." James huffs on righteously in this vein, demanding whether the edifying and entertaining properties of such a subject have not, egad, really been exhausted. Perhaps he reaches the nadir when he enquires with supercilious rhetoric: "If we are to write the natural history of the prostitute on this extended scale, on what scale shall we handle that of her betters?"[19]

As time passed and James's understanding kept pace with his inherent tendencies, he began to discover in Daudet a truly delightful talent—that quality which Zola had abruptly recognized in his laconic estimate: "Avant tout, c'est un poète."[20] In 1882, he distin-

guishes Daudet from his French colleagues as a note-taker, and in
doing so varies just slightly his earlier insistence on observing
imaginatively: Daudet *feels* as he sees, and expresses that feeling "in
quick, light irony, in jocosity, in poetry. . . . He discovers every where
the shimmer and murmur of the poetic."[21] The principal essay on
Daudet, in the following year, repeats the same appreciative tone:
Daudet achieves a most satisfactory fusion of the real and the poetic.
What he gives us, James affirms, is "the transmuted real"; and he adds
a poetic flourish of his own as he says it is "the fruit of a process that
adds to observation what a kiss adds to a greeting." It was perhaps
the effect of the poetic touch that helped James to alter his attitude
to the infamous Sidonie Chèbe. For in this later essay he returns to
that piece and, while still objecting to the little horror, he finds a
more mature explanation of his disgust. The new comment bears
comparison with his final estimate of Nana.

In *Fromont Jeune* . . . the horrid little heroine is a mechanical doll,
with nothing for the imagination to take hold of. . . . The reader's
quarrel with Sidonie Chèbe is not that she is bad, but that she is not
felt, as the aesthetic people say.[22]

One determining influence that helped James to accept the
Naturalist's unabashed frankness may have been the threat of the
imposition of moral legislation from the Grundys. He might himself
object to the extended treatment of prostitutes but, like Voltaire, he
would defend with his life the right of a novelist to undertake such
a treatment. In reviewing *La Fille Elisa* in 1877, he commends Goncourt's just condemnation of critics who would forbid the writer to
publish anything that could not be read by young ladies. And in his
essay on Turgenev, following the Russian's death, he fully sympa-
thizes with Turgenev's pointed observation that the demand for
moral concessions and abdications never comes from the artists
themselves. Serious art, James would maintain, has no concern with
the conventionally moral: it is irresponsible—or responsible only to
its own integrity as a faithful representation of actual life. The only
duty of a novel, he felt, was to be well written; that merit included
every other of which it was capable. Under that persuasion he might
certainly cherish even the boldest Naturalist novel, if only it were
artistically done.

This was the point, then, to which James had been brought during the years between his brief introduction to the grandsons of Balzac and the beginning of the decade of the eighties. It is the point from which he was about to embark upon the second period of his literary career. He had by this time come close to sharing fully the aesthetic persuasions of the Realist-Naturalist group. At the beginning of 1884, he would write to Howells of his current situation.

I have been seeing something of Daudet, Goncourt and Zola; and there is nothing more interesting to me now than the effort and experiment of this little group, with its truly infernal intelligence of art, form, manner—its intense artistic life. They do the only kind of work, today, that I respect; and in spite of their ferocious pessimism and their handling of unclean things, they are at least serious and honest. The floods of tepid soap and water which under the name of novels are being vomitted forth in England, seem to me, by contrast, to do little honour to our race.[23]

He had made his peace.

CHAPTER III

The Bostonians

The *Portrait of a Lady*, published in 1881, marks the end of James's first period; his second may properly be said to begin with the publication of his critical essay "The Art of Fiction" in 1884. There is a clear distinction between the two periods. During the first, James's fiction exhibits the dominant influence of Hawthorne. His subject, especially in his major fiction, is the International Theme, and the treatment is controlled by American sympathy and concern. All the early heroes—Roderick Hudson, Christopher Newman, Daisy Miller, Catherine Sloper, Isabel Archer—are American, and they are made to visit Europe so that their peculiar Americanism can be graphically defined and evaluated. The experience of Europe is always somewhat threatening, and our sympathies are for the most part with the vulnerable hero. (*The Europeans* merely shows the obverse of the same coin.) During the second period, the influence of Hawthorne is replaced by that of Zola, Daudet, Turgenev, and Maupassant. The International Theme is absent from his major fiction for two decades, just as he was himself absent from America for that length of time. American sympathy and concern are replaced by European as controlling features in the treatment.

Now *The Bostonians* may seem to be an exception to this. Its locale and all its characters are American. Yet the treatment is satiric; the attitude is objective and unsympathetic, as we might expect from an author who had left America for more congenial shores. The very nature of this novel is singularly appropriate for James's first major

42

work of his new phase: *The Bostonians* is more American in appearance than any of his other novels and at the same time more critical of his homeland. It most distinctly reinforces the break that James had made: it finished his business with "them" at home, so to speak, and cleared the ground for him to begin his new ventures. He had to show his unappreciative compatriots what he could do and that he was serious and capable as a dedicated artist.

In his notebook James referred to *The Bostonians* as "an attempt to show that I *can* write an American story."[1] That expression captures both the sense of showing the homefolks what they were losing in his expatriation and also the sense of determination to succeed professionally and make his mark in his chosen field. The note of determination further separates the second period of James's career from the first: he becomes much more definitely the professional, much more conscious of the position he must assume as a man of letters. His fortieth birthday (April 1883) had made him acutely aware that his youth was behind him, and that it was certainly time for him to establish himself in his career.

Signs that the first period was drawing to a close are visible in various of his writings during the late seventies. The note of farewell to early preoccupations is unmistakably discernible in his critical biography *Hawthorne* (American Men of Letters Series, 1879). The book is in part a graceful tribute to his first master, yet it takes fully into account what James then felt to be Hawthorne's principal weakness—his insufficient realism. The other theme that James develops largely in this book is the more serious and general failure of America to afford a sufficiently fertile milieu to nourish any but the most exceptional artistic talent. The artist's only solution to the problem posed by the barren native ground, James clearly implies, is expatriation. This problem had been stirring within him for some time. Early in 1871, for example, he wrote to Charles Eliot Norton complaining that America would yield its secrets only to a really grasping imagination—"This I think Howells lacks. (Of course *I* don't!)"[2]—and regretting that to write well of this country one must be really a master and "unfortunately one is less." Then his novel of 1875, *Roderick Hudson*, takes up the problem again and tries fictionally the solution of expatriation for its artist-hero. In his *Hawthorne* James spells out in devastating detail what he felt to be the emptiness of the American scene:

No sovereign, no court, no personal loyalty, no aristocracy, no church, no clergy, no army, no diplomatic service, no country gentlemen, no palaces, no castles, nor manors, nor old country houses, nor parsonages, nor thatched cottages, nor ivied ruins; no cathedrals, nor abbeys, nor little Norman churches; no great Universities nor public schools—no Oxford, nor Eton, nor Harrow; no literature, no novels, no museums, no pictures, no political society, no sporting class—no Epsom nor Ascot![3]

William Dean Howells, of course, was not in sympathy with his friend's unpatriotic strictures or with the idea that expatriation was at all indicated for an American artist. His review of *Hawthorne* took James to task for his pessimistic view of the situation. James's reply, in a letter at the beginning of 1880, reasserts his belief and gently tosses a challenge to Howells.

It is on manners, customs, usages, habits, forms, upon all these things matured and established that a novelist lives—they are the very stuff his work is made of; and in saying that in the absence of those 'dreary and worn out paraphernalia' which I enumerate as being wanting in American society, 'we have simply the whole of human life left,' you beg (to my sense) the question. I should say that we have just so much less of it as these same paraphernalia represent, and I think they represent an enormous quantity of it.[4]

James affirms that he will be refuted only by the appearance of an American novelist who really belongs in the company of Balzac and Thackeray. He commends Howells for not feeling the want of all the "paraphernalia" and adds, provocatively, "on the day you make your readers . . . do the same, you will be the American Balzac." (He surely felt that he had stacked the cards.)

Following his own advice, James set out for Paris in the autumn of 1875 to meet the writers of the young French school. It is sometimes thought, consequently, that the second phase of his career began with that sojourn. Edmund Gosse and after him William C. Frierson have contended that James's next novel, *The American*, represents his initial venture in the Naturalist mode as it inaugurates the Experimental novel in English.[5] But all the evidence indicates that the departure in 1875 was a false start. If it did take him a long step in the direction of his desired goal, he was nevertheless off the mark too soon. Whether he was aware of the fact or not, he was not yet quite ready to make the definite break he intended—and was indeed determined inevitably to make.

Now there is some evidence of French influence in James's work of the seventies, but that is comparatively minor and scarcely at all derived from the Flaubert group. Hawthorne remains the dominant influence in the first book James published, *A Passionate Pilgrim and Other Stories* (1875).[6] Of those stories, "The Last of the Valerii" shows some debt to Prosper Mérimée, but the allegorical theme derives from *The Marble Faun.* *Roderick Hudson* is also largely indebted to that novel, although it owes something to *L'Affaire Clémenceau* of Dumas *fils,* which James had reviewed for the *Nation* in 1886. *The American* benefits from James's having read Turgenev's *A Nest of Noblemen* (1858). But to call it the first experimental novel in English requires overlooking the cape-and-sword atmosphere that drenches its Gothic conclusion, and the strong echoes of the murky mystery of *The House of the Seven Gables,* which obviously mark it as Hawthornesque romance.

After the publication of *The American,* however, the Hawthorne influence does begin to wane. And at about that time James began work on *The Portrait of a Lady.*[7] There, Hawthorne has been replaced by George Eliot and Ivan Turgenev as principal contributing influences. In view of that change it might seem reasonable to consider *The Portrait* as marking the beginning of James's second period. Insofar as it is indebted to the work of the great English realist and a member of the Flaubert group, it does forecast what we can expect in James's future work. Yet it is quite distinctly the culmination of the work of his first period, and can most satisfactorily stand as the terminal opus of that period. To begin with, *The Portrait of a Lady* grew up amidst his early productive years: its inception coincided with the publication of *The American,* as a letter to his mother in 1878 clearly indicates. And from the moment of its inception James apparently knew that it would be a major work—the first master piece, which would bring to an end the years of apprentice and journeyman work, "those untried years" as he called them.[8] Furthermore a regular series of important events befell James between the years of that novel's publication and 1884, events which serve to mark a distinct break between the earlier time and the later, as they cut his immediate ties to his homeland and helped thrust him into the European literary scene.

Two of his admired colleagues in the field of fiction, Gustave Flaubert and George Eliot, died in 1881. That double loss seemed to have a double effect on him: it made him sensible of the fact that he was himself no longer young, and it encouraged him to return and attempt to reestablish the relationship with his own kin and country—as though to settle himself and be sure of his roots. Having completed *The Portrait* abroad, he returned to America. After some months at home he recorded in his notebooks the double effect I mention:

I am 37 years old, I have made my choice, and God knows that I have now no time to waste. My choice is the old world—my choice, my need, my life. . . . it is an inestimable blessing to me, and a rare good fortune, that the problem was settled long ago, and that I have now nothing to do but to act on the settlement.—My impressions here are exactly what I expected they would be, and I scarcely see the place, and feel the manners, the race, the tone of things, now that I am on the spot, more vividly than I did while I was still in Europe. My work lies there. . . . I feel as if my time were terribly wasted here![9]

In January, 1882, he was hastily summoned to Cambridge from a visit in Washington by word of his mother's final illness. Her death touched him deeply. It seemed to him as if the whole family structure had been shaken: "She was our life, she was the house, she was the keystone of the arch. She held us all together, and without her we are scattered reeds."[10] The structure was indeed tottering, for before the year was out James's father had also died. And the reeds were certainly scattered: the two younger boys had already left home and William was married. James's home was effectually broken up. Nothing now held him there, nothing now need hold him. He was completely free at last to realize his own solution to the old problem of the American artist's dilemma, free to undertake the journey of indefinite expatriation. He was certainly spurred on in that resolve by the unfavorable impression his native land had made upon him. References to the lack of taste and the poverty of manners, the generally uncongenial atmosphere, recur as a refrain of lamentation through the notebook entries during this time. It was, then, with a feeling of release that he finally set out at the end of the summer of 1883 for Europe—as much like one fleeing the thing he fears as like one seeking the thing he loves.

Another blow was to fall, however. On his arrival in England he was met with the news that his friend and colleague Ivan Turgenev was dead. In less than three years the three contemporary writers whom he most esteemed—two of them had influenced his latest novel—

were lost to him. That loss must have struck him sharply and encouraged him to draw even closer to those who remained as fellow workers in the same literary vineyard.

One more combination of circumstances completes the series of events which marks so definitely the line between James's first and second periods. To the generally unfavorable impression made upon him by the American scene was added the disappointment he experienced at the failure of his attempt at play-writing. During the months following his mother's death he adapted his popular *Daisy Miller* for the Madison Square Theater. The play was never produced. Here was a bitter pill to swallow, even though he tried to wash it down with the philosophical explanation to himself that he had, after all, learned a good deal about the theatrical world. The effect of that disappointment, fortunately, was not discouragement but a greater determination than ever to persevere in "experiments, in studies, in attempts," and to make his mark as a man of letters. "I see many opportunities ahead," he wrote in his notebook; "I must make some great efforts during the next few years. . . ."[11]

James was further encouraged in his determination to become a successful professional artist by the example of Zola, whose Naturalism was by this time (1884) in command of the literary scene in Europe. James was now ready to enter that scene and, if possible, to play a stellar role. Early that year he wrote from Paris to tell William of his activity and especially of his renewed association with the members of the Flaubert group: "Seeing these people does me a world of good, and this intellectual vivacity and *raffinement* make an English mind seem like a sort of glue-pot."[12] When Walter Besant's essay on fiction appeared as part of the current discussion of prose fiction, it seemed to James that the moment he had been waiting for had arrived—the moment for entering the lists in a really professional way. He wrote, in reply to Besant, his own essay on "The Art of Fiction." Its nature and scope boldly announce the position he had arrived at and show the emergence of the influence he had absorbed. With this crucial essay he distinctly inaugurated the second period of his career.

This period, which continues until James's entry into the theater in 1890, really divides into two halves. The earlier half features the critical essay "The Art of Fiction," and two major novels, *The Bostonians* and *The Princess Casamassima* (published simultaneously in 1886), as well as several important pieces of short fiction. The latter half includes the significant critical essay "Guy de Maupassant" (1888), and the major novel *The Tragic Muse* (1890), and also some short fiction. These later years, 1887-90, are distinguished from the earlier half of the period by evidence of the resurgence of James's interest in the theater and a discernible shift or modification in aesthetic theory. But the whole period is very much of a piece, and this separation into two halves serves mainly as a convenience for discussion.

"The Art of Fiction"

What has come to be recognized as James's most important single essay was originally published in *Longman's* magazine in September 1884. A rejoinder to Besant's discourse on the same subject, it is of course somewhat polemical in nature; and it provoked in its turn a reply from Robert Louis Stevenson, "A Humble Remonstrance." James's reaction to this last was to write very cordially to Stevenson, suggesting (quite correctly) that the two of them were in more agreement than disagreement. He modestly explained also that his pages in *Longman's* were only half of what he had to say, that he was merely making a plea for liberty against Besant's restrictions on the writer. The truth is, however, that the essay touches on much more than the modest "half" of the aesthetic question James granted in his letter to Stevenson.

The various points he makes in the essay may be fairly subsumed under the two headings Freedom and Responsibility. His opening gambit is to object to Besant's "attempting to say so definitely beforehand what sort of an affair the good novel will be."[13] James maintains that we can properly hold the novel to but one obligation, and that is that it be interesting. He clearly accepts Zola's definition of a work of art as "un coin de la création vue à travers un tempérament." And he would encourage the reader to recognize the valid implication in that—that writers, like other individuals, differ, and must therefore be expected to see life in their own somewhat peculiar way. The reader must be willing, then, to let writers be themselves and to grant them their own *personal* impression of life—that is, to see what they *can* see. We dare not legislate what a writer may or may not see, what he may or may not write about, if we expect honesty. Grant the writer his freedom of choice, James urges, and let him write as he wishes. And here he is echoing Zola's plea, "Par grâce! laissez-le écrire comme bon lui semble." Let him do what he wants; judge him on how he makes it turn out. Critical appraisal, apparently, is to concern itself with technique—with how, not what, things are done.

James insists that the province of art is all life, all feeling, all observation, all vision. In doing so, he is obliged to confront again the question he had wrestled with earlier (and not always successfully) —the question of morality and art. He begins with an attack on Besant's praise of novels that display a "conscious moral purpose" and the implied condemnation of "immoral" novels. He claims flatly that in a discussion of aesthetics the moral question is out of place: questions of art are questions of execution, the question of morals is another affair. Suppose you wanted to paint a moral picture, he asks; how would you go about it? He points out that the confusion of the moral with the aesthetic results in the so-called "good" novel, which features the Happy-ending and distributive justice. The trouble with such novels, obviously, is that they are simply untrue to life. Ironically, then, the "good" novel is the result of moral weakness and appeals to moral cowardice: it masks the truth of life. James thus maneuvers himself into a position whence he can turn the tables on Besant and his novel of conscious moral purpose; he can level the charge of immorality against the "good" novel, by pointing to its moral dishonesty. And worse, the moral dishonesty is compounded by moral hypocrisy: there is a traditional difference, he maintains, between "that which people know and that which they agree to admit they know, . . . that which they feel to be a part of life and that which they allow to enter into literature."[14] This is the line Zola took in his defense of *Germinie Lacerteux:* "Le crime est donc d'avoir dit tout haut ce que beaucoup d'autres pensent tout bas." Real moral energy is exhibited by the artist who will survey the whole field of life and report it honestly.

James adds one condition to this argument. He does not want to be understood to say that subject does not matter. Like Turgenev, for example, he would maintain that there are trivial subjects and serious subjects; the virtue of the latter (and this is almost their definition) is that they give a greater amount of information about the human mind. Nevertheless, to return to the important matter of artistic freedom, one must not try to urge upon the writer this or that subject as being "serious," or to prohibit him from touching others as being "trivial." He makes the observation that the deepest quality of a work of art will always be the quality of the artist's mind. And that, James feels, sufficiently covers the moral question.

Quite apparently, the aesthetic assumption prompting this plea for liberty is that the business of the art of fiction is to capture and present life as it really is. That assumption is explicitly stated several times in the essay. If the novelist is to represent life faithfully, he must of course be free to look at all of it—to see life steadily and whole. The documents of fiction, James says, are precisely those of history; they are life as it is lived. To catch the very note and trick of life is the novelist's business, and he does well to make generous use of his notebook to record what he observes. Once observed, life must be fully and faithfully rendered, made visible and palpable and audible: "the air of reality (solidity of specification) seems to me to be the supreme virtue of a novel—the merit on which all its other merits . . . depend."[15]

In such passages as this we detect the tone of voice of the man who had found Hawthorne not enough of a realist, who had assisted at the discussions among the "votaries of realism" at Flaubert's, who had seen Zola (for example) with his reams of notes taken *sur le vif* in preparation for some new piece of fiction. Yet there are two refinements to the recognized argument that we must not fail to notice; first, that James cherishes the *selective* eye of the observant artist. He does not ask for mere reproduction, but for the creation of "the illusion of life." Second, he requires that the selective eye be guided by the idea that fiction creates that illusion with a view to *interpretive* expression. The artist attempts to render the look of things, to be sure, but above all "the look that conveys their meaning." James's principle is that fiction must give its reader as nearly as possible the impression that life itself gives, but most important it must give the something more that makes that life seem understandable. Fiction must create a meaningful and significant impression of reality.[16]

Finally James has several words to say about the integrity of the work of fiction—its organic nature and its ultimate independence from its creator. He decries the critical tendency which fragments the novel by distinguishing too sharply among description, dialogue, narration, incident, etc. He claims that he cannot conceive of description which is not in intention narrative, of dialogue which is not descriptive, and so on: all the parts function together in being what he calls "illustrative." A novel, James insists, "is a living thing, all one and continuous, like any other organism, and in proportion as it lives will it be found, I think, that in each of the parts there is something of each of the other parts."[17] What he is driving at, of course, is not so much the reciprocal aid of the various parts functioning together, as rather the inviolable wholeness of the work of fiction. Each piece of the novel contributes to the expression of the idea that is itself, in turn, inseparable from the means which express it. Form and content are one.

The organic integrity of the novel enables it to stand alone, to be self-expressive, dramatically immediate. It tells you nothing; it merely shows you what it is. "Soyons exposants et non discutants," Flaubert had exhorted his fellow writers. James agreed. His particular horror was the novelist who violated the integrity of his work by intruding himself as the omniscient and omnipotent author. Such violation was not simply an aesthetic fault, it was virtually a moral fault: it was the refusal to take the art of fiction seriously. The author's intrusion will seem to plead for the work he has created and at the same time, paradoxically, it will deny the very vitality it might have had. Let him keep his hands off, James urges; let the created being stand alone and alive. And once again we can detect the aesthetic principles of Flaubert behind this attitude of James's—that familiar principle which demands that the artist be invisible and all-powerful in his work, like God in His creation, *qu'on ne le voie pas!*

The essay concludes with a rousing word of encouragement to the aspiring young writer, gathering up the various points it has raised and reasserting its twin themes of Freedom and Responsibility. "All life belongs to you . . . try and catch the colour of life itself . . . your first duty is to be as complete as possible—to make as perfect a work."

"The Art of Fiction" is an important document in James's career: it is a formal and "professional" statement of aesthetic principle which indicates unequivocally his attitude to his craft at that crucial moment of his development. It indicates furthermore that the influence of the Flaubert group is alive and active in his thoughts. During the months which preceded the composition and publication of this essay, James was deeply involved in the preparation of the two major novels which begin his new phase of artistic endeavour. A logical expectation is that he was preparing them in accordance with the very principles enunciated in "The Art of Fiction." He thought highly of the two novels in preparation and had great hopes for them. To his friend Perry he described them as "the two best things I have done."[18] The two best things were *The Bostonians* and *The Princess Casamassima.*

II

In April of 1883, just a few months before he was to embark on indefinite expatriation, James set down in his notebook the transcription of a letter to his publisher, Osgood. It briefly described a new novel, as yet nameless, about the American scene—particularly Boston. He had been gathering the material for this novel almost unconsciously during most of his adult life, and he had been storing up impressions more or less consciously since his return to America late in 1881. According to his notebooks, the impressions were on the whole what he had anticipated—unfavorable. They confirmed in him, as I say, the determination to escape his native shores as soon as possible. These noted impressions persist in their unflattering nature and seem a fitting introduction to his plan of the new novel. It would be a remorseless exploitation of Boston. In the sketch he sent to Osgood, James explains that his intention is to write a very *American* tale, very characteristic. The most salient and peculiar feature of American social life, he has decided is "the situation of women, the decline of the sentiment of sex, the agitation on their behalf."[19]

Among the principal characters of the novel there is, first of all, a severe young spinster, Olive Chancellor, of solid, well-to-do, bourgeois Boston stock, very sensitive and "high-strung" and chiefly alert to the demands of Duty. She is keenly (if not hysterically) interested in the woman's movement. Her distant cousin from Mississippi, Basil Ransom, is her opposite in every respect; he is the easy mannered, conservative Southern gentleman, rather impoverished from the recent civil war, and decidedly masculine in outlook and interests. Between these two principal characters is introduced the heroine of the novel, Verena Tarrant. The letter to Osgood describes her as "a daughter of old abolitionists, spiritualists, transcendentalists, etc." She is young, innocent, naive, and attractive; her special talent is "inspirational" speaking. The three principals meet early in the novel at the home of Miss Birdseye, an ineffectual, disorganized little old woman who subscribes to all causes and at whose domicile a small group of the devotees of the woman's movement have gathered. Verena is persuaded to speak inspirationally on the subject of female emancipation. Basil Ransom finds her very appealing, personally— not as a speaker. And Olive Chancellor is completely overwhelmed by the sapphic creature. She effectively takes Verena under her wing; she wants to protect and develop her, ostensibly that she may better serve the cause, but clearly also because she is strongly attracted personally to the girl.

Here is the eternal triangle, similar to Sartre's version of it in *Huis Clos*, which provides the frame of the story. Olive appeals to Verena's sense of devotion and duty, both to the movement and to Olive herself. She has virtually purchased the girl from her mountebank father, Dr. Selah Tarrant, a mesmeric healer; and she demands of Verena that she renounce all usual worldly affections and limit herself exclusively to the woman's movement. Her general demand is couched, appropriately, in Mephistophelian terms: "Entsagen sollst du, sollst entsagen!" Her specific demand of Verena is "Promise me not to marry!"[20] Under Olive's jealous influence and guidance Verena enjoys the beginning of a promising career as an inspirational speaker.

At every turn Basil Ransom pays his unambiguous addresses to Verena. He thinks a great deal of her; tells her flatly that the woman's movement and her connection with it are all humbug and nonsense; wants her to be his own private inspiration as Mrs. Ransom. The contest between Olive and Basil reflects the dramatic conflict within Verena herself, who discovers more and more as the novel progresses that her own inclination is toward Ransom. And the novel concludes with the coincidence of her recognition of that inclination, the truth of her own heart, and Ransom's final determination to grasp what he wants. He seizes and carries off the willing Verena from the very scene of her most promising public performance, leaving the frantic Olive holding the bag.

The novel does full satiric justice to its intended "remorseless exploitation" of the vulgar world of publicity and the newspapers. Selah Tarrant and the effeminate Matthias Pardon serve that purpose admirably. It also gives effective dramatic expression of the horror of the powerful force of money as a tool for exploitation and manipulating human beings. And it exposes to ridicule the queer assortment of reformers and agitators who flutter and cringe ineffectually through its pages. As James had planned, *The Bostonians* is "a tale purely American" and full of the impressions he had gathered at first hand. It is a bit surprising, then, to read in his notebook the flat and unequivocal statement "Daudet's *Evangéliste* has given me the idea of this thing."[21] That indebtedness is reiterated, at least by implication, in subsequent notes for the novel.[22] There has been a general reluctance to take James at his word (although there is no reason why one always should in such matters). Some critics feel that James got nothing but the initial impulse from Daudet's novel; others suggest that the note itself is a distraction and claim that his real debt is to Hawthorne's *The Blithedale Romance;* and most recently it has been suggested that Howells' *Dr. Breen's Practice* and even the *Antigone* are the likeliest sources.[23]

Now it is not by any means an easy matter to say with certainty just what materials buzzing in an artist's mind were actually the elements responsible for inspiring a given work. In the present case, however, if we compare the finished novel with the works mentioned above we may be able to arrive at some clear notion of the contributive literary elements. All the works listed, as well as one or two heretofore overlooked, may have had a share in the matter. For all are concerned with some of the main themes and interests of *The Bostonians:* the theme of strong personal influence—mesmerism, animal magnetism, or whatever; movements for reform; the conflict between the impulse of human love and the demand of duty to a cause or to a particular person—parent, close companion, etc.

The Blithedale Romance has a strong claim to our attention. Points of similarity to *The Bostonians* suggest themselves at once. The familiar central triangle involving Zenobia, Priscilla, and Hollingsworth, and the remarkable relationship of the two women are set against the background of reform movements—both the social experiment at Blithedale and Hollingsworth's program of rehabilitation. There is further the matter of mesmeric influence in which Westervelt, Zenobia, and the Veiled Lady are mysteriously concerned, and the strange influence that Zenobia exerts willy-nilly on the passive Priscilla. The significance of these similarities is sharply curtailed, however, when we consider their component parts in detail. A second look at the pair of women in each novel reveals a marked difference between them—the stern and severe Olive Chancellor is quite unlike the luscious Zenobia, and the vital and vibrant Verena has little in common with the pale and submissive Priscilla. The nature of the personal influence in question here is also different in the two stories: —almost diametrically opposed in effect. Zenobia's influence on Priscilla threatens (and that, surely, is the proper verb) to humanize the girl, to turn her into a real flesh-and-blood woman capable of actually loving and being loved by Hollingsworth. Olive's influence threatens to turn Verena away from any such possibility. In one or two instances Hollingsworth seems to forecast Basil Ransom. He expresses a sentiment, once, that Ransom constantly affirms: he says to Zenobia, "woman is the most admirable handiwork of God, in her true place and character. Her place is at man's side. . . ."[24]And his act of snatching Priscilla away from her public appearance is like Ransom's carrying off Verena at the close of *The Bostonians*. But that act by no means resolves the problem in *Blithedale*, as it gratefully does in James's novel. Hollingsworth's winning of Priscilla can hardly be taken to represent a triumph—certainly not a triumph over the forces that contribute to the decline of the sentiment of sex; quite the contrary! Priscilla is surely the most unwomanly woman to escape from Hawthorne's pen, and Hollingsworth's union with her seems to leave him a broken man. It is almost as though she were his "snow image," brought indoors. Ransom's bold gesture, on the other hand, promises to bring him the enjoyment of a vigorous if not opulent life with his delightfully feminine Verena. And their union unquestionably means a triumph over the reformers' mistaken zeal, a reaffirmation of the sentiment of sex.

Similarities there are; the danger is to claim too much for them. Too great a claim will blind us to the contribution which several other stories may have made to the creation of *The Bostonians*. For example, two short stories: Turgenev's "A Strange Story" (1869) and James's own "Professor Fargo" (1874), which is indebted to it, are both concerned with "animal magnetism." Turgenev's tale is about the magnetic influence which the hero Vasily, a religious fanatic, wields over Mademoiselle Sophie, daughter of a Russian noble: he persuades her to leave the comfort of hearth and home and to accompany him in his crusade and share in his hardships. In James's story, the "spiritual magnetism" of Professor Fargo succeeds in winning the deafmute daughter of Colonel Gifford away from her father's clutches. The ingredients of the father-daughter couple and of mesmeric influence, particularly in "Professor Fargo," are much nearer to what we find in *The Bostonians* than are the comparable features of *Blithedale*.

In making his case for the contribution of Howells' *Dr. Breen's Practice*, Mr. Oscar Cargill points out that it was coupled with *The Portrait of a Lady* in a review in 1881, and argues that it therefore could well have been in James's mind when he was planning his next novel, *The Bostonians*. The heroine of the title is a "doctoress," like James's little Dr. Mary J. Prance, and she also has an admiring ladyfriend. The relationship between the two ladies, however, promises

nothing like what we find in James's novel; and there are no other
notable similarities. There is another of Howells' novels, published a
year earlier than *Dr. Breen's Practice,* which has been overlooked as
a contributive influence on *The Bostonians: The Undiscovered Country* had at least as much to offer James as any of the other stories
mentioned above.

In *The Undiscovered Country* we find the father-daughter pair: Dr.
Boynton exercises mesmeric influence over his charming Egeria.
There is also the lover of Egeria, young Ford, who is comparable in
many respects to Basil Ransom; he is quiet, handsome, and of modest
means, and he aspires to be a writer. The novel has no counterpart
to Olive Chancellor, but a similar antagonist element is provided by
the community of celibate Shakers into which Egeria is placed and
from which Ford must persuade her to fly into his arms. Like Ransom,
Ford offers his beloved the delights of normal human love and marriage; like Ransom he has to contend with the antipathetic pressure
exerted on her to renounce such pleasure. Howells convinces us that
Egeria was "made for love," as James would write of Verena,[25] and
that she does perfectly right in finally accepting her lover—as we feel
of Verena's acceptance of Ransom. The dramatic situation, the principal concerns of the plot, and the thematic emphasis of *The Undiscovered Country* are quite close to what we find in *The Bostonians;*
and the number of points of similarity in character and structure is
greater in this instance than in any of the others we have considered.

Surely all these stories were simmering genially in the crucible
which brewed *The Bostonians.* Yet James claimed flatly that Daudet's *Evangéliste* had given him the idea of the thing. Now *L'Evangéliste* is the story of a fresh and appealing young woman, Eline
Ebsen, the dutiful daughter of a widowed mother. She is dearly loved
by a *petit-fonctionnaire,* M. Lorie-Dufresne, to whom she is attracted
and for whose motherless children she feels a great fondness. As
Verena Tarrant is "made for love" so was Eline "née pour la matér-
nité."[26] But just as the promise of fulfillment of Lorie-Dufresne's
hopes and of Eline's natural and wholesome bent seems on the way
to realization, there is introduced the bleak and nefarious influence
of the reforming crusade of Mme Jeanne Autheman and her *dames
évangélistes.* Mme Autheman takes Eline from her home and her
lover, and exercises a fierce and ruthless sort of persuasion on her to
win her for the evangelistic cause. James had objected to Daudet's
development of Jeanne Autheman—

She seems to me terribly, almost grotesquely void. She is an elaborate portrait of a fantastic Protestant, a bigot to the point of monstrosity, cold-blooded, implacable, cruel. . . . But Mme Autheman strikes me as quite automatic; psychologically she is a blank. One does not see the operation of her character. She must have a soul, and a very curious one. . . . but we know nothing about Mme Autheman's inner springs, and I think we fail to believe in her.[27]

Her similarity to Olive Chancellor is nevertheless striking. Although, unlike Olive, she is married, her wedded state only serves to reinforce the bitter irony of her pronounced antipathy to men. Jeanne's influence on Eline is calculated to harden the girl against the attractions of men—indeed, against all associations that involve human love. Her guiding principle is, like Olive's, that of renunciation: "Ce qu'il [Jesus Christ] exige, c'est un renoncement complet aux splendeurs, au bien-être, à toutes les affections du monde."[28] Her specific exhortation much stronger than Olive's "Promise me not to marry," is the laconic "N'aimez point!"[29]

In both novels the reform movements which Jeanne and Olive represent respectively are inhuman and perverse in their conscious endeavor to stifle the passion of normal human love. Jeanne's influence as the arch opponent of love is pervasive: it is directly responsible for the suicide of her generous and unfortunate husband; it wrenches the lamenting Welshwoman away from her husband and children; it separates the faithful servant Sylvanire from her devoted Romain the locks-keeper; and it tears Eline away from her mother and her beloved Lorie-Dufresne. Further emphasis to this theme is dramatically given by the Reverend Assandon and his somewhat shrewish wife; he is the only character in the novel who can register any effective gesture of opposition to Jeanne Autheman. He denies her the sacraments in his church. As a result of this intrepidness he regains the love of his wife, although he has clearly lost all else; but what doth it profit a man . . . ?

The power of Mme Autheman results from the tremendous wealth of the Autheman bankers, which she has inherited. Significantly, the power of money is prominently employed in the stifling of love. Jeanne Autheman's gold has as effectually bought Eline from her family as Olive Chancellor's payment to Selah Tarrant purchased Verena. Lorie-Dufresne is powerless against the Autheman forces, and he is defeated.

With this we come to the principal difference between the two novels. *L'Evangéliste* is in intention tragic, while *The Bostonians* is comic satire. But the truth each novel variously expresses is, at bottom, one. Daudet could count on his readers' recognition of the tragedy in the defeat of normal human love by the strange force of the fanatic Protestant, who employed to this end the gold won by the money-lending family of Jewish Authemans. James would have to persuade his readers of the rightness of Ransom's triumph over the perverse forces of the woman's movement; that he would attempt by rendering as recognizably absurd the votaries of the movement and by suggesting (and none too subtly) the streak of perversion in Olive's attraction to the lovely Verena. A final difference between the two novels is, of course, the absence of the "magnetic" father in *L'Evangéliste.*

Yet the similarities—major themes and emphasis, the nature and arrangement of principal characters, and the features of the central dramatic conflict—are numerous and striking. In most respects, *The Bostonians* is much closer to Daudet's novel than to any of the other stories (individually or in combination) mentioned above as contributive influences. This fact encourages acceptance of James's simple admission of specific indebtedness to Daudet. There is, however, one additional characteristic of *The Bostonians* which further heightens its resemblance to *L'Evangéliste;* it was written under the general influence of French literary Naturalism—it is James's initial attempt to write a novel in the naturalistic mode.

We might consider *The Bostonians* under three principal headings. There is, first, the attempt to situate the action in a recognizable and convincing "here and now." The events narrated in the novel are supposed to have taken place during the decade which preceded its publication, and the scenes of action are represented with a sufficient abundance and accuracy of detail to create the "palpable provable world" of Balzacian or of Naturalistic fiction. Also, more attention is now given to accurate description of characters—their appearance, gestures, clothing, mannerisms of speech—and of the particular setting in which they live and function than is to be found in James's earlier work. The intention is, of course, to give density to the people and places, to the slice of life with which the novel is concerned. Secondly, there is the technical aspect of the novel, those devices which James employed to increase the illusion of reality in his fiction by representing life "without rearrangement" as far as possible and by fashioning the novel to give it as selfsufficient an air as he could —to make the novel "tell itself," dramatically and without apparent manipulation and explanatory intrusion. And third, there is in the novel's attention to the heredity of its heroine and the related environmental influences, the strong implication of James's interest in Zola's conception of the novel as an experiment.

To begin with James's representation of his characters, we notice that the novel opens with a description of the principal male character, Basil Ransom, followed within half a dozen pages by descriptions of Olive Chancellor and her sister, Adeline Luna. Two features of these and subsequent delineations of character are that they are by no means simply detailed factual catalogues: James's creative imagination always plays about the more important details and enlivens them with impressionistic support. And further, the descriptions are always strategically placed with a view to the novel's total effect and to its principal business: they are placed according to their calculated function in the organic whole that is the novel. Here, then, is Basil Ransom as he presents himself initially to Mrs. Luna. And it is important that the initial view of him be hers, for, as we soon learn, she is the type of woman who has an eye for the male figure.

Mrs. Luna glanced at him from head to foot, and gave a little smiling sigh, as if he had been a long sum in addition. And, indeed, he was very long, Basil Ransom, and he even looked a little hard and discouraging, like a column of figures, in spite of the friendly face which he bent upon his hostess's deputy, and which, in its thinness, had a deep dry line, a sort of premature wrinkle, on either side of the mouth. He was tall and lean, and dressed throughout in black; his shirt collar was low and wide, and the triangle of linen, a little crumpled, exhibited by the opening of his waistcoat, was adorned by a pin containing a small red stone. In spite of this decoration the young man looked poor—as poor as a young man could look who had such a fine head and such magnificent eyes. Those of Basil Ransom were dark, deep, and glowing; his head had a character of elevation which fairly added to his stature; it was a head to be seen above the level of a crowd, on some judicial bench or political platform, or even on a bronze medal. His forehead was high and broad, and his thick black hair, perfectly straight and glossy, and without any division, rolled back from it in a leonine manner. These things, the eyes especially, with their smouldering fire, might have indicated that he was to be a great American statesman; or, on the other hand, they might simply have proved that he came from Carolina or Alabama. He came, in fact, from Mississippi, and he spoke perceptively with the accent of that country.... This lean, pale, sallow, shabby, striking young man, with his superior head, his sedentary shoulders, his expression of bright grimness and hard enthusiasm, his provincial, distinguished appearance, is, as a representative of his sex, the most important personage in my narrative.[30]

There, quite solidly specified, is Ransom—his stature and posture, his dress (including the simple assertation of the small red stone), his face and head in striking detail. The portrait is heightened by illustrative comment and simile which are double-edged, that is they are descriptive yet subtly evaluative at the same time. To emphasize the "character of elevation" of his head, James writes, "it was a head to be seen above the level of a crowd"; and that not only indicates rather extraordinary height, but also subtly suggests figurative superiority as well. And his pompadour coiffure, "in a leonine manner," manages to lend something of leonine strength of purpose and nobility to the head, as well as a clearer notion of its appearance. The sentence full of near oxymoron which concludes the quotation above, is a fitting complementary statement to balance the introductory simile: he is a bit puzzling, but in an attractive way, to Mrs. Luna— and to the reader, who is caught up by the paradoxical figure and is eager to learn more.

We know how he looks and have seen his first gesture—which is itself revealing of character—that of picking up a book. James concludes his introductory picture of Ransom by giving us a notion of his speech: "he prolonged his consonants and swallowed his vowels, ... was guilty of elisions and interpolations, and ... his discourse was pervaded by something sultry and vast, something almost African in its rich, basking tone, something that suggested the teeming expanse of the cotton field."

The first paragraph of chapter two contains the initial portrait of Olive Chancellor—or rather the first draft of her portrait, to which touches will be added later. For it is not given to us in a block, as Ransom's was, but is interspersed with comments on her movements and on Ransom's thoughts about her. Of course her actions and gestures are part of her development in the story. This is her appearance to Ransom:

She was habited in a plain dark dress, without any ornaments, and her smooth, colorless hair was confined as carefully as that of her sister was encouraged to stray. She had instantly seated herself, and,

while Mrs. Luna talked she kept her eyes on the ground. . . . this pale
girl, with her light-green eyes, her pointed features and nervous
manner, was visibly morbid; it was as plain as day that she was
morbid. Poor Ransom announced this fact to himself as if he had
made a great discovery. . . .[31]

The plainness and colorlessness and nervous severity of the young
spinster emerge distinctly from this comparatively brief sketch. The
sketch is subsequently filled in by such touches as that provided a few
pages later, which tells us that Olive was "refined" but chilling: her
sharp physiognomic features and especially her eyes, that suggest
"the glitter of green ice," are complemented by the detail "She had
absolutely no figure, and presented a certain appearance of feeling
cold."[32] This is the figure who is to stand for the perverseness of the
woman's movement—the chill, unmarried, strikingly single, young
Bostonian who represents principally the decline of the sentiment of
sex. Ransom is later to think, "Olive Chancellor's sex (what sex was
it, great heaven? he used profanely to ask himself)."[33]

But the portrait is not complete until it is framed, or rather until
it is placed against an appropriate background. Like the Naturalists,
James felt that the setting, the particular milieu in which a character
is placed, should be a significant part of the characterization—that it
should be a sort of continuation of the character and should thus
further explain him. Thus, we find Olive, the typical Bostonian, at
home to receive her cousin Basil; and as the third chapter opens we
are given a description of her parlor. It is not a very full description,
but the salient details are significant: the numerous books—"everywhere, on little shelves like brackets (as if a book were a statuette)"
—placed as though to be looked *at* (as distinct from *into*) and even
perhaps to be worshipped, the curtains festooned "stiffly," the attraction to German rather than French—a detail rich in subtle
suggestion of the manly and rigorous teutonic spirit rather than of the
more feminine pliability of the romantic.[34] The details of her parlor
augment our impression of Olive, and we can share Ransom's impression: "he had never seen an interior that was so much an interior as
this queer corridor-shaped drawing-room."[35] Even more richly
suggestive is the view from Olive's parlor window. It is a view that
strikes us as realistically accurate, as convincing; we feel that it quite
satisfactorily situates Olive in Boston, on the Back Bay. Yet it is at the
same time clearly enough an extension of her—reflects directly upon
her character and develops it further for us: it is indeed Olive's view,

her peculiar view not only of Boston but of the world in general.

The western windows of Olive's drawing room, looking over the water, took in the red sunsets of winter; the long, low bridge that crawled, on its staggering posts, across the Charles; the casual patches of ice and snow; the desolate suburban horizons, peeled and made bold by the rigor of the season; the general hard, cold void of the prospect; the extrusion, at Charlestown, at Cambridge, of a few chimneys and steeples, straight, sordid tubes of factories and engine-shops, or spare, heavenward finger of the New England meeting house. There was something inexorable in the poverty of the scene, shameful in the meanness of its details, which gave a collective impression of boards and tin and frozen earth, sheds and rotting piles, railway lines striding flat across a thoroughfare of puddles, and tracks of the humbler, the universal horsecar, traversing obliquely this path of danger; loose fences, vacant lots, mounds of refuse, yards bestrewn with iron pipes, telegraph poles, and bare wooden backs of places.[36]

James achieves here something very like the effect T. S. Eliot sought in his brief line—"Rocks, moss, stonecrop, iron, merds." The chill, spare, desolate, rotten scene is, once again, Olive's view; its effectiveness is in its reflexive illumination of her character; it completes the bleak Miss Chancellor.

Verena Tarrant, the third of the three principal characters of the novel, appears on the scene late in chapter four. But her description is withheld until the dramatically appropriate moment—the occasion of her first performance in the novel as an inspirational speaker. Then, with all eyes upon her, and especially those of Basil and Olive, she is fully described. She is different, perhaps exotic, yet with an air of innocent freshness and naturalness, and quite attractive.

. . . she was certainly very pale, white as women are who have that shade of red hair; they look as if their blood had gone into it. There was, however, something rich in the fairness of this young lady; she was strong and supple, there was color in her lips and eyes, and her tresses, gathered into a complicated coil, seemed to glow with the brightness of her nature. She had curious, radiant, liquid eyes (their smile was a sort of reflection, like the glisten of a gem), and though she was not tall, she appeared to spring up, and carried her head as if it reached rather high. Ransom would have thought that she looked like an Oriental, if it were not that Orientals were dark; and if she had only had a goat she would have resembled Esmerelda. . . . She wore a light-brown dress, of a shape that struck him as fantastic, a yellow petticoat, and a large crimson sash fashioned at the side; while round her neck, and falling low upon her flat young chest, she had a double chain of amber beads.[37]

One of the strongest notes in the portrait is that of oddity, of a rather bizarre mixture of parts that don't match. We easily sympathize with Ransom's perplexity: "she had the sweetest, most unworldly face, and yet, with it, an air of being on exhibition. . . . If she had produced a pair of castanets or a tambourine, he felt that such accessories would have been quite in keeping."[38] The note of oddity is carried further, of course, by Verena's milieu, the Tarrant household. But the question of the proper setting for Verena is, after all, what the novel is all about.

Since the other two main characters in the novel are bent on winning Verena, each has reason to feel that she doesn't belong where she is. Olive Chancellor feels that the wonderful Verena is precisely the girl she has been looking for as a companion—a girl of the people. Verena is attractive because she is different, because she is fresh and innocent and spontaneously charming, and because she is passive and pliable; and then, as I say, she is a simple girl of the people—just what Olive's conscience requires. When she finally visits the Tarrant home—to see Verena in her peculiar setting—she finds it "as bad as she could have desired; desired in order to feel that (to take her out of such a *milieu* as that) she would have a right to draw her altogether to herself."[39] The milieu includes of course Verena's odd parents, the ineffectual and mildly pretentious mother, the leering and unctuous father in his eternal waterproof, as well as the very house itself, "Tarrant's temporary lair."

. . . a wooden cottage, with a rough front yard, a little naked piazza, which seemed rather to expose than to protect, facing upon an unpaved road, in which the footway was overlaid with a strip of planks. These planks were embedded in ice or in liquid thaw, according to the momentary mood of the weather, and the advancing pedestrian traversed them in the attitude, and with a good deal of the suspense, of a ropedancer. There was in the house nothing to speak of; nothing, to Olive's sense, but a smell of kerosene; though she had a consciousness of sitting down somewhere—the object creaked and rocked beneath her—and of the table at tea being covered with a cloth stamped in bright colors.[40]

A strong impression of the temporary, the unsubstantial, the illfounded and rickety, of the altogether precarious and miserable emerges sharply from this setting. It exactly catches the flavor of the whole Tarrant existence of seamy improvidence and crass humbuggery. And Verena's own relation to all of this is in one sense unreal —although she is quite innocent of that knowledge, as she is indeed of most. She is "submissive and unworldly,"[41] and accepts the only life she has known with a perfect absence of critical scrutiny. It is no wonder that Olive thinks of her as strange, as belonging to "some queer gypsy-land or transcendental Bohemia."[42]

That queer land is epitomized to some extent by the initial gathering at Miss Birdseye's, the occasion of Verena's first performance in the novel. In a way this is the most significant setting in the book: not only the first but also the most typical gathering of the tacky participants in the woman's movement in the novel, it sums up and focuses all the quackery and nonsense of ill-advised reform movements generally. It is the dwelling of Miss Birdseye, adherent to all movements for reform and especially, now, to the woman's movement—indeed, she is almost the goddess of reform humbug, or at least the earthly vicar of that goddess. And here, appropriately, occurs the debut of Verena, the innocent American girl who is to be won or lost to the woman's movement. A most solid and satisfying setting it is. The temple of these modern vestal virgins (married or male or not!) is cluttered with a whole series of quite fully developed portraits: of Selah Tarrant, of the imposing Mrs. Farrinder and her appendage ("she had a husband and his name was Amariah"), the newspaperman Matthias Pardon, the brittle and sexless but somehow admirable little doctress Mary J. Prance, and Miss Birdseye herself. James has here accomplished what he so admired in Balzac—the feat of sketching fully a whole cluster of characters, no matter how minor their role, to give a thick and convincingly real representation of a world bustling and richly populated. The chiefest of those at the first reunion is of course Miss Birdseye, the presiding genius. She deserves full quotation, but a glimpse or two must suffice:

She was a little old lady with an enormous head; that was the first thing Ransom noticed—the vast, fair, protuberant, candid, ungarnished brow, surmounting a pair of weak, kind, tired-looking eyes, and ineffectually balanced in the rear by a cap which had the air of falling backward, and which Miss Birdseye suddenly felt for as she talked, with unsuccessful irrelevant movements . . . a mere sketch of a smile, a kind of installment, or payment on account. . . .
She always dressed in the same way: she wore a loose black jacket,

with deep pockets, which were stuffed with papers, memoranda of a voluminous correspondence; and from beneath her jacket depended a short stuff dress. The brevity of this simple garment was the device by which Miss Birdseye managed to suggest that she was a woman of business, that she wished to be free for action.[43]

A wonderfully ridiculous, pathetic, laughable, lovable old biddy. And she belongs in the apartment we find her in: as James points out, it "completed Miss Birdseye herself, if any thing could be said to render that office to this essentially formless old woman. . . ." Her parlor is described as long, loose, empty, and bare, as white, flat, and featureless—as though to afford convincing proof of the statement that Miss Birdseye "had never had any needs but moral needs."[44]

This queer transcendental Bohemia, furthermore, is itself recognizably situated in Boston. Quite enough of the actual city is captured in the novel to convey a sharp sense of it and to permit, therefore, something of the little stain which is centered at Miss Birdseye's to seep and spread into the larger urban (if not urbane) environment of the actual Boston. We encounter the ubiquitous jangling horsecars, the hotels, and the swarming streets; but we also breathe the very atmosphere of the city James wanted particularly to *bafouer*—the clamor for publicity, the diminished respect for privacy, the blare of cheap advertising—symbolized in the galling figure of the intrepid newspaperman. The passages devoted to the evocation of Boston are, again, judiciously placed to be functionally active in the novel; they are by no means merely decorative. When the scene shifts from Boston to New York, as it does on a few occasions, James gives detailed descriptions of selected sections of the city. Central Park, as one of the predominant and therefore familiar features of the city, is naturally chosen to provide part of the recognizable authentic background to the drama. More than that, however, James's treatment of the Park makes it functionally contributive to the novel's expression. Basil and Verena find themselves in this situation: Verena is playing truant, for Olive's understanding was that she should spend an hour with Ransom, not wander about with him half the day, as she does; furthermore, Verena had visited Central Park the day before—but properly in a carriage and with Henry Burrage. Thus the scene between Basil and Verena not only sharpens our sense of the conflict between him and the woman's movement (and, indeed, of the same conflict within the girl herself), but also between him and Henry Burrage as suitors for Verena. This setting is fully enough described

—the dimensions of the Park, the kind and arrangement of its details, its immediate surroundings—but its features do more than represent it realistically: by their very nature they serve to comment on the situation and on the developing character of the heroine. Consider this concluding passage of a long descriptive paragraph:

... they even considered the question of taking a boat for half an hour, ... and after having threaded the devious ways of the Ramble, lost themselves in the Maze, and admired all the statues and busts of great men with which the grounds are decorated, they contented themselves with resting on a sequestered bench, where, however, there was a pretty glimpse of the distance and an occasional stroller creaked by on the asphalt walk.[45]

The "devious ways of the Ramble" and the Maze are obvious enough reflections of their gentle, not quite aimless yet mildly perplexing pursuit; the reference to the busts of great men is a subtle reminder of the motif of the decline of the sentiment of sex (and how encouraging that Verena should share with Basil in admiring them!); the comfortable solitude of the sequestered bench—only emphasized by the creak of an occasional stroller—quietly but eloquently expresses the nature of the pleasure these two potential lovers are sharing on this "stolen" afternoon. One is even tempted to linger over the barely hinted promise of the almost cinematographic "pretty glimpse of the distance."

The total scene of the novel is augmented by descriptions of Harvard College and especially of Memorial Hall. These are not so devotedly functional as most of those we have been considering, yet the presence of Basil Ransom before the Civil War Memorial serves to emphasize his role as the outsider—the Southerner, at that moment and especially in that place inescapably the alien if no longer the enemy, becomes more intelligible to us. The description of Marmion on the Cape, late in the novel, manages to capture the predominant atmosphere of retirement and unbuttoned ease, sparseness of population and laxness of arrangement, as well as presenting us with a clear notion of the actual appearance of the place—

Ransom regarded the place as a town because Dr. Prance had called it one; but it was a town where you smelt the breath of the hay in the streets, and you might gather blackberries in the principal square. The houses looked at each other across the grass—low, rusty, crooked, distended houses, with dry, cracked faces and the dim eyes of small-paned, stiffly-sliding windows. Their little dooryards bristled with rank, old-fashioned flowers, mostly yellow; and on the quarter that stood back from the sea the fields sloped upward, and the woods in which they presently lost themselves looked down over the roofs.[46]

James's description catches the whole flavor and aroma of the sleepy resort town, and further provides an appropriate setting for the quiet death of old Miss Birdseye (one notices the dry cracked faces and the dim eyes of the houses, and the old-fashioned flowers) as well as a suitably Arcadian escape for Ransom and Verena. The quiet scene at Marmion is also an excellent means of contrast to the scene of explosive activity that is to follow—it is the lull before the storm that surrounds the production of Verena at the Music Hall and the dramatic climax of her escape with Ransom at the last moment.

In *The Bostonians* James has realistically "done" (as he would say) Boston, Cambridge, Marmion, and to some extent New York. His intention, like that of the Naturalists, was to create a palpable, provable world for his characters to move in. Similarly, he had tried to give roundness and density to those characters by ample description of their person, postures, and gestures, of the peculiarities of their dress and of their speech, of their dwellings and of the scenes which they habitually frequent. The aim always is to achieve the air of reality, to create a successful illusion of actual life. Associated with his handling of description is a series of technical devices employed in the telling of the story, devices which have as their aim the enhancing and sustaining of the air of reality, of preserving the necessary illusion.

James had, as we noted, accepted Flaubert's dictum that the artist should be "invisible et tout-puissant": he recognized that the appearance of the omniscient and omnipotent author in his work threatens always to destroy the illusion of reality—which is the novelist's immediate concern. Among the various devices which James employed to give his stories the air of self-sufficiency, of telling themselves, we might mention first of all what he himself called "point of view." Now he used that term in two senses: in looking at the germ of a story he would turn it about, examining the various facets and the attendant possibilities for drama and for artistic interest to determine which aspect seemed the most promising—which face should be turned toward the reader, or from what point of view the thing should best be approached.

But it is the second sense of the term which principally concerns us here—that is point of view used to mean the angle of vision *within* the story, used to mean "narrative authority." While James is never absent from his stories—excepting first-person narratives, of course —he is usually careful that his intrusions are not those of the recognizable omniscient author: in the telling of his tales he makes extensive use of attributed authority, of restricted omniscience (if that mild barbarism be permitted), of the *point of view* of one or more of his *dramatis personae.* He pretends to know about only the one character, tells us what that character sees and hears, and what that character thinks or can deduce about his observations. This device serves as a means of focusing the scene of action for the reader, of limiting and defining it; it also makes the character in question (the focusing character)—rather than the author—seem to be the authority whose word we are taking. Throughout most of *The Bostonians* James adheres pretty rigorously to this technique of narration. If we refer to the various quotations above cited as examples of James's descriptive technique, we notice that in virtually every case the description is given to us, not on the authority of the author, but on that of one or another of the *dramatis personae.* We first see Ransom as he appears to Mrs. Luna—he is given to us from her point of view, and on her authority; Olive Chancellor is presented from Ransom's point of view, and so is the description of her parlor and of the view from her parlor window; and so on. Now, so far as the presentation of Verena Tarrant is concerned, it comes to us principally from the points of view of both Basil and Olive; and we get somewhat different impressions of the girl, to be sure, depending upon whose point of view (whose authority) is functioning at the moment.

There is, too, this added advantage that the device serves as a means of *reflexive* characterization: we learn about Ransom from what he sees in Verena, and about Olive from what she sees. Now this does not lead to the situation of the several blind men confronted with an elephant—which turns out to be variously like a rope, like a tree, like a wall, etc. Olive and Basil (in this instance) see the same things but differ in their interpretations of or reactions to them, or their attention selects different items to dwell on and we get a complete view of the girl by combining the details chosen by the two observers. And since Verena is observed occasionally by others, since she comments on and expresses herself and is sometimes the subject of discussion between various of her observers, we have no more trouble distinguishing the real Verena than we do anyone or anything in actual life. The point is, of course, that we are not conscious of the author's *telling* us how she appears or how we should see her, as we should be without this technique of narration. Furthermore, as the various "focusing" characters expose her for us they are also exposing themselves at the same time.

An extension of the technique of point-of-view, of "limited omniscience," is to be found on those occasions when James wants to shift from one point of view to another. This is a simple matter when dialogue can be made to intervene; the narrative that leads up to the dialogue may be given from one character's focus, and that which follows given from another's—of the last speaker in the dialogue, say. When the shift must be made within a long narrative passage, however, another strategy is called for. James's system is, to put it most simply, to bring a particular object sharply to the center of vision of the two characters in question—between whom the shift of focus is to be made. A good example of this strategy is to be found in Chapter 33 of the novel; it is the beginning of the great day in Central Park which Basil and Verena share, and the particular passage begins with Verena's point of view focusing the action—she and Basil stand at the window watching the departure of Olive, who has agreed to let them alone.

. . . at that moment Olive passed out of the house and descended the steps *before her eyes.*

Olive's figure, as she went by, was, *for Verena,* full of a queer, touching, tragic expression . . . and *Basil Ransom's companion* privately remarked how little men knew about women, or indeed about what was really delicate, that he, without any cruel intention, should attach an idea of ridicule to such an incarnation of the pathetic, should speak rough, derisive words about it. Ransom, in truth, today was not disposed to be very scrupulous, and he only wanted to get rid of Olive Chancellor, *whose image,* at last, decidedly bothered and bored him. *He was glad to see her go out. . . .*[47]

Verena has guided our eye to the figure of the departing Olive; Ransom picks up the same sharply focused figure without interrupting our visual attention—almost without breaking our line of vision. The shifting of focus is facilitated by the use of the locution "Basil Ransom's companion" instead of the usual "Verena": Basil is, so to speak, being eased surreptitiously into place. Then Verena's thoughts, as she watches Olive, glide easily to Ransom's opinions; the virtually invisible hand of the author picks up the question of those opinions, actually slipping into Ransom's point of view (and the flavor of the two sentences in question is quite that of dialogue—one easily imagines the actual exchange between Basil and his companion.) James completes the transition by finally bringing Basil Ransom's actual view of the departing Olive into play as the focusing agent with the final clause of the quotation. This device is familiar to readers of Virginia Woolf, who adopted it, developed it, and used it extensively in her fiction.

One additional word about James's device of point-of-view in *The Bostonians* must be devoted to his use of Verena Tarrant as a focusing character. Since the novel is largely a contest between Basil and Olive for the young charmer, and since Verena's own volition as a determining factor in the contest comes into play only rather late in the novel, it is perfectly appropriate that James does not "go behind" Verena (to use his term)—that is, give us her thoughts (except for her own speaking of them) at any great length, or permit her point of view to focus the action for us—until that volition is strengthened sufficiently to express itself. Verena's point of view does not function as part of the narrative technique of the novel until the beginning of Chapter 31 (there are forty-two chapters). In this as in other matters of technique James has kept the demands of the organic whole of his novel constantly in view.

In "The Art of Fiction" James had complained that he could not accept the practice of speaking of dialogue, description, narration, etc., as distinct and separable features of fiction: he saw the novel as being all of a piece, an organic whole with all sections working in concert to a single end. We have noted how James's descriptive passages benefit from his technique of point-of-view to serve in some degree of reflexive characterization of the observing or focusing character; and also that description and dramatic development are carried on simultaneously (for example, in the scene between Basil and Verena in Central Park). We noted further that the selection of the focusing character for a given scene depends regularly on the dramatic necessity of the development of the novel as a whole—e.g. the choice of Mrs. Luna's view for the initial representation of Basil Ransom; and the withholding of Verena's point of view until that moment in the novel when her volition has unmistakably awakened, when her "view" of things has finally come really to matter.

A related technique which James develops and employs exten-

sively in *The Bostonians* is one that I call "narrative in idiom": it is
simply a passage of narration-cum-description couched in the language or idiom peculiar to the character whose point of view is
currently being employed—it is a kind of literal indirect discourse.
It is, thus, a combination of elements, and often very effective. A good
example of this technique is to be found in the early scene at Miss
Birdseye's, when Basil and Dr. Prance are together and the doctress
is describing for the visitor from Mississippi the various notables
present.

He had given her a chance, vainly, to start some topic herself; but he
could see that she had no interests beyond the researches from
which, this evening, she had been torn, and was incapable of asking
him a question. She knew two or three of the gentlemen; she had seen
them before at Miss Birdseye's. Of course she knew principally the
ladies; the time hadn't come when a lady-doctor was sent for by a
gentleman, and she hoped it never would, though some people
seemed to think that this was what lady-doctors were working for.
She knew Mr. Pardon; that was the young man with the 'side-whisk-
ers' and the white hair; he was a kind of editor, and he wrote, too,
'over his signature'—perhaps Basil had read some of his works; he
was under thirty, in spite of his white hair. He was a great deal
thought of in magazine circles. She believed he was very bright—but
she hadn't read anything. She didn't read much—not for amusement;
only the 'Transcript.' She believed Mr. Pardon sometimes wrote in
the 'Transcript'; well, she supposed he *was* very bright. The other
that she knew—only she didn't know him (she supposed Basil would
think that queer)—was the tall, pale gentleman, with the black mus-
tache and the eyeglass. She knew him . . . but. . . . If he should come
and speak to her—and he looked as if he were going to work round
that way—she should just say to him, 'Yes, sir,' or 'No, sir,' very coldly.
She couldn't help it if he did think her dry; if *he* were a little more
dry, it might be better for him. What was the matter with him? Oh
she thought she had mentioned that; he was a mesmeric healer, he
made miraculous cures. . . .[48]

The whole passage is strongly redolent of Dr. Prance's speech, or
her characteristic idiom: it is flat, skeptical, sardonic, and just sufficiently punctuated with certain Yankee locutions (as James noted
them) to identify her as a distant cousin of Daisy Miller. Her idiom
provides the grateful tincture of vitriol necessary to etch in the various characters upon whom her critical eye happens to fall—the
women of the movement, Pardon the intrepid newspaperman, Selah
and of course Verena Tarrant. The technique is, as I say, a kind of

indirect discourse, yet the sense of conversation, of dramatic dialogue, is strongly present—as can be seen especially in the last sentence of the quotation. And furthermore, it gives the feeling of
dialogue in a dramatic setting: one is kept perfectly aware of the
attendant activity, aware that the conversation is by no means a
sequestered one but that the mesmeric healer threatens to approach
them at any moment. All this gives us Dr. Prance's rather caustic view
of the meeting and its assisting members; and as we have her vision
of it all, we realize that she is at the same time unintentionally exposing herself to us by a kind of reflexive characterization. When we look
again at the opening sentence of the quotation, however, we see that
it is ultimately Basil Ransom's point of view which focuses the whole
scene: what we are given, then, is his view of Dr. Prance's view of
things. The conclusion to the scene, the last sentence of the chapter,
reminds us of this fact: we read Ransom's appealing conviction that
"It was certain that whatever might become of the movement at
large, Doctor Prance's own little revolution was a success." She had
just left to return to her "lab." We like this self-possessed little woman's view of the assorted nuts that comprise the Birdseye gathering,
and we consequently approve of Ransom's amused approval of her.
If it seems that the action has not been greatly advanced during this
particular interlude, we must recognize that the scene has been realized and vitalized for us by James's technique, and that the drama has
continued to develop.

All of this indicates James's attempt to be convincingly real, to
catch the very note and trick of life, without apparent rearrangement, of which his novel pretends to be a factual report. The influence of the Naturalists' theory and practice is evident here. The
influence of Zola in particular, and especially of his theory of *le
roman expérimental,* is also apparent in the new attention paid to the
force of heredity and environment as determining agents in the life
of the principal characters (especially of Verena) of *The Bostonians.*
It is important to notice that the same influence is visible in some of
James's principal tales of this period. Several of them exhibit an
"experimental" aspect—in Zola's sense: it is as though the author had
begun by asking himself "What would happen if a character with
such and such an hereditary complement and background as X's
were placed in a milieu exhibiting these particular characteristics?"
Mr. William C. Frierson is quite correct in his assumption about these
matters as they touch James:

No doubt when Zola published *Le roman expérimental* he expounded the theories which had been developed by the naturalists in Paris, and with which Henry James was thoroughly familiar. The experimental novelist would 'show what a certain "passion" aroused under certain circumstances and in a certain environment, will result in as regards the individual and society.'[49]

The tale "Lady Barberina" will serve as an example of James's "experimental" stories of this period. He had sent a brief sketch of the tale to his publisher along with his outline for *The Bostonians,* so it may be safely assumed that the two pieces were closely associated in James's mind. The best resume of the tale is found in James's notebooks:

The name of the thing to be *Lady Barberina.* I have already treated (more or less) the subject of the American girl who marries (or concerning whom it is a question whether she *will* marry) a British aristocrat. This story reverses the situation and presents a young *male* American who conceives the design of marrying a daughter of the aristocracy. He is a New Yorker, a good deal of an Anglomaniac and a "dude"; and as he has a good deal of money she accepts him and they are united. The 1st half of the tale goes on in England. In the 2d the parties are transported to New York, whither he has brought his bride, and it relates their adventures there, the impressions made and received by the lady, and the catastrophe.[50]

The resume does not suggest that "Lady Barberina" is either more or less of an "experiment" than any of James's international stories. A look at the text of the story, however, reveals an important distinction. There, the heroine's heredity and the domestic and social environment in which she has been raised are given special emphasis. As the young American, Jackson Lemon, assesses the value of his proposed acquisition,

it came over him more than ever that it had taken a great social outlay to produce such a mixture. Simple and girlish as she [Lady Barberina] was, and not particularly quick in the give and take of conversation, she seemed to him to have a part of the history of England in her blood; she was a *résumé* of generations of privileged people, and of centuries of rich country life.[51]

The reader is made to feel—by James's presentation of the Canterville family and their home at Pasterns—that Jackson's impression is quite right. Her inheritance, background, and social experience have rendered Lady Barberina incapable of adjusting, as we say, to the new environment of American life—she is *determined* to react negatively. It is also clear that Jackson Lemon is virtually determined to set the whole affair into motion. He is as strong willed as Daisy Miller, the wilfully ignorant little heroine who rushes needlessly to her death in Rome. At the outset he recognizes the risk he may be running in attempting to make an American wife of Lady Barberina, but the possible success to be won makes it seem well worth while. But as he continues to press his suit for the girl and finds himself confronted with the cordial Canterville request that their solicitors (theirs and Jackson's) arrange the matter of settlement, his new-world hackles stubbornly raise themselves. He will marry her only on his own terms, he insists, promising of course to treat his wife always with handsome generosity—but not under the stress of legal coercion. "Jackson Lemon was conscious that if he should marry Lady Barberina it would be because it suited him. . . . He believed that he acted in all things by his own will—an organ for which he had the highest respect."[52]

As the story develops it emphasizes the fondness of such a belief in free will by demonstrating how Lemon is influenced, provoked, determined by the force of the Canterville traditions (of which Lady Barberina appeared to him to be the accurate *résumé*) and of the opinion of Mrs. Freer, to grant the demands for legal settlement—to grant indeed almost anything—if only he can "do what he wants." That phrase has in context a sadly ironic flavor; and the irony runs through James's account: "Jackson's strength of purpose was shown in deciding to marry Lady Barberina on any terms. It seemed to him, under the influence of his desire to prove that he was not afraid—so odious was the imputation—that terms of any kind were very superficial things."[53] Thus Lemon has won—a Pyrrhic victory! The catastrophe is realized in Lady Barberina's rigid unhappiness in America, and in her finally returning to England and refusing to consider accompanying Jackson back to America. We share Jackson Lemon's recognition of the bind he has got himself into:

During these last weeks it had come over him, with a quiet, irresistible, unmerciful force that Mrs. Dexter Freer had been right when she said to him, that Sunday afternoon in Jermyn Street, the summer before, that he would find it was not so simple to be an American.

Such an identity was complicated, in just the measure that she had foretold, by the difficulty of domesticating one's wife. The difficulty was not dissipated by his having taken a high tone about it; it pinched him from morning till night, like a misfitting shoe. His high tone had given him courage when he took the great step; but he began to perceive that the highest tone in the world *cannot change the nature of things.*[54]

Or rather we share his sad dismay that, in spite of all, he has gotten into a mess. His own responsibility was simply to act "under the influence of his desire. . . ." We have seen, thus, "what a certain 'passion' aroused under certain circumstances and in a certain environment, will result in as regards the individual and society." It may be argued that the case of Daisy Miller might have been expressed in just these terms. The point is that it was not. The emphasis in that story is quite other: the question of heredity is not raised; Daisy is indeed as free to pursue her way as she pretends to be, while Jackson Lemon's sense of free will is perfectly illusory. Daisy will not be dissuaded from doing what she wills (of course she is somewhat perversely encouraged in that direction by being told there are things she ought not contine doing); Jackson is obliged to meet the terms proposed. He acts under the influence of his passion; what he believes to be his exercise of choice is merely his acceptance of the determined line of action. There is here, perhaps, a broader reflection on the general American notion of freedom: that it is a complex fate to be condemned to American freedom.

The Bostonians is another, full-scale, example of the experimental story—James's first *roman expérimental.* It offers us the "case" of Verena Tarrant, the naive girl with her peculiar heredity, her strange progenitors and upbringing, who is introduced consecutively to the contradictory influences of Olive Chancellor and Basil Ransom and driven by her particular passion (of which she only gradually becomes aware during the course of the novel) to a determined end. James is very careful to indicate that Verena's heredity is a matter of importance: he devotes several passages to a discussion of it, as it is commented upon by many of the characters in the novel. At Verena's first entrance on the scene with her parents, Miss Birdseye takes note of them and reflects that as a daughter of a mesmeric healer and a product of old abolitionist stock Verena "would probably be remarkable as a genius."[55] James reinforces this notion a little later, but raises a question even as he does so: "Though it would have seemed eminently natural to you that a daughter of Selah Tarrant and his wife should be an inspirational speaker, yet, as you knew Verena better, you would have wondered immensely how she came to issue from such a pair."[56] The suggestion is that while the bizarre parents seem to account for Verena superficially viewed, there remains something in the girl apparently perculiar to her alone. James tells us that her ideas of enjoyment were very simple, as is appropriate to the serious-ness of purpose of the bleakly waterproofed Selah and his abolition-ist-descended wife; yet as we learn in what the simple ideas of enjoyment consist, we see that Verena is her mother's daughter after all. James explains that "she enjoyed putting on her new hat, with its redundancy of feather,"[57] and it turns out that Mrs. Tarrant also harbors certain frivolous tastes in the matter of "simple enjoyment": she is grateful for her daughter's association with Olive Chancellor because of the social possibilities thus opened to the girl. Mrs. Tarrant is even more fascinated by Olive's sister, Adeline Luna: "She had seen all the people who went to lectures, but there were hours when she desired, for a change, to see some who didn't go; and Mrs. Luna, from Verena's description of her, summed up the characteristics of this eccentric class."[58] And after Olive has begun buying Verena from her parents on the installment plan, the consequent new-found ease afforded Mrs. Tarrant expresses itself in a certain mild redun-dancy of decoration—like Verena's feathered hat. The better we know Verena, the more she seems to be the daughter of the feminine soul that has pined beneath Mrs. Tarrant's spare exterior.

Olive is eager to recognize something anomalous in Verena's being the daughter of the Tarrants. She is glad that Verena is a girl of the people, and relieved to find her poor house in Cambridge sufficiently ramshackle; but since "She had come to consider the girl as a wonder of wonders, to hold that no human origin . . . would sufficiently account for her," it is certainly understandable that she should feel Verena's "springing up between Selah and his wife was an exquisite whim of the creative force."[59] The importance of Olive's attitude is that it indicates her own justification of her desire to "rescue" Verena and mould her into what she wishes the girl would be—to see she is not condemned (as Olive would say) by her progenitors.

Now a similar observation is made by Basil Ransom, yet his strikes us as the more accurate in that he recognizes that Verena is not such an anomaly as Olive sees her—even though he is as eager to find reason for saving the girl.

He understood her now very well (since his visit to Cambridge); he saw she was honest and natural; she had queer, bad lecture-blood in her veins, and a comically false idea of the aptitude of little girls for conducting movements; but her enthusiasm was of the purest, her illusions had a fragrance, and so far as the mania for producing herself personally was concerned, it had been distilled into her by people who worked her for ends which to Basil Ransom could only appear insane. She was a touching, ingenuous victim, unconscious of the pernicious forces which were hurrying her to her ruin.[60]

James adds a word, at the outset of Chapter 31, that seems to settle the matter. He describes Verena driving up Fifth Avenue with Olive,

smoothing her gloves, wishing her fan were a little nicer, and proving by the answering, familiar brightness with which she looked out on the lamp-lighted streets that, whatever theory might be entertained as to the genesis of her talents and her personal nature, the blood of the lecture-going, night-walking Tarrants did distinctly flow in her veins. . . .[61]

The impression left with us is that hereditary influence does matter in the case of Verena Tarrant, and that one main aspect of the Tarrants' hereditary bequest has been strongly seconded by her earlier experiences in the environment provided by her parents. Chapter 10 tells us a good deal about the irregular life of the Tarrants and something of their history. Verena's share in all that is summed up in the next chapter:

She had been nursed in darkened rooms, and suckled in the midst of manifestations; she had begun to 'attend lectures,' as she said, when she was quite an infant, because her mother had no one to leave her with at home. She had sat on the knees of somnambulists, and had been passed from hand to hand by trance-speakers; she was familiar with every kind of 'cure,' and had grown up among lady-editors of newspapers advocating new religions, and people who disapproved of the marriage-tie.[62]

The influence of the precepts and example of her lugubrious father has been quite significant in Verena's development—his commitment and devotion to publicity and the public life, especially his fond admiration for newspapers and advertising. Selah as a private person has almost no perceptible existence, for "Even in the privacy of domestic intercourse . . . Selah's nature was pitched altogether in the key of public life."[63] This has perhaps been the keynote of Verena's milieu and chief among the pernicious forces which Ransom considers to be hurrying her to her ruin. And he sees Olive not simply as the latest influential item in the list, but actually a continuation of that represented by Selah, as she guides Verena's "passion"—even more perversely than the parents—into those channels Olive feels to be the best.

Ransom, then, becomes the antagonistic force in Verena's environment. He appeals to what he considers her best self and intends to offer her passion an opportunity for its most natural expression. In her freshness, innocence, and naivete, that "moral spontaneity" which James had cherished in his young compatriots like Minny Temple and Clover Hooper, Ransom finds much to be salvaged and redeemed. Verena's passion is, in the broadest sense, charity—*caritas;* she is genial and generous, submissive and pliable, ready to give of herself—or let herself be taken—for any cause that promises to help improve the lot of the unfortunate. It is the passion of selfless human love. But the influence of the "queer, bad lecture-blood," the guidance of Selah, the Greenstreet Tradition, and her fond mother's silly expectations added to Olive's hopes for her, encouraged by the Burrages, have become a compelling force to direct Verena's passion into a particular channel. The combined hereditary and environmental influences have made her feel that the public expression of that passion in the cause of the downtrodden sex is the most acceptable and laudible contribution of herself and her talents that she could possibly make.

The effect of Ransom's dogged and solitary efforts is to persuade Verena to consult other tendencies in her nature. There are, to be sure, other tendencies in that nature, although she has neglected and repressed them by allowing Olive as she had others to dominate her and direct her wishes and actions. It is clear that in agreeing to "renounce"—and for the most part to renounce serious male companionship—Verena is acting in opposition to some of the fundamental elements of her nature. When she and Olive spend a musical evening in Henry Burrage's rooms at Harvard, Verena is markedly touched:

It would be very nice to do that always—just to take men as they are, and not have to think about their badness. It would be very nice not to have so many questions, but to think they were all comfortably answered . . . sit there and listen for ever to Schubert and Mendelsohn. *They* didn't care anything about female suffrage! And I didn't feel the want of a vote to-day at all, did you?[64]

Ransom's visit to Cambridge to see her, their long day together in New York, and finally his persistent month at Marmion accumulate to speak to that part of Verena's nature that is not innately inimical to men. More and more Verena recognizes that she is really attracted to Ransom; more and more she feels the appeal of his suggestion that she devote herself—privately—to him alone. Finally, that part of her nature, in which her sentiment of sex surely resides, succeeds in its demands; finally Verena understands the passion that has moved her from the first—the passion of *caritas*.

It was simply that the truth had changed sides; that radiant image began to look at her from Basil Ransom's expressive eyes. She loved, she was in love—she felt it in every throb of her being. Instead of being constituted by nature for entertaining that sentiment in an exceptionally small degree (which had been the implication of her whole crusade, the warrant for her offer to Olive to renounce), she was framed, apparently, to allow it the largest range, the highest intensity. It was always passion, in fact; but now the object was other. . . . Why Basil Ransom had been deputed by fate to exercise this spell was more than she could say—poor Verena, who up to so lately had flattered herself that she had a wizard's wand in her own pocket.[65]

There must, after all, have been something in the blood of the Greenstreets to account for Mrs. Tarrant's interest and fascination in Adeline Luna and for her constant expectation that her daughter would marry, even though Matthias Pardon comes closest to her notion of a probable son-in-law. There is even the suggestion that Selah has within him something of the sense of human love, although it has been seriously perverted—like so much else in the novel.

The result of the experiment of *The Bostonians* is that what we are moved to call the best in Verena's nature, her true self, has been realized. The role of heredity and of environment past and current has been important in the experiment. Verena's behavior was largely determined by those two forces. This is not to say that she has been simply a passive victim of those forces, for the novel is obviously concerned with the gradual awakening of her volition in conjunction with the gradual increase of her self-awareness. She grows aware of how her dominant passion had been perverted and was being further how her dominant passion had been perverted and was being further perverted by the queer influence of Olive Chancellor and all she represents. Verena is brought finally to the point where she can choose to accept her attraction to Basil Ransom—and to act on that choice. As the Southerner hurries her bodily away from the jaws of the demanding public, Verena is able to say "Ah, now I am glad!" The experiment has come to its gratifying conclusion.

The Bostonians has come to occupy rather a peculiar place in the James canon. Since it is the only one of his major novels to be omitted from the New York edition which James selected and edited early in this century, a mild stigma has somehow attached to it. Even Mr. Quentin Anderson in his provocative *The American Henry James* maintains that the novel does not really belong in the canon. It has not been completely neglected, nor has it been so much underrated as improperly evaluated. Consequently, it seems necessary to say a word or two about James's achievement in *The Bostonians* and to reconsider the question of its typicality.

It is, to begin with, an impressive satire of certain features of American life in James's day—is, indeed, one of James's funniest books. It successfully exposes the quackery and fuzzy-headedness of foolish addiction to various kinds of faddish movements and causes. The wonderful creature Miss Birdseye serves as an admirable example of this, as she manages to sum up and symbolize in her own person all the ineffectual and disorganized muddlery of good intentions gone haywire: "a confused, entangled, inconsequent, discursive old woman, whose charity began at home and ended nowhere, whose credulity kept pace with it, and who knew less about her fellow-creatures, if possible, after fifty years of humanitary zeal, than on the day she had gone into the field to testify against the iniquity of most arrangements." "She was heroic, she was sublime, the whole moral history of Boston was reflected in her misplaced spectacles...."[66] Yet she is protected by her creator: we have a real fondness for the futile old soul and are truly moved by her quiet death—even though we laugh heartily at her, as when she confronts Basil Ransom with the earnest woman's-movement question, "Do you regard us, then, simply as lovely baubles?"[67] The satiric portrait was sharply enough etched to provoke a stern rebuke from brother William for Henry's having put Eliza Peabody into his novel under the name of Birdseye.[68]

Selah Tarrant serves James's purposes well also in this respect. His constant toothy leer, his eternal waterproof that engulfs him like a set of wings to enhance his similarity to a vulture, the unsavory atmosphere of his "associations" at Cayuga and of his manipulative cures effected among the ladies, and finally his willingness to let Olive purchase his daughter, all combine to make him a memorable morsel. The ability of the various reform movements to absorb a creature like Selah Tarrant testifies not only to their fondness but ultimately to their capacity for skull-duggery and actual moral evil. In company with Matthias Pardon, he also aids James's hearty satire of the importunity of the press, the craze for publicity, the attendant destruction of personal privacy.[69] That such an institution could flourish, that such unabashed vulgarity and cheek could succeed in the society which *The Bostonians* depicts—these are facts which amply attest not only to the decline of the sentiment of sex but to the collapse of respect for human dignity as well. It is difficult, then, not to feel some sympathy with Basil Ransom even at those moments when his criticism of that society is most scathing.

The whole generation is womanized; the masculine tone is passing out of the world; it's a feminine, a nervous, hysterical, chattering, canting age, an age of hollow phrases and false delicacy and exaggerated solicitudes and coddled sensibilities, which, if we don't look out, will usher in the reign of mediocrity, of the feeblest and flattest and the most pretentious that has ever been. The masculine character, the ability to dare and endure, to know and yet not fear reality, to look the world in the face and take it for what it is—a very queer and partly very base mixture—that is what I want to preserve, or rather, as I may say, to recover. . . .[70]

The satire, of course, by no means depends simply on the character sketches and occasional aphoristic utterances that sum them up. James's ideas are quite satisfactorily *fleshed* out and embodied in the whole work, in the living organism that is the novel. The main line of plot development, embracing the central contest between Olive Chancellor and Basil Ransom for Verena Tarrant, and the supporting activity of Matthias Pardon and (more seriously) Henry Burrage as competitive suitors for Verena's hand, serves to express dramatically the perverseness of such a Cause as the woman's movement and of the decline of the sentiment of sex. Matthias Pardon is not really a serious candidate—although he is Selah Tarrant's obvious favorite as being able to offer Verena apparently limitless publicity through his

association with the newspapers. Yet he deserves a place beside
Henry Burrage, for both these suitors would publish Verena as much
as Olive could desire—and that, clearly, is their principal qualification as husbands for the girl. But most striking, because most central
in the novel, is the perverse attraction of Olive to Verena. The lesbi-
anism, latent though it may be, is unmistakable in Olive's characterization. All of this—the suitors and their qualifications—on the one
hand expresses the idea that Verena is being sought either as a tool
to be employed for the Cause, or for the gratification of what is
presented as perverted passion. On the other hand there is the antagonistic but normal and healthy (as we say) attitude of Basil Ransom, the alien, aristocratic conservative who wants Verena merely for
herself. We remember the shock of Verena's early recognition that
Ransom's interest in her, unlike the interest of all the others, is purely
personal: "See here, Mr. Ransom, do you know what strikes me? . . .
The interest you take in me isn't really controversial—a bit. It's quite
personal!"[71] As the novel progresses Verena realizes more and more
that the opportunity Ransom offers her—normal, human, personal,
private love and marriage—is really what her most essential nature
craves. And she finally accepts it.

Ransom is a strong conservative, of course, and extremely dubious
of the current state of the democratic society, which he sees as
gullible and especially vulnerable to any trash-talking but floridly
rhetorical rouser: "fluent, petty, third-rate palaver, conscious or unconscious perfected humbug; the stupid, gregarious, gullible public,
the enlightened democracy of his native land, could swallow unlim-
ited draughts of it."[72] Yet he is, as the novel has dramatically expressed it, the only possible alternative to the foolish and perverse
forces which threaten to dominate Verena. He will have no truck
with that. And he is unmistakably male; the sentiment of sex has not
declined in him: he is indeed the one eligible and qualified *male*
figure in the novel. Olive is perfectly aware of that fact, and it is the
main reason why she recognizes him as her chief adversary and fears
his power. Consequently, the triumphant union of Basil and Verena
is precisely the conclusion the novel has been aiming at. It provides
a fitting and optimistic ending to the satirical treatment of the problem.

While *The Bostonians* is certainly concerned with its perfectly
apparent topic—the woman's movement and all that—and with the
satiric handling of that topic—i.e. the exposure to ridicule of certain

recognizable American types and tendencies; at bottom, neverthe-less, it is concerned with those problems of human relationship which James's fiction always examines.[73] The typical Jamesian themes, the developing Jamesian ethic with its recognizable and constant *summum bonum* and its direst evil, all are here successfully incarnate in the thick envelope of his novel's realistic surface. In *The Bostonians*, as in the stories which preceded and would follow it, the familiar forces are arrayed against each other: the demands of Duty, the nagging dictates of Conscience, the stern literal judgement of the Pharisee are set in opposition to natural Impulse, the promptings of Spontaneity (the urgent whisper of Emerson's Whim), the require-ment of clear-eyed Consciousness and honest Self-knowledge. And these forces contend for domination of the hero's soul. The question here, typically, is whether the respect for human integrity will be honored, whether the natural development of a human individual will be permitted and encouraged, or whether the evil of "emotional cannibalism," of the cash nexus for human intercourse will finally prevail. Olive Chancellor obviously represents the demands of Duty and Conscience—that is almost the first piece of information we are given about her. The strength of her appeal to Verena becomes increasingly the appeal of Duty. "You are my conscience," Verena tells her.[74] And she turns for help to Olive as to her conscience, particularly in her effort to combat her natural impulse to turn to Ransom. She knows where her duty lies—with Olive and the Cause. And she does owe her duty to Olive, all right, for Olive has made Verena her own by right of purchase. Similarly Olive recognizes with regret her duty to permit the Burrages to take Verena over from her: theirs is the greater "right" as they possess the greater material wealth. But as Verena's eyes are opened, as she comes to understand more fully the whole situation in which she is involved and to recog-nize more clearly what are the demands of her essential being—when, in a word, her consciousness is fully awakened, she can accept the alternative offered by union with Ransom to all the essentially dehumanizing and fundamentally selfish forces that have engulfed her.

As is usually the case with the Jamesian heroine—a young and inexperienced American girl who is innocent, naive, fresh, and vul-nerable—Verena Tarrant has had to learn to recognize the evil of the world and to find the means of coming to terms with that evil so as to live successfully, not to retreat from it but to confront it boldly and refuse to be its victim. (James could not praise a fugitive and cloistered virtue.) In his "international stories" James was able to avail himself of an admirably appropriate metaphor for the expression of his ideas about the development of the human soul, about the means of successful adaptation to the human condition: his innocent heroine (the main character is typically a young woman) comes from the New World of America, comparatively free of convention and nude as to significant manners of behavior, yet of good heart and honest impulse ("moral spontaniety"). She is introduced to the world of experience in Europe—ancient, knowing, heavily conventional, and strongly girt with traditional patterns of behavior. The Old World, the world of experience, must be faced (in James's view as in Blake's) if the heroine is to develop and mature; the risks are grave, but the reward is commensurate with the risks. The greatest reward is self-knowledge, clear-sightedness, a real understanding of oneself and of the world one must live in; it represents a triumph over the world gained by means of rejecting its merely worldly prizes.

The metaphor of *The Bostonians* is, of course, quite like what I have just described—with the difference that it employs only the American scene. The same terms are apparent here as in the international stories, except that there is some slight rearrangement among them. Verena is the familiar Jamesian innocent heroine; the world of experience into which she introduced is the world of "reforms" and "causes," and the woman's movement: there she is victimized and made use of, bought and sold, exposed to the glare of rude publicity, her personal integrity disregarded. The evil in that humbugging, immoral world she must recognize and reject, as the heroine of the international stories must in the old world of Europe. The one sharp difference here is that the aristocratic, high-mannered, traditional aspect of that world is represented by the figure who appears as Verena's savior—Basil Ransom. It is his chivalrous behavior that most obviously underlines this aspect of his role, but also one is made to feel that behind him lies a long pedigree, a gentle society, traditions and conventions and a way of life not vastly different from the life of Europe as the Jamesian heroine finds it. But the Civil War has effectively ended that way of life which Ransom represents, and its principles are embodied only in his present self (as Faulkner's Ike McCaslin is intended to embody in himself the virtues of the vanishing wilderness). His chivalrous manner often rings hollow in the novel, as do the manners of some of James's Europeans and Europeanized Americans in the international stories. As the novel describes the development of Verena's self-knowledge, it offers a parallel development in the case of Ransom—his gradual discarding of the superfluous chivalrous manner. It falls away in his confrontations with Verena, is most useful and "necessary" in his dealings with Olive, and is most easily provoked by Adeline Luna. Ransom's chivalry suffers its supreme test on the crucial occasion of Verena's most triumphant public appearance: Mrs. Luna tries to keep Basil at her side and prevent him from going into the auditorium to see Verena precisely by appealing to his chivalry: "Is that the way a Southern gentleman treats a lady?"[75] He leaves Adeline, shrugging off the demands of chivalry when the more natural and personal demands are stronger.

In the international stories there is often a note of sadness attendant on the success won by the American hero or heroine: that success so often appears to be a kind of failure—at least as "the world" measures success and failure. The victory of Isabel Archer in *The Portrait of a Lady* is the maturity she ultimately achieves, her clear-eyed consciousness of her true self and of the nature of the world— and also of her love for Ralph Touchett, who dies after contributing to Isabel's awakening. Yet that novel has often been read as just the opposite, as the story of the failure of an obstinate girl who has made her bed and now must lie in it. The novel certainly lacks the conventional "happy ending" that would announce it as the story of a victory. One wishes somehow that Isabel's future held some obvious promise of the more conventional tangible joys—rewards—that we are accustomed to recognize. In fact, it seems that James's international stories have always been striving toward some workable compromise between the two opposites in conflict—a fusion of American and European, let us say. American naked innocence needs to be clad in the garment of traditional European manners; conversely, mere manners need to be filled out by the good and innocent heart of the unspoiled American. Not that one can simply clap the two together —that shotgun wedding produces a character like Gilbert Osmond, who has given up virtually all of his original self to manners alone: he is not conventional but "Convention itself." The innocent requires the clothing of manners which suit it, which permit it to express itself in a civilized way. That union, then seems to have been a constant aim in James's international fiction; but he never satisfactorily effected that compromise until he wrote his masterful *The Golden Bowl*. But in *The Bostonians* James did manage something similar in the union of Verena and Basil—the former losing her naivete and gaining the sophistication and self-knowledge necessary to recognize the evil of her world and to understand her true self, the latter losing the superficial manner of his inherited chivalry (though remaining a gentleman) and thus achieving a greater naturalness and honesty. This is, of course, not exactly or not completely the equivalent of the compromise aimed at in the international fiction: and that is because, first, the antinomies are not exact equivalents and, second, because *The Bostonians* is purely American. There is sufficient similarity between this purely American tale and the international stories, however, for us to recognize that the same Jamesian pattern informs both.

A final word must be added on the conclusion of the novel. From all that has been said thus far about the contest for Verena and, increasingly, within Verena herself, it should be quite apparent that the tendency of the novel is in the direction of the girl's realizing what is natural and necessary for her own fulfillment—union with Basil Ransom. Yet the final pair of sentences of the novel seem to raise a question about that fulfillment:

But though she was glad, he presently discovered that, beneath her hood, she was in tears. It is to be feared, that with the union, so far from brilliant, into which she was about to enter, these were not the last she was destined to shed.

Some readers have found here ground for the belief that Verena has not made a happy choice, that in accepting Ransom she has accepted something of a brute. Even so brilliant a critic as Mr. Irving Howe seems to be of that persuasion. At the end of his Introduction to the novel (Modern Library edition) Mr. Howe writes—

What James thought of Ransom's pretensions, what he made of the whole affair, how thoroughly he maintained the critical and ironic tone throughout the book, is suggested in this hint that Ransom and Verena, married at last, would live unhappily ever after.

Now it is true, to be sure, that in *The Bostonians* James was as careful as he usually was to protect his villains and to avoid whitewashing his heroes—was careful, in a word, to eschew the black-and-white manner of melodrama. Thus, Basil Ransom is by no means free of faults or full of virtue; but his virtues are quite sufficiently sane— particularly as antidote to the noxious nonsense to which they are opposed in the novel—to provoke reasonably full sympathy in the intelligent and impartial reader. And it is not entirely irrelevant to point out that in many instances Ransom's ideas are very close to those expressed by James himself.

The truth is that all the natural impulse of the novel is directed toward the "happy-ending" James gives it. Indeed, so optimistic does the conclusion appear that James must have wished to qualify it somewhat by suggesting that the prospect before Verena and Basil was certainly no rosier than it is for most young couples anticipating matrimony. The final pair of sentences simply prevent the novel from ending with a broad Pollyanna grin; furthermore, they keep the story within the necessary bounds of faithful realism. To the end, *The Bostonians* maintains its fidelity to the aim of creating a convincing illusion of reality.

Chapter IV

Hyacinth and the Princess

The Princess Casamassima began its serial run in the *Atlantic* just a few months after *The Bostonians* had begun to appear in the *Century.* Both were published in book form in 1886. They are true companion pieces, especially as they are both principally concerned with movements for reform and to a large extent with the common folk. The immediately obvious difference between them is that in *The Princess* the reform movement is a much more serious affair than it is in the satiric *Bostonians.* In spite of its title, *The Princess Casamassima* is the story of the tragic career of Hyacinth Robinson, illegitimate son of a French working-girl and (perhaps) of an English aristocrat. He is brought up, by a poor dressmaker, like a little gentleman and schooled with subtle hints that he has the best English blood in his veins even though he lives in Cockney London. His character seems to attest both to the aristocratic blood of his putative father and to the French blood of his poor mother (who was jailed for the murder of a Lord Frederick, to whom Hyacinth's paternity is attributed); he has the tastes of a gentleman and a fondness for things French. He is introduced, through fellow workers, to the subterranean anarchist movement and finally pledges himself to do whatever may be required of him to further social improvement. At the same time he finds himself put in touch with the aristocracy by meeting a couple of gentlewomen who interest themselves in the betterment of the working class; one of them, the Princess Casamassima, is herself already associated with the anarchist movement. Through his acquaintance with the Princess, the education and nourishment of Hyacinth's taste carry him forward to his dramatic dilemma: his position in life and his oath to the anarchists bind him to the workers' cause, yet his artistic temperament and his love for the aristocratic life of culture and *gentilesse* make him antipathetic to any movement aimed at upsetting that world of beauty and levelling it down. He cannot betray his oath; he cannot be false to himself. When the moment arrives for his pledge to be redeemed Hyacinth can exercise but a single option. He commits suicide.

James explains in his Preface that the idea for the novel came to him as a result of his habit of strolling through the streets of London —the idea, specifically, of some small and obscure but intelligent creature, underprivileged but sensitive enough to be aware of the privileged life that seemed forever denied him. Hyacinth Robinson "sprang for me," James says, "out of the London pavements." The social climate in which Hyacinth exists—the general turmoil of social unrest and anarchist demonstrations—similarly sprang at James from the actual atmosphere of London during the eighties and, indeed, from the whole atmosphere of the western world. The spirit of 1789 was still very much alive and threatening the *status quo* on both sides of the Atlantic; and the threat was dramatically realized simultaneously in the Haymarket Tragedy in Chicago as well as in the Trafalgar Square riots in London in the very year of the novel's publication. There is ample evidence in James's letters from that period that he was quite aware of the stormy threats of upheaval in the social order, especially as they were manifested in Europe. He met a number of Russian exiles in England and may have been introduced to the anarchist Prince Kropotkin at Turgenev's in 1880.[1] Lionel Trilling finds generous evidence of the influence of James's experience of the times in *The Princess Casamassima* and suggests that *The Revolutionary Catechism* of Bakunin and Nechayev might be taken as a guide book to the novel.[2] In any case James had apparently had the experience necessary to create an authentic picture of society touched by revolutionary turmoil. And in those letters of his which discuss popular unrest James exhibits an interesting ambivalence of attitude. His sympathy with the aristocracy is apparent as he recounts to Grace Norton the Irish Dynamiters' blowing up of Westiminster Hall and the Tower; yet in a letter to her brother he condemns the upper classes in England as being worse than the French aristocracy before the Revolution. On the other side he of course recognizes the grinding poverty and abject misery of the lower classes that would perfectly justify their rising in revolt; yet he feels it is not really the simple poor but gangs of roughs and thieves who are actually responsible for the damage done. Behind all of this, to be sure, is James's fear lest the old England he had known and loved would be no more. These divided sympathies and, finally, that basic apprehension of irreparable loss are reflected and magnified in Hyacinth Robinson.

If the hero of the novel sprang out of the London pavements, the heroine, who gives her name to the title of the novel, returned to James from the pages of his early *Roderick Hudson*—the beautiful Christina Light, who became the wife of the Prince Casamassima. She must have recommended herself to James's imagination as a character admirably suited to represent and embody all the sweets in the shop-window of the world into which little Hyacinth would peer longingly. The Princess would naturally represent the great world through her aristocratic marriage; but because of the unhappy nature of that forced marriage, which alienated her from family and "appropriate" friends, she could also naturally make the social connection with a simple book binder, Hyacinth. Her capriciousness, explained again by her singular background, would make her meddling with commoners and anarchists understandable; and since that capriciousness does not extend so far as utter bitchiness, she would not risk losing completely the reader's sympathy. She was made to order for the role required in the new novel.

James expresses some doubt in the Preface to *The Princess* about the advisability of "resurrecting" characters from earlier works, although precedent for the practice had been well established by Balzac and Zola, to mention but two. Yet he admits he felt the demand of the *disponible* Christina to be allowed to live again. The fact is, of course, that he had originally given her such an abundance of vitality in *Roderick Hudson*—"The multiplication of touches had produced even more life than the subject required," James modestly observes[3]—that her possibilities were by no means exhausted. And as I say, she was perfectly suited for the part.

These, then, were the chief ingredients simmering in James's artistic crucible—the boy of the streets, the atmosphere of revolution, and the Princess with left over life to live. The very combination of ingredients is strongly reminiscent of the similar combination in a novel by James's friend and colleague Turgenev, *Virgin Soil;* and when we look at James's finished novel we notice additional similarities emerge. He had reviewed the French translation of *Virgin Soil* for the *Nation* in 1877, and included a description of Turgenev's hero, Nejdanov, that reads like a preliminary sketch for his own Hyacinth Robinson. Although there is no reference to Turgenev's novel in what has survived of James's notes for *The Princess*, it would seem that his memory of it must have been subconsciously active during his writing of the novel. It is reasonable to assume that this work of Turgenev's, like those of the other members of the Flaubert group, would have been lying near the threshold of James's conscious mind at that time. The similarities between these two novels are sufficiently marked to encourage scholars to claim that James was heavily indebted to his Russian friend in this instance—that *The Princess* is considerably derivative and imitative. A sounder view, however, recongizes that what James actually derived from *Virgin Soil* (although he was apparently unaware of it) was a kind of pattern or skeletal framework upon which to hang his own material—the sensitive illegitimate hero, the women who surround him as representatives both of the aristocracy and of the people, the fraternal comrade, the revolutionary movement, and the denouement in suicide. A close comparison of the two novels reveals that, real as James's indebtedness was, the obvious similarities are superficial and narrowly structural. Their skeletons are like, but the meat of the two and finally the essential spirit, are distinctly different.

Both heroes are natural sons of an aristocratic father and a lower-class mother; yet, while Nejdanov is educated and cared for by his father's family, Hyacinth receives no recognition whatsoever from Lord Frederick's family. Both heroes believe that it is the inheritance of certain aristocratic traits from their paternal line which interferes with their dedication to the revolutionary cause; yet this idea, which is given little attention in *Virgin Soil*, becomes a dominant and persistent theme in *The Princess*. Turgenev makes us feel that while Nejdanov wants to work for the people, his heart really isn't in it: he is the fastidious romantic idealist whose sympathy with the people is mainly theoretic. James, on the other hand, exploits fully the dual heritage of Hyacinth, making him a virtual battleground on which the opposed sympathies of his aristocratic and commoner heredity struggle for possession of his soul. That is the central conflict of the novel.

The women with whom the hero is associated in the respective novels also exhibit certain superficial similarities. In *Virgin Soil* there is the simple and sturdy Mashurina, faithfully devoted to the cause and to her love of Nejdanov. Her healthy solidity and coarseness and her association with the people make her similar to Millicent Henning, the muse of Cockneyism in *The Princess*. Yet Milly has far more spunk, pride, and vital charm than the stolid Mashurina, and the mutual affection of Milly and Hyacinth is quite a different relationship from that of Mashurina and Nejdanov. The ultimate distinction is that whereas the Russian girl is a dedicated revolutionary, Milly dearly wants the social ladder undisturbed—so that she may climb it!

Then there is Madame Sipiagina, a wealthy married woman, rather good- than ill-natured but basically cold and indifferent—a flirt who wants simply to make a conquest of Nejdanov. In some ways she is like James's Princess Casamassima, admittedly a *capricciosa*. Madame Sipiagina finally interferes spitefully in Nejdanov's affairs and is a principal contributor to his demise; the Princess, however, at least thinks she wants to aid Hyacinth and the cause. Moreover, Christina goes much further in making her contribution to the anarchist movement than the chill Madame Sipiagina could manage. Nejdanov is momentarily attracted by the fascinating basilisk Sipiagina but leaves her for his "true love"; Hyacinth is attracted by Christina also, but there is never any strong suggestion of the possibility of romantic involvement between them, and, furthermore, part of Christina's attraction is as a representative of the great world of taste, of beauty, of the finer things for which he hungers desperately.

The third woman in Nejdanov's life, Mariana, has a distinctly representative role: she represents the people, the miserable, poor, and oppressed of the whole of Russia. Nejdanov is as much in love with her as he can be with anyone—as much as Hamlet is in love with Ophelia, Turgenev encourages us to believe—and of course that love is made symbolic. They run away together, but they do not marry, and Nejdanov is unable to bring himself to consummate their union. His recognition of the insufficiency of his love is equated with his recognition of the insufficiency of his devotion to the revolutionary cause. He commits suicide, and his dying gesture is to unite Mariana and his stout friend Solomin.

The most marked point of resemblance in the two novels is the similarity between Solomin and James's Paul Muniment. The Russian is strong, level-headed, and sure of himself, and his generally benevolent attitude to the idealistic and sensitive young hero makes him seem like a steadying older brother. He has, then, very much the appearance and function of Paul Muniment in James's novel. Also,

Solomin's attitude of tolerant amusement at some of the futile thrash-
ing around of the more frenetic revolutionists is very like Muniment's
attitude at the meetings in the "Sun and Moon." Both men remain
sympathetic and understanding as they see the waning of revolutionist dedication in the respective heroes. Finally, each replaces the
hero in the life of his lady friend. As Nejdanov dies he begs Solomin
and Mariana to join hands: he recognizes that Solomin's quiet determination and strength of purpose qualify him as the fitting consort for
the symbolic Mariana. In James's novel, Hyacinth simply finds that
Paul Muniment has willy-nilly diverted the attention of the Princess
to himself as a more desirable representative of the people than the
aristocratic little book-binder. Hyacinth's suicide follows this association of Paul and Christina.

The Princess Casamassima is distinctly English in attitude and
character while Turgenev's novel is Russian; James gained a sharper
definition of the central tension by reducing the number of women
intimately involved in the hero's life to two; at the same time he
achieved a richer and more complex problem for his hero by developing the dimensions of the conflicting elements within him; and
the different placing of the suicide alters the focus of the hero's
dilemma and renders it more acutely affecting. I think that *The Princess* has more direct social relevance, speaks more directly to the
broad implications of revolution, than does *Virgin Soil;* and Hyacinth's role in contributing to the expression of those implications is
comparatively larger than Nejdanov's. The indebtedness admitted,
The Princess Casamassima remains definitely original and peculiarly
Jamesian in essence.

James's descriptive technique in *The Princess* is again, as it was in
The Bostonians, quite in keeping with the principles he had expressed in "The Art of Fiction." To set the scene for Hyacinth's tragic
adventures he would try to give an impression of "life *without* rearrangement," to convey convincingly "the air of reality." To paint that
picture vividly James had only to call upon his experience of the
London he knew and to render carefully the impressions he had
gained and the features he had noted. He had taken note of the scene
in both senses of the phrase, of course: he had taken it in with his
quick and eager eye, but he had also recorded a good deal in his
Notebooks. He was convinced of the value of the Naturalists' practice
of note-taking and followed their example. Consequently, he was
able to set the scene solidly and credibly in *The Princess:* the streets

of Cheapside and Camberwell, the river and dockside, Crookenden's bindery, the pubs, and even Greenwich are "done." Not just the look of them, with their bustling activity or contrasting quiet, but the sound and smell and flavor as well—their whole atmosphere has been noted and rendered impressively. The great grey Babylon is unmistakably *there,* palpable and provable.

One of the earliest and most impressive passages of description in the novel presents the prison in which young Hyacinth's unfortunate mother has been incarcerated and where she lies dying. Amanda Pynsent has brought the boy for his only visit. They approach the "dusky mass . . . sprawling over the whole neighborhood with brown, bare, windowless walls," and enter to find their dreadful expectations realized. We share their experience of the grey stony courts, unlighted staircases, uncanny corners and recesses of the draughty labyrinth; we stare amazed at the inmates, "dreadful figures, scarcely female, in hideous brown misfitting uniforms . . . marching round in a circle"; and follow Amanda

into the circular shaft of cells where she had an opportunity of looking at captives through grated peep-holes and of edging past others who had temporarily been turned into the corridors—silent women with fixed eyes, who flattened themselves against the stone walls at the brush of the visitor's dress. . . . Here were walls within walls and galleries upon galleries; even the daylight lost its colour and you couldn't imagine what o'clock it was."[4]

The sense of overwhelming depression and horror increases until they arrive at the infirmary and are taken to the bedside of the wretched Florentine Vivier. The lengthy description serves to establish the awful, solid fact of the woman's incarceration—the dominant mass of the building seen externally, the dingy and devious interior, the frightful dehumanized inmates; it also conveys the profound impression which the visit makes on the sensitive mind of Hyacinth. We feel that James had benefited, in this instance, from "the principle of the Note." In a letter of 1884 to T. S. Perry, indeed, James tells of a visit to Millbank prison to collect notes for this scene; he adds, significantly, "you see I am quite the Naturalist."[5]

What we found to be true of the descriptive passages in *The Bostonians* is similarly true of those in *The Princess Casamassima:* in accord with the principles of "The Art of Fiction," James regularly fashions his descriptions to answer the total demands of his novel.

They always do more than merely render the appearance of things, and they are all functionally integrated parts of the organic whole. The visit to the prison dominates the first section of the novel and appropriately closes that part of the story devoted to Hyacinth's childhood. The situation of his mother is likewise the dominant fact of his childhood: it casts a pall over all the rest of his life and thus lends a note of tragic foreboding to the whole action of the novel. Furthermore, the technique of description here is calculated to contribute to the characterization of Pinnie: the prison is given to us from her point of view, and while the awfulness is emphasized by her reaction to the scene, that very reaction enables us to recognize the terrible responsibility she feels that she has taken upon herself as well as her apprehension of guilt at exposing her sensitive little charge to such an experience. (It has impressed him, all right, for the memory of it is vividly present at the closing moments of his life.) The scene, then, is realistic, economically functional, and fully integrated.

It is difficult to do justice to the extensive descriptive treatment of the London setting without numerous lengthy quotations from the novel; but some excerpts may serve to suggest what James has done. A fairly representative passage occurs in Chapter 5, when Hyacinth is strolling on a Saturday night toward Milly's dwelling in Buckingham Palace Road.

... the smaller shops and open air industries were doubly active, and big clumsy torches flared and smoked over handcarts and costermongers' barrows drawn up in the gutter ... he lost himself in all the quickened crowding and pushing and staring at lighted windows and chaffering at the stalls of fishmongers and hucksters. He liked the people ... who wandered about disinterestedly and vaguely, their hands in empty pockets, watching others make their bargains and fill their satchels, or staring at the striated sides of bacon, at the golden cubes and triangles of cheese, at the graceful festoons of sausage, in the most brilliant of the windows. He liked the reflexion of the lamps on the wet pavements, the feeling and smell of the carboniferous London damp; the way the winter fog blurred and suffused the whole place, made it seem bigger and more crowded, produced halos and dim radiations, trickles and evaporations on the plates of glass.[6]

There is something reminiscent of Zola in such passages as this, even though it lacks the ponderous weight of Zola's impressive mass of detail, indeed of catalogue. It is not quite the equivalent of *le ventre de Paris,* yet there is enough suggestion of quantity and variety in the selection of details and their manner of presentation (e.g. the string of parallel phrases and clauses) to render the scene fully. All the bustle and clutter is conveyed; the murky duskyness of the air is emphasized by the flare of the smoky torches and the damp reflection of the lamps. The whole atmosphere is captured; we can feel the scene, as most of the senses are appealed to by the presentation. The passage also lets us know Hyacinth's fellow-feeling with the common people, "his brothers and sisters," and for their typical habitat and customary activity. But his attitude is romanticized, his view rosy-hued and idealistic: his brothers and sisters (as he sees them) are quaintly the picturesque poor. This is of a piece with the rest of the early development of Hyacinth: he loves London and its people and will therefore be ready to aid in gaining a better life for them. What is primarily a description of setting functions ultimately as preparation for the moment when Hyacinth will grasp the opportunity to work for revolution and for the results that will follow from that act. Here is an illustration of James's idea that a novel is not a series of different kinds of writing: "I cannot imagine composition existing in a series of blocks, nor conceive . . . of a passage of description that is not in its intention narrative . . . [etc.]."

The potential revolutionaries, the common workers from whom the movement must recruit its forces, gather regularly at the public ordinary, The Sun and Moon. James's descriptive treatment of that setting is again arranged to express its total atmosphere. He does not give us the dimensions of the pub or number the tables and chairs or mention the decor, yet we are made aware of the muffled din of muted conversation punctuated by the occasional outburst of rhetorical interrogation or observation accompanied by a thump on the table. All our senses are involved by the description: "The filthy air reached the place in the damp coats of silent men and hung there till it was brewed to a nauseous warmth, and ugly serious faces squared themselves through it, and strong-smelling pipes contributed their element in a fierce dogged manner. . . ."[7]

The function of a passage like this one, describing the group at the Sun and Moon, is obvious enough: it shows us the London workers, the fund upon which the revolution must draw, in all their depressing chaos; but it also shows Hyacinth's reaction. Before the end of the chapter in which this scene occurs, he has himself sprung upon one of the tables to deliver an impassioned speech of exhortation in which he declares himself ready to undertake all for the cause of social improvement. As the chapter (and Book II) ends he is whirled away for a secret confrontation with Hoffendahl, and to him he gives the pledge of his life for the anarchist movement. The impression conveyed by the whole of this lengthy passage may be that some change has occurred in the habitues of the pub—an increased readiness for revolutionary activity that would fully justify Hyacinth's vital pledge. In fact, however, it is only Hyacinth's sense of a change that is expressed to us: "though the note of popularity was still most effectively struck by the man who could demand oftenest, unpractically, 'What the hell am I to do with half a quid?' it was brought home to our hero on more than one occasion that revolution was ripe at last."[8] We are forced to recognize that Hyacinth has by no means made a rational commitment, but has been swept off his feet emotionally—by the pressure of circumstances.

To give an idea of the completeness with which James has "done" London—and particularly the life of her streets—we might look at his depiction of the area into which the Princess has, in a spasm of asceticism and strict economizing, taken lodgings. We have it on the authority of Hyacinth, the informed observer of such matters, that Madeira Crescent is not squalid, but simply had "that petty parochial air, that absence of style and elevation, which is the stamp of whole sections of London. . . ."

Hyacinth could see as they approached it that the window-place in the parlour, on a level with the street door, was ornamented by a glass case containing stuffed birds and surmounted by an alabaster Cupid. . . . The long light of a grey summer evening was still in the air and Madeira Crescent wore a soiled, dusty expression. A hand-organ droned in front of a neighbouring house and the cart of the local washerwoman, to which a donkey was harnessed, was drawn up opposite. The local children as well were dancing on the pavement to the music of the organ, and the scene was surveyed from one of the windows by a gentleman in a dirty dressing-gown, smoking a pipe, who made Hyacinth think of Mr. Micawber.[9]

Here again the activity, the sights and the sounds are presented clearly—not so much as Zola would have done it, but rather in the style of Flaubert: careful selection of a few graphic details serves to catch the scene and its particular atmosphere. The dustiness, the humdrum daily round, the greyness of life at its ravelling edges are all amply suggested by the donkey-drawn washerwoman and the

figure in the dressing-gown fondly looking out for something to turn
up. The drone of the hand-organ and even the dancing of the children (the innocent amusement of the unknowing young) heighten
the impression of the deadliness of the scene. We feel the full justness
of Hyacinth's summing up of the house and street—a setting that
combined every quality that should have made it detestable to the
Princess Casamassima.

The description of Madeira Crescent, complemented by an account of the interior of the low, stucco-fronted house, adds to the
characterization of Christina and indelibly marks a stage in her progress as a sympathizer with the underprivileged—as well as a step (as
she pretends to hope) toward an active role in the anarchist movement. The whole passage also further develops Hyacinth for us as it
is presented from his point of view—another example of reflexive
characterization. We recognize the effect of Hyacinth's education—
his experience of the Princess and her way of life for example at the
lovely country house of Medley (which provides a striking contrast
to her house in Madeira Crescent)[10] and his experience of the gay
boulevards, the theatres and palaces and museums of Paris. And we
realize, as we share Hyacinth's view of the Crescent, that both sides
of the sharply conflicting natures within him have now been fully
developed, and that they are about to bring him to an impasse or tear
him apart in their strife.

In James's description of the various characters in the novel he
employs many of the devices we have just been considering. In a
sense, of course, the whole novel is devoted to the characterization
of its hero. Strictly speaking, however, definite passages of fairly
direct description sketch him out for us. We first see Hyacinth at age
ten, a diminutive little chap with golden curls and dark blue eyes. In
Chapter 5 we find the initial description of him as the young man
whose career we shall follow through the novel. He appears no larger
in stature than he had promised to be: his figure is slight, his chest
narrow, his complexion pale, and he has dense curly hair, a high
forehead, large eyes, a fair moustache, and a delicate hand—which
impresses Milly Henning as the hand of a gentleman. For of course
the view we have of Hyacinth is refracted through Milly's vision. She
has returned to Lomax Place after an absence of several years to look
up her old playmate. What she sees constitutes a descriptive rendering of Hyacinth that is quite fully detailed, quite solidly factual; but
those details are pregnant and the facts suggestive, so that we not

only perceive the physical presence of Hyacinth but also are enabled to draw several pertinent inferences about him which are verified as the novel progresses. But there is another, perhaps less obvious, set of facts here which do not pertain immediately to Hyacinth and which are quite as real and relevant and theoretically quite as "provable" as the former set: they are the facts which the observer, Milly, reveals about herself as she takes careful note of the attractive young hero.

Miss Henning observed that when he first appeared he wore his little soft circular hat in a way that left [his] frontal locks very visible. He was dressed in an old brown velveteen jacket and wore exactly the bright-coloured necktie which Miss Pynsent's quick fingers used of old to shape out of hoarded remnants of silk and muslin. He was shabby and workstained, but an observant eye would have caught the hint of an "arrangement" in his dress.... There was something exotic in him, and yet, with his sharp young face, destitute of bloom but not of sweetness, and a certain conscious cockneyism that pervaded him, he was as strikingly as Millicent, in her own degree, a product of the London streets and the London air. He looked both ingenuous and slightly wasted, amused, amusing and indefinably sad.[11]

What is involved here, so far as Milly is concerned, is a kind of psychological realism, an early stage in the development of a technique that culminates (for James) in *The Ambassadors* and ultimately leads to the narrative technique of James Joyce and Virginia Woolf and numerous others. Of course the use of an observer is a device that allows the author to veil his omniscient presence so that the scene seems to be presented directly and immediately—without, that is, the interference of the mediate narrating author. But in instances like the one in question, where the observer is not only reporting the appearance of another character but also adding interpretations and impressions of her own—that is, reacting to that character—the scene takes on quite a dramatic aspect, for what we are witnessing is actually the interaction of the two characters before us. Here, then, is a good example of the quality of "dramatic immediacy" which Joseph Warren Beach noted as a special feature of James's fiction.

It might fairly be said that Amanda Pynsent is also involved in the drama of the scene. An acute reader will notice that in the passage quoted Milly's function as observer does not persist to the very end: she quits that function after the sentence referring to Hyacinth's necktie ("which Miss Pynsent's fingers used of old to shape ... ")—

but just how long after? Is the reference, in the subsequent sentence, to "an observant eye" Milly's reference? Is it James's? Is it possibly Amanda's? The second-last sentence of the quotation is hardly Milly's, for it compares her and Hyacinth in a way she was not—at least at that moment—capable of doing. But it might be Amanda's. The passage quoted is immediately followed by a direct statement of Miss Pynsent's; so that what we have seen is James's subtle technique of shifting his focus from Milly's to Amanda's point of view.

The whole context from which the quotation is taken is comprised of direct discourse intermixed with descriptive passages like the one in question, and most certainly involves Amanda with the other two in the dramatic situation. But it is apparent that the particular passage quoted contributes fully to the maintenance of the dramatic quality of the whole section of the chapter and to its strict coherence by skillfully and subtly shifting from one point of view to another—without skipping a beat! And all of this is presented in the guise (so to speak) of a rather traditional realistic description of Hyacinth Robinson.

James develops his hero in *The Princess*, as he had done in *The Bostonians*, by developing his peculiar setting—which accounts for him quite as much as his clothing or the company he keeps. Hyacinth's setting is, to be sure, the whole of London, whose streets he had loved to walk from his tenderest years. More strictly, his setting is Lomax Place and, most immediately, the meagre dwelling of the good Pinnie. That dwelling is described in full and pregnant detail, and again appropriately via the observant eye of Milly Henning. If she has returned in part to look up Hyacinth she has also returned to look down upon her old neighborhood: she wants to impress the inhabitants of Lomax Place with her rise in the world and to emphasize her difference from them—and from what she herself had been or at least promised to become. Her eye is liable, then, to emphasize the less flattering aspects of the scene before her; but even as it does so it numbers the items in the scene with some clear objectivity.[12] She notes the washed out yellow stuff covering the old familiar sofa, the pincushions, needlebooks, pink measuring tape, and the same old collection of fashion plates "crumpled, sallow and fly-blown." She notes Amanda herself, bristling with needles and pins stuck all over the front of her dress; the absence of rustling fabrics, the solitary presence of the skirt of a shabby dress witness the state of Amanda's business. The scene is quite self-explanatory. The washed-out and unchanged furnishings, the signs of Pinnie's ceaseless yet ineffectual industry impinge painfully on our senses. Poor Amanda herself, a sort of declining Mrs. Tiggy-Winkle, stands in the center, a symbol of her "show room," as if to underline the fact that she now has nothing to show. The presentation is sufficient without any comment, even from Milly—yet her impression of things hangs heavy in the air.

When Amanda appeals to Hyacinth, newly entered, to side with her against Milly—"Miss 'Enning wouldn't live in Lomax Place for the world. She thinks it too dreadfully low."—we wince at his sharp reply: "So it is; it's a beastly hole."[13] The effect of the description of Hyacinth's dwelling is at first to divide our feelings about him, but finally to enable us to understand his predicament the better. We realize easily enough how that setting must work on the sensitive young man whose taste is forming already and whose yearning for "finer things" we already know. The setting functions as the extension and explanation of his character, of that identity which Hyacinth will try to escape later in the novel; on the other hand it represents a part of him which he cannot, and to some extent will not want to, deny—a part to which he is bound by ties of profound sympathy and affection. His sharp judgment on this dwelling and Lomax Place generally—"it's a beastly hole"—shocks us because we know the effect it has on Pinnie and seems therefore to smack of ingratitude. Yet almost at once, by a kind of "double-take," we see that Hyacinth's reaction is complex and at bottom humane. That reaction is composed of revulsion from the squalid life, a desire to escape it himself but also a desire to help those whom he cares for to want to escape it as well. It is a beastly hole for Pinnie as well as for Hyacinth; the recognition that it is so must precede any possible move to work for change, for improvement—for revolution.

The passage in question is, thus, fully functional and is one of many similar. A full consideration of James's development of Hyacinth's setting leads us to the London streets (always), to Crookenden's bindery where he finds satisfaction of his need for gainful labor and of his artistic yearnings, to the poor apartment of his friends the Muniments and to the modest house of the Poupins. Indeed, we should be led to consider a great deal of London as the novel presents it in order really to comprehend the setting which completes Hyacinth.

We must also consult the company he keeps. Of particular importance is the pair of young women with whom Hyacinth is principally involved—Milly and the Princess. Milly deserves a whole section to herself, for she is surely one of James's most successfully realized characters. As the novel began serial publication, James's new friend, Robert Louis Stevenson, wrote immediate approval, singling out Milly for special comment: "As for your young lady, she is all there; yes, sir, you can do low life, I believe."[14] She does make her palpable presence felt: she is indeed "all there"—round and firm and fully realized. Milly is, like the other main characters, developed gradually in a series of scenes throughout the novel. The first full-scale description of her occurs when she returns to visit Lomax Place. James wisely begins the passage dramatically by allowing Milly to introduce herself with the frank avowal, "Well, I enjoy beautiful 'ealth." The description bears out the truth of her statement as it lists her physical features—her bold, good-natured eye, her abundant brown hair, and the flaunting whiteness of her smile. "Her head was set on a fair strong neck and her robust young figure was rich in feminine curves. Her gloves, covering her wrists insufficiently, showed the redness of those parts in the interstices of the numerous silver bracelets that encircled them, and Miss Pynsent made the observation that her hands were not more delicate than her feet."[15] Amanda continues her observation by noting that Milly is a bundle of contradictions— that in spite of her magnificence she is common, and yet has about her something fresh, successful, and satisfying.

There are plenty of details here to fill out all three dimensions of the healthy Miss Henning; and there is a fair share of interpretative comment on her in Miss Pynsent's observation. It was a happy stroke of James's to give us the benefit of Amanda's point of view: she is by no means biassed in the young woman's favor—as a mere man might be—and she is critical but just in her appraisal. The measure of appreciation that Amanda can permit herself here strikes with the greater force as we recognize the opportunity Milly has given for antipathy. In addition, the details manage to express—even beyond Amanda's interpretation—the mixture of qualities in Milly: they indicate the determined rise of which she is so proud, yet reveal the persistence of those characteristics that will forever mark her relation to the fair lady who is her younger literary cousin, Liza Doolittle the Dustman's daughter. James does not keep strictly to Amanda's point of view. The burst of rhetoric in the final sentence of the paragraph of description is beyond her capacity, and one may well feel here the exuberant presence of the omniscient author—momentarily gripped by the passion of Pygmalion:

She was to her blunt, expanded finger-tips a daughter of London, of the crowded streets and bustling traffic of the great city; she had drawn her health and strength from its dingy courts and foggy thoroughfares and peopled its parks and squares with her ambitions; it had entered into her blood and her bone; the sound of her voice and the carriage of her head; she understood it by instinct and loved it with passion; she represented its immense vulgarities and curiosities, its brutalities and its knowingness, its good-nature and its impudence, and might have figured, in a an allegorical procession, as a kind of glorified townswoman, a nymph of the wilderness of Middlesex, a flower of the clustered parishes, the genius of urban civilisation, the muse of cockneyism.[16]

Milly is so roundly rendered, so satisfyingly real and full of vital actuality that some readers will reject any suggestion that her role in the novel is at all representative. Yet it seems hard to miss the encouragement James has given here to consider that she represent, at least for Hyacinth,[17] all the bustling contradictory populace of London— "the people," in whose cause he is soon to enlist. It is as true for Milly as it is for Hyacinth that all of London is her setting: even as the foregoing quotation suggests, London is an extension and explanation of her while she in turn sums it up and epitomizes it.

The other side of Hyacinth Robinson is attracted to Christina, the Princess Casamassima. Quite obviously, she is not rendered in the way Milly is: her physical presence is never so solidly specified, never made so tangible and dense. The facts we are given about the Princess are mainly the facts of Hyacinth's impression of her. We first meet her, for example, in the dimly lit box at the theater and see her through Hyacinth's already dazzled eyes. We do make out certain features—her dark eyes and thick, delicate hair with two or three diamond stars in it, a string of pearls, and a rococo fan. But these specific factual details seem almost drowned in the welter of exciting impressions that flood in upon the fascinated little bookbinder. Hyacinth sees her as "fair, shining, slender, with an effortless majesty." He is not sure of her eyes: "they are dark, blue or grey, something not brown." She makes him think of something antique and celebrated. "Purity of line and form, of cheek and chin and lip and brow, a colour that seemed to live and glow, a radiance of grace and eminence and success—these things were seated in triumph in the face of the Princess, and [Hyacinth] questioned if she were really of the same substance with the humanity he had hitherto known. She might be divine, but he could see she understood human needs. . . ."[18]

Now those details are about as realistically accurate and objective as the dimensions of Keats' "magic casements." What we are faced with here is that other order of facts I mentioned earlier—facts that have to do with Hyacinth's soul, that describe his state of mind. Those are real enough and quite clearly expressed. The quotation offers, then, another example of the kind of psychological realism that James was becoming interested in developing. The Princess is not the solid creation that Milly is, yet she is vitally present to us (in passages like this one) because of the convincing reality of Hyacinth's acute awareness of her.

It is important for the general aims of the novel, furthermore, that we never quite see the Princess as a sharply defined objective entity: it is Hyacinth's perception of her that we must see clearly. She is a fairy princess in his eyes, and redolent of all the good things of the gentle life for which the artistic soul of Hyacinth hungrily yearns. Her role is as representative as Milly's, so far as he is concerned. To make her too definite and palpable would threaten to destroy the quality of fairy princess—which we must be able to perceive as Hyacinth does. If we were allowed to see clearly and unmistakably that she is not the ideal aristocratic beauty that she seems to him, the dramatic irony would be so strong as to crush our sympathy for Hyacinth and gravely alter our interest in Christina. She must remain rather vague and dim in outline.

If the presentation of Christina herself is somewhat vague and impressionistic, the settings in which she typically appears are rendered in careful and generous detail. And James frequently indicates that her milieu is indeed intended to complete and explain her: "Hyacinth had time to count over the innumerable *bibelots* . . . involved in the character of a woman of high fashion and to feel that their beauty and oddity revealed not only whole provinces of art, but refinements of choice on the part of their owner, complications of mind and—almost—terrible depths of temperament."[19] Particularly revealing (to Hyacinth, at least) is the impressive house at Medley. The library, for instance, is especially striking in its array of genial comforts: the vast writing table alone—with its paper and pens, inkstands and blotters, seals, stamps, candlesticks, reels of twine, paperweights, and book-knives—indicates the opulent profusion of *things*, the rich abundance of comfortable conveniences available to accommodate life's every demand. Here is a perfect synecdoche for life at Medley and, moreover, for the whole of life as the Princess lives it. Here is *la dolce vita*, an existence of luxury and indolence.

We understand Hyacinth's fairy princess much better, seem to see her more clearly, as a result of this view of her in her appropriate setting. And we likewise easily understand the tremendous appeal such a figure has for Hyacinth. The impressive fact of Medley permits us to gauge the descent in Christina's life when she moves to the house in Madeira Crescent. The contrast is great enough to permit us to sympathize with Hyacinth's sense of shock: how can his Princess bear so to demean herself? He regards her sacrifice as a *tour de force*. The reader may well feel that the sacrifice (even if not so great, after all, as Hyacinth reckons it) does indicate a certain seriousness in Christina's desire to give up everything and so merit the respect of the revolutionists. So the reader will in his turn experience some shock at Paul Muniment's comment to the Princess "You've a great deal left for a person who has given everything away." That observation indicates the limits of Paul's sympathy with Christina and of his appreciation of the sacrifice involved. In a way he is right: she has a great deal left, including her maid-servant Assunta and her Italian cook; but Paul judges her sacrifice absolutely, Hyacinth with perhaps more justice relatively.

But the question of whether Paul or Hyacinth is right has no real relevance here. The point is that Christina has impressed Hyacinth with what he considers her great self-denial; the further point is that she remains for us a bit of a puzzle in her new situation. Is she once again simply being capricious, we wonder, or is she truly serious in making what sacrifices she *can?* We are uncertain and consequently can more readily sympathize with Hyacinth's uncertainty about her —which is, of course, at the very heart of his dilemma. In this instance the novel has expressed what it must not explain: our impression of the situation is as real (as uncertain and complex) as our impression of it would be in actual life.

The three principal characters, then, are developed vividly in these various ways. Around them clusters a host of secondary characters who are themselves fully individuated, vivified, and provided with their explanatory setting. They share the responsibility for the sense of the crowded and varied human scene of London which James has managed to create in the novel: the kind avuncular Vetch, Amanda's friend and neighbor in Lomax Place; Paul Muniment and his invalid sister Rosie in their cramped quarters in Audley Court; Crookenden and his bindery and his tidy family; Captain Sholto in his adequate bachelor quarters; Eustache Poupin and his wife in their cozy home; the willowy Lady Aurora of Belgrave Square. And behind or among these characters there is the crowd of minor figures, brought individually into brief sharp relief by a choice graphic detail as they are drawn forward from the crowd to play their momentary roles: the imposing Mrs. Bowerbank, a high-shouldered towering woman suggesting squareness; the impassive Herr Schinkel with his perpetual pipe and untidy bandage; Lady Marchant and her daughters from Broome; etc. It is certainly true, as Lionel Trilling says in his essay on *The Princess Casamassima*, that "James is at the point in his career at which society, in the largest and even the grossest sense, is offering itself to his mind. . . . The social texture of his work is grainy and knotted with practicality and detail."[20]

To achieve that grainy and knotted quality, James attended especially to the full rendering of his scene of action; he attempted to capture and express the whole atmosphere by describing not only the look of things but their feel and taste and smell and sound as well. The last of these requires a special word. I illustrated something of James's attention to the sounds of his scene by indicating the nature of the typical remarks of the habitues of the "Sun and Moon." But throughout the novel there is abundant evidence of James's care to give the most authentic ring to the speech of his characters—not simply what they say, that is, but their peculiar manner of saying it. To begin with, the speech of many of the characters is marked by the cockney "a"—Milly's first home is in Lomax "Plice," which she considers a "shime"; their speech is also marked by the mute "h" where one expects an aspirate, so that Milly's name becomes " 'Enning," 'eaven 'elp us! But along with this feature of the cockney pronunciation we find those turns of phrase that we recognize as typical of that class to which Hyacinth's earliest friends belong. For example, there is this exchange between Pinnie and Mrs. Bowerbank about the boy Hyacinth:

". . . And do he have his tea that way by himself, like a real little gentleman?"
"Well, I try to give it to him tidy-like, at a suitable hour," said Miss Pynsent guiltily.

The peculiar grammatical fault and the phrase "tidy-like" give this bit of dialogue quite an authentic ring. Of course, this is just what Zola had attempted: to capture the real sound and the true flavor of the people he put into his fiction, to achieve compelling authenticity.

And we know that he provided himself with copious notes of particular idioms with the aim in mind of reproducing the real thing in his fiction. James followed the Naturalists' practice. In his Notebooks for the period during which he was preparing *The Princess Casamassima* we find entries like this:

August 22nd [1885]. Phrases of the people ... "that takes the gilt off, you know." ... a young man—of his patron, in a shop ... "he cuts it very fine." ... " 'Ere today, somewhere else tomorrow: that's 'is motto."[21]

These characters of *The Princess,* born within sound of Bow Bells, share the stage with French, Germans, Italians; and James's attempt to convey the peculiar flavor of the speech of these others led him to use the conventional devices similar to the vowel modification he used to portray the cockney speech. Herr Schinkel, for example, is regularly made to say "lofe" for "love" and "bett" for "bed." Another device, closely associated with these, is the sprinkling of characteristic phrases from the native tongue of a given character through his conversation. Thus, Mme. Poupin calls Hyacinth "mon petit," and exclaims at some silly remark, "En v'là des bêtises!" And Madame Grandoni easily agrees, with "Natürlich," or soothes the estranged husband of her friend Christina by calling him "caro mio." A judicious sprinkling of such phrases manages to suggest the foreign nature of the conversation—without carrying Naturalism to its *reductio ad absurdam.*

But there is an extension of these rather conventional devices in the novel, an innovation which seems particularly effective. It consists, apparently, in the use of a stilted form of English to suggest the character's unfamiliarity with the English tongue. Actually these particular passages are literal translations from the character's mother tongue. Consider Poupin's frequent (with a shrug) "What will you have?" The English "What do you expect?" etc., is inadequate as a rendering of Poupin's French-flavored conversation. Similarly, Madame Poupin's turn of phrase in such comments as "He's the person we have seen in this country whom we like the best," or again". . . not as good as good as anyone in the world? I should like to see!" are literal translations of idiomatic French. And Herr Schinkel's laconic remark to Hyacinth, "Your way, not so?" is a literal translation from the idiomatic German. The point here is not, of course, that one must be able to recognize the actual native phrase behind the stilted English, but rather that this strategy of using the literal translation captures as authentically as possible the peculiar flavor of the speech of the character in question—and further, that an ear of average acuteness will detect the unmistakably French, or Italian, or German, treatment of the words and appreciate the fidelity of rendering.

Finally, a word on the ultimate extension of the device I have just mentioned, which is to be found in the scene at the prison between Hyacinth and his dying mother: Florentine Vivier's speeches are with one exception all in her native French. This is, if you like, the last word in Naturalistic verisimilitude—as if some Victorian literalist were to turn *Romeo and Juliet* completely into Italian! But James has not quite done that. The effect of that long and touching scene is, in addition to the almost overwhelming realism of Florentine's idiom, to drop a grateful veil over a scene of heart-rending pathos and subdue its horror, to provide a suitable means of containing the highly charged emotional content of the scene. Consequently, this extreme use of the idiom is a very felicitous stroke. James has even provided a little hint of what he was doing, a signal to appreciation, as he permits the attendant Pinnie to feel "that this separation of language [between Florentine and Hyacinth] was indeed a mercy."[22]

There is another aspect of James's narrative technique as seen in *The Princess Casamassima* that was influenced by the theory and practice of the Naturalists. In discussing *The Bostonians* I mentioned those narrative devices of James's which are aimed at creating a self-sufficient story—a story that appears to be free of dependence upon an explanatory and manipulating author—and chief among them the use of point-of-view narration. This later novel also offers ample evidence of the technique of point of view as an effective means of reducing the role of the omniscient author and enhancing dramatic immediacy. Seldom, if ever, are scenes or characters presented to us objectively—that is, in the old traditional manner of the story-teller to his audience. Usually we have an observer before us who views the setting or personage to be described. He acts as the focus: we see things through him and get the scene and its details on *his* authority—not, apparently, on the authority of the omniscient author. Occasionally, in this novel, much less frequently than in *The Bostonians,* James has resorted to the little rhetorical ruses that seem to deflect the burden of authority from the narrator. In a scene between Christina and Hyacinth at her Mayfair dwelling, for example, we read: "By the time he had been with her half an hour she had made the situation itself easy and usual, and a third person who should have joined them at this moment would have noticed nothing to suggest that friendly social intercourse between little bookbinders and neapolitan princesses was not in London a matter of daily occurrence."[23] The hypothetical "third person" functions exactly like the locution "I do not know whether" which precedes an idea that the author wishes to implant without appearing to do so on his own authority. In all those passages quoted above as illustrations of James's descriptive technique we noticed the presence of an observer, a focusing agent or authority; and we also noticed the additional function of this practice as a means of *reflexive* characterization—as, for instance, the description of Hyacinth in which Milly in part reveals herself by the details she notices and the observations she makes on them. Of course it is Hyacinth Robinson's point of view which predominates in *The Princess,* for it is principally his story: his way of seeing things, the impressions they make on him are what matter most in the novel. How Hyacinth sees his puzzling world is, indeed, at the very heart of the problem in the novel; and I will turn to that matter in a moment.

One more example of James's narrative technique must be given first, however, an example which further illustrates one of the principles enunciated in "The Art of Fiction." There James had said that he could not conceive "in any novel worth discussing at all, of a passage of description that is not in its intention narrative, a passage of dialogue that is not in its intention descriptive, . . . [etc.]. A Novel is a living thing, all one and continuous. . . ." Certain passages of *The Princess,* as of *The Bostonians*, combine the features of dialogue, narration, and description (or, more exactly, characterization). One such involves Rosie Muniment and Hyacinth; the invalid has undertaken to explain Lady Aurora.

She had made their acquaintance, Paul's and hers, about a year before, through a friend of theirs, such a fine brave young woman, who was in St. Thomas's Hospital for a surgical operation. . . . Paul had to admit that her ladyship was beyond anything that any one in his waking senses would believe. She seemed to want to give up everything to those who were below her and never expect any thanks at all. And she wasn't always preaching and showing you your duty; she wanted to talk to you sociable-like, as if you were just her own sister.

. . . her ladyship thought Rosy's Paul the very cleverest. . . . Rosy wouldn't spread such a rumour as that in the court itself, but she wanted every friend of her brother's (and she could see Hyacinth was a real one by the way he listened) to know what was thought of him by them that had an experience of intellect.[24]

Perhaps the main purpose of this segment is to narrate the history of Lady Aurora as it involves the Muniments; but it has all the flavour of Rosy's natural manner of speaking—it is a kind of direct indirect-discourse—and is, then, another example of what I have called "narrative-in-idiom"; since it also conveys the sense of dialogue (notice, for instance, the parenthetical clause in the last sentence of the quotation) the passage has definitely a dramatic quality. It is as though this passage, in appearance narrative, were being enacted before our eyes. In addition to that, of course, it manages to contribute to the characterization of the bright-eyed little magpie Rosy.

As all these examples from *The Princess Casamassima* illustrate, James was in fact following rather closely the precept and pattern of French Naturalist literature. His technique of describing both characters and setting, and the narrative art directed to constructing a story that would seem independent of the traditional story-teller and thus succeed in creating a satisfactory illusion of reality are features clearly apparent in *The Princess*, and they amply attest to the influence of the Flaubert group.

The influence, furthermore, of Zola's ideas about *le roman expéri-mental* is especially evident in *The Princess Casamassima*. This story of a modern Hyacinthus, fatally suspended between two loves, offers the clearest example of the Jamesian experimental novel. Nowhere else in James's work does the determining effect of the heredity and the environment of the hero play so large a role. The hereditary influences are more explicitly present here than in the other two major novels of the eighties, and the environmental forces to which the hero is exposed correspond to the hereditary more closely here than elsewhere. It is a complex little case for experimental examination. Hyacinth Robinson is a combination of two pairs of antagonistic (in the terms of the novel) elements—French and English, commoner and aristocratic blood. The first element in each pair comes to him from his mother, the second from his father (we are led to believe). His experience places him in a series of *milieux* in each of which he is exposed to the influence of various combinations of those elements: each of these encounters realizes one or more aspect of his hereditary mixture. And at every turn of the action, the question of Hyacinth's heredity is raised before us and its importance to him is emphasized.

Hyacinth is raised in an environment which is English and commoner, although Pinnie keeps alive the whisper of an aristocratic background. Through Anastasius Vetch, the paternal neighbor, he makes the acquaintance of the Poupins (French and commoner), and through them, in turn, he meets Paul Muniment (English commoner). These latter two contacts also resurrect the republican strain of his maternal grandfather, the earlier Hyacinthe. Poupin and Muniment strengthen that association by introducing him to the group of reformers at the "Sun and Moon." At Muniment's he makes his first contact with the English aristocracy in the willowy form of the Lady Aurora Langrish. And not long after that Hyacinth meets the Princess Casamassima, an even more exalted representative of the aristocracy, and one with whom he is quickly made to feel that French is the aristocratic *lingua franca*. It is as though the environment were arranged to transmit direct appeal to the corresponding hereditary elements within Hyacinth, and at the same time to provoke reaction from those hereditary elements to which they are opposed. The "experiment," we might say, is set up to discover what will become of the character in which these potentially conflicting elements are confined, especially when he is placed in an environment where the same elements will act upon him from without. James very neatly framed the purpose of the experiment when he wrote in the preface to the novel that "the reward of a romantic curiosity would be the question of what the total assault, that of the world of his work-a-day life and the world of his divination and envy together, would have made of him. . . ."[25] An initial answer to that question is that it makes of Hyacinth a most perplexed young man. The elements within him are mixed but not fused, and those assaults are equivocal. To begin with, Hyacinth is by no means sure of who or what he is. When he first meets Paul Muniment, early in the novel, he is presented with the mild dilemma of deciding his national identity. Muniment suggests, "Perhaps you're French." Hyacinth pauses. He thinks of his mother, her suffering in an alien land; and as he feels that all of that would make him French, he is immediately made conscious of other, different qualities—"He had a father too, and his father had suffered as well. . . ." He can only answer Paul lamely with, "Oh, I daresay I ain't anything!"

As important for Hyacinth as the question of his national identity, certainly, is the question of his social affinities. A long section of the final chapter of Book First indicates that the republican, revolutionary strain in his blood is responding to the stimulus of the same strain in his environment: he feels he is indeed the grandson of his mother's father, whose very name he bears. Yet the doubt intervenes at last, as he cannot forget the aristocratic strain that he believes is in him as well.

He had no need to reason about it; all his nerves and pulses pleaded and testified. His mother had been a daughter of the wild French people—all Pinnie could tell him of his parentage was that Florentine had once mentioned that in her extreme childhood her father, his gun in his hand, had fallen in the blood-stained streets of Paris on a barricade; but on the other hand, it took an English aristocrat to account for him. . . . the reflexion that he was a bastard involved in a remarkable degree the reflexion that he was a gentleman.

A thousand times yes, he was with the people and every possible vengeance of the people. . . , but all the same he was happy to feel he had blood in his veins that would account for the finest sensibilities.[26]

"A thousand times yes . . . but"—and the equivocal note is sustained. And that note persists through the closing episode of Book First as Hyacinth takes Milly out for the evening. Their little romance reflects Hyacinth's sympathy with the common people she represents; but notice that he squires his Muse of Cockneyism not to the music hall but to the theater—indulging his tastes like a little gentleman.

Book Second begins by introducing an influence that will heighten the tension we have already seen in Hyacinth. At the theater to which he has taken Milly he is made acquainted with the glamorous Princess Casamassima. He has already met Lady Aurora, but in the sober and homely setting of Paul Muniment's. Yet the vibrations which that earlier association had gently aroused are newly awakened now, and he is acutely aware that the new element in his environment—the distinctly aristocrat—touches an eagerly responding chord in his hereditary make-up. Two results are produced: first Hyacinth is flattered to learn that these two aristocratic ladies share his interest in the popular cause; and second, the contrast between the luxurious ease of the quotidian aristocratic existence and the grinding poverty of the lower classes sharpens his sense of pity for the underprivileged. His new experience, then, tends to confirm his tendency to participate in the movement for reform. At the close of Book Second Hyacinth rises at the "Sun and Moon" to make his impassioned plea for action that results in his being whisked off to meet the mysterious Hoffendahl and to utter the oath that effectively mortgages his life. He has shown himself a true son of the people, "*ab ovo* a revolutionist."

But there is no easing of tension for him subsequent to his commitment to the cause. Book Third at its very outset establishes a striking dramatic contrast for Hyacinth: hard on the heels of his success as a pledged revolutionary follows his success in Society—in that Society of which the Princess is so exalted a representative. He has accepted her invitation to visit the sumptuous country house of Medley, that most appropriate of settings which serve as the extension and explanation of his fairy princess. Hyacinth is there as more than spectator, for he is able to share in the magic life of beauty and ease, and the aristocratic strain in the blood of Lord Frederick's son cries out in eager response. He is given reason to feel, moreover, that he really belongs in such a setting, as he successfully meets the social test provided by the visit of Lady Marchant and her daughters: "This was the first time a young gentlewoman hadn't been warned, and as a consequence he appeared to pass muster."[27] And as if to emphasize Hyacinth's attraction to the way of life he feels he was born to lead, James creates a mild little romance between him and the Princess. The result of this turn of events is, of course, to involve Hyacinth more inextricably than ever in the wretched dilemma that has plagued him from the outset. He tells Christina his whole brief story up to the fateful encounter with Hoffendahl. He does not say that he pledged himself to the cause, but rather "I gave my life away." He adds that he now finds himself pitying not the unhappy poor, but the rich, the happy. The Princess closes this exchange with an apt and touching observation. "Fancy the strange and bitter fate: to be constituted as you're constituted, to be conscious of the capacity you must feel, and yet to look at the good things of life only through the glass of the pastry cook's window!" Indeed!

A harsher note of discord is added to this ideal environment at Medley with the reappearance of Captain Sholto, the sometime friend of the Princess. Hyacinth's dilemma is further confused and complicated as Sholto reminds Hyacinth that he has intruded on the bookbinder's relationship with Milly Henning. A surprising pang of jealousy is aroused in Hyacinth, and he suddenly feels that Milly's

"mingled beauty and grossness, her vulgar vitality, the spirit of con-
tradiction yet at the same time of attachment that was in her, had
ended by making her indispensable to him."[28] To confound matters
further, Sholto reveals that his own interest in the anarchist movement was feigned—"I believe those on top of the heap are better
than those under it, that they mean to stay there, and if they're not
a pack of poltroons they will"[29]—an interest merely assumed to aid
in his role as virtual pander to the Princess, whose interest in turn he
regards as gross caprice.

The death of Pinnie effectively ends Book Third by calling Hyacinth away from the idyll at Medley. Her death serves to awaken in
him a sense of guilt at having neglected his fond foster parent, at
having forsaken his own; yet at the same time it marks the severing
of a bond that has held him to Lomax Place and to the people.

Our sense of Hyacinth's separation from "his own" is increased as
Book Fourth transports him across the Channel—chiefly to Paris.
There the environment will surely awaken a sympathetic response
from the French stream in Hyacinth's blood; but the crucial question
at this stage of the experiment is whether the "great grey Babylon"
will speak more loudly to the grandson of the republican revolutionary or to the little aristocrat who sprang to life at Medley. Eustache
Poupin has armed Hyacinth with several letters of introduction to
socialist friends in the French capitol. But there, as at Medley, it is
the appeal of luxury and good living and rich culture—the delights
of the theatre, the treasures of the Louvre, the gay life of the Boulevards—that speaks most urgently to Hyacinth. The letters from Poupin remain undelivered. But Hyacinth has a letter of his own to
attend to, a long explanation of his complete disaffection: "Dear
Princess, I may have done you good, but you haven't done me much.
. . . I may have helped you to understand and enter into the misery
of the people—though I protest I don't know much about it; but
you've led my imagination into quite another train."[30] The environmental pressure has done its work: the influence of the Medley milieu
and of the pleasant Paris setting, in which it is now recalled, have
provoked the telling response of Hyacinth's paternal strain (as we are
encouraged to believe it to be).

He returns to London to face Poupin and to see again the Princess
in her new dwelling and measure her progress—or decline. She
seems to him now to be merely playing with life, to be in truth the
capricciosa Madame Grandoni has always called her. And at the same

time he is reminded of his own position as suspect and dubious in the eyes of his old friends of the "Sun and Moon." As though to heighten at once our sense of the dubiety of Hyacinth's position and our feeling of suspense over the disaster imminent in Hyacinth's Damoclean oath, Book Fourth ends with Vetch's plea to the Princess to intercede on Hyacinth's behalf and prevent the sacrifice which he suspects is to be demanded of the young man. Oddly enough, a figure from Hyacinth's original plebian setting is here seeking from the exalted representative of aristocratic society intercession with the anarchists. A strange reversal of roles. But then the whole variegated scene of the novel has been full of reversals and inversions and topsi-turviness which have tumbled Hyacinth unmercifully about. Small wonder that the Princess says of him to Vetch, "He changes constantly and his impressions change," and again "He's a strange mixture of contradictory impulses. . . ."[31]

There remains only for the last two books (actually the final fifth of the novel) to provide the denouement of this tragic drama—although it is less a denouement than an alexandrine cutting of the knot which looses the cataclysm. The first two books of the novel have provided the rising action, the next two the falling action, with the climax occurring in Book Third, where the *peripeteia* and what there is of *anagnorisis* closely coincide with classical propriety. Only the resolution is needed to complete the tragic pattern. Early in the last book there is a long passage of resumé which reiterates the hereditary influence and the environmental pressure to which Hyacinth has been subjected and which he has tried vainly to understand. That passage prepares for Hyacinth's final collapse.

. . . There was no peace for him between the two currents that flowed in his nature. . . . He had a high ambition: he wanted neither more nor less than to get hold of the truth and wear it in his heart. . . . but to whatever quarter he turned in his effort to find it he seemed to know that behind him, bent on him in reproach, was a tragic wounded face. The thought of his mother had filled him with the vague, clumsy fermentation of his first impulses toward social criticism; but since the problem had become more complex by the fact that many things in the world as it was constituted were to grow intensely dear to him, he had tried more and more to construct some conceivable and human countenance for his father—some expression of honour, of tenderness and recognition, of unmeritted suffering, or at least of adequate expiation. To desert one of these presences for the other—that idea was the source of shame, as an act of treachery would have been; for he could almost hear the voice of his father ask him if it were the conduct of a gentleman to take up the opinions and emulate the crudities of fanatics and cads. . . .[32]

The one truth that Hyacinth does grasp is that he cannot bring himself, in spite of all (or rather because of all), to contribute to the downfall of a class and a way of life he believes are responsible for much of the beauty that civilization has produced. He sees that he can never fulfill his oath and, on the other hand, that he cannot betray that oath: in either case he would have to be false to himself. The whole complication, then, is so arranged as to fix Hyacinth in immobility. When he finds himself at last apparently bereft of his fairy princess, betrayed (in one way or another) by Paul Muniment, and evidently forsaken by Millicent Henning, he has no choice left. Or rather he is faced, like Emma Bovary, with a single undeniable option. And so we have our results: the brutal experiment grinds to its logical and inevitable conclusion with Hyacinth's suicide.

Now the impact of the environment on Hyacinth is never so clear and unambiguous as this digest of the plot may make it seem. One of the dominant themes in the novel, indeed, is precisely the equivocal and puzzling nature of that environment: Hyacinth is constantly perplexed by his experience of a world that seems too often inverted or perverted. (The topsy-turviness is frequently emphasized by the metaphoric language of dialogue and narrative.) To put it baldly, Hyacinth is never quite sure of who's who. The problem begins with the introduction of the aristocracy, who seem mainly to be opposed to their own class: Lady Aurora frankly eschews the pleasures of Inglefield Park and Belgrave Square to hob-nob with Paul and Rosy Muniment and interest herself in the cares of the common people. Hyacinth is introduced to the Princess Casamassima by Captain Sholto, whom he has known as a frequenter of the anarchist gatherings at the "Sun and Moon"; she too seems deeply interested not only in the lot of the common people but even in their movement for social reform: she assures Madame Grandoni that "we're living in a fool's paradise, that the ground's heaving under our feet," and the old lady replies, "It's not the ground, my dear; it's you who are turning somersaults." The final turn of the screw is applied by Hyacinth's discovery that not only is his fairy princess interested in popular reform movements, but that she has actually preceded him in association with

Hoffendahl, the shadowy power behind the anarchist association!

Even the common folk, if not quite opposed to their own kind, are eager enough to maintain the existing hierarchy—the *status quo* which Hyacinth is trying to recognize. Milly wants the established order left alone so that she can rise in it. Rosy Muniment is its staunch defender: she scolds her brother, "You'll make a great mistake if you try to turn everything around." Yet even the solid Paul Muniment "seemed capable of turning revolutionists themselves into ridicule for the entertainment of the revolutionized."[33] The strange social inversion, as it seems to Hyacinth, most immediately touches him in the persons of the two women in his life; his perplexed comparison between then underlines his mild dismay. For example:

Millicent . . . seemed to answer in her proper person for creeds and communions and sacraments; she was more than devotional, she was individually almost pontifical. . . . The Princess Casamassima came back to him in comparison as a loose bohemian, a shabby adventuress. . . . The Princess wanted to destroy society and Millicent to uphold it.[34]

The puzzling nature of the society in which he moves, the equivocal stimuli of his environment, make it very difficult for Hyacinth to realize his ambition to "get hold of the truth and wear it in his heart." He cannot quite trust the impulses of his sympathies nor can he be perfectly sure of his "natural" affinities when the apparent objects of them are themselves uncertain in their identity. And that in turn most seriously vexes the problem of Hyacinth's decision about his own identity. His whole history, after all, is in a remarkable way similar to that of Tom Jones: his career, like Tom's, carries him through various sections of society in what is actually a quest for himself. "Who am I really?" is the constant, nagging question that faces him at every turn. The question arises more frequently and more poignantly during the first half of the novel, but it is never completely quieted. Milly Henning introduces the question as early as the fifth chapter, when she has returned to Lomax Place to re-enter his life. "Come now, who are you?" she boldly demands; and Hyacinth can give no answer other than lamely to announce that he is a "forwarder" at a bookbindery. Again, fifty pages before the end of the novel, Milly returns to the same question, if somewhat indirectly: "I don't believe you half the time know what you do mean yourself. I don't believe you even know with all your thinking what you do think. That's your disease."

Hyacinth's response is evasive, even in its apparent frankness, yet pitifully revealing.

"It's astonishing how you sometimes put your finger on the place," he now returned with interest. "I mean to think no more—I mean to give it up. . . . It confers no true happiness. Let us live in the world of irreflective contemplation—let us live in the present hour."[35]

We remember that on meeting Paul Muniment Hyacinth is presented with the question of his identity, that "He didn't really know," and that he finally confessed "I daresay I ain't anything!" Old Pinnie was always pleased, for her part, at Hyacinth's sometimes flashing out the proud remark that he was not what he seemed; but the trenchant irony of such an allusion strikes the reflective Hyacinth himself: "He was not what he seemed, but even with Pinnie's valuable assistance he had not succeeded in representing to himself very definitely what he was."[36] The question comes up yet again when he meets the Princess Casamassima; when she asks him about his family he can only reply dully that he has none—"None at all. I never had."[37] And perhaps most striking, because of its crucial situation in the novel, is Hyacinth's contemplation of himself in the mirror in his room at Medley: "in a place where everything was on such a scale it seemed to him more than ever that Mademoiselle Vivier's son, lacking all the social dimensions, was scarce a perceptible person at all."[38]

On occasion this theme is enhanced by James's use of a theatrical metaphor to reinforce the dubiousness of Hyacinth's real identity. At her first view of the mature Hyacinth, for example, Milly thinks he looks like an actor and in a moment has told him he ought to be in the theater "in a fancy costume"—"Hyacinth was on the point of replying that he didn't care for fancy costumes, he wished to go through life in his own character; but he checked himself with the reflection that this was exactly what he was apparently destined not to do. His own character? He was to cover that up as carefully as possible; he was to go through life in a mask, in a borrowed mantle; he was to be every hour and every day an actor."[39] But to admit that one is masked, that one is acting out a role, is to imply that one's real self—one's "own character"—is hidden beneath. If this is true of Hyacinth, his problem is that he cannot quite distinguish what if anything is hidden beneath his mask, or, worse, that the mask may actually represent his real self. His problem is rather like that of

Sartre's Kean; it is also like that of James's Lambert Strether, who, when present at the theater with Maria Gostrey, apparently cannot tell whether the life on stage or the life in the stalls is the more real. Hyacinth experiences a similar illusion when he is first introduced to the Princess Casamassima in her box at the theater: "so pleasant was it to be enthroned with fine ladies in a dusky, spacious receptacle which framed the bright picture of the stage and made one's own situation seem a play within a play."[40] If Hyacinth is acting, living a play, still "he had not succeeded in representing to himself very definitely what he was."

The emphasis throughout the novel is so placed as to minimize any impression that Hyacinth is at all simply a passive victim of the forces that toss him to and fro. He is made to seem very much the conscious agent in his own tragedy, as he is constantly questioning, attempting interpretation, trying to understand those forces to which he feels himself exposed. We find our attention directed less to what his mixed heredity and complementary environment are doing to him and much more to what he is making of those potential influences— how he is choosing to be affected by them. Hyacinth's keen awareness of his situation, James said in the Preface, provides the "interest."

This in fact I have ever found rather terribly the point—that the figures in any picture, the agents in any drama, are interesting only in proportion as they feel their respective situations; since the consciousness, on their part, of the complication exhibited forms for us their link of connexion with it. . . . Their being finely aware—as Hamlet and Lear, say, are finely aware—*makes* absolutely the intensity of their adventure, gives the maximum of sense to what befalls them.[41]

But that is only one half of the story, for in *The Princess Casamassima* the technique (as described in the foregoing quotation) virtually becomes the subject. The subject is really Hyacinth's consciousness of bearing certain hereditary strains and the question of what that consciousness will oblige him to do and decide to be. For instance, we never really *know*, as Hyacinth himself never really knows, whether Lord Frederick was in fact his father. The posited *fact* is always Hyacinth's belief about his inheritance, about the significance of items in his *milieu* and their relevance to him—whoever he decides he is. He is thus far less the typical victim of his heredity and environment, and much more the victim of his own conceptions. Hyacinth therefore seems to exercise more influence on his own fate than other heroes of experimental novels; and it seems that his own choices produce the consequences which entangle him in his final tragic dilemma. In this respect he is perhaps as close to the hero of George Eliot's novels as to the hero of Zola's. But I would in any case insist on the distinction between the Jamesian and the Zolaesque experimental novel—and particularly in this case, of *The Princess Casamassima*—because the peculiar development and role of the hero's consciousness of himself and of his situation seems rather definitely to forecast James's technique in *The Sacred Fount* and *The Ambassadors*. Nevertheless, the data with which Hyacinth is perpetually concerned remain his mixed heredity and the strangely matching environment in which he finds himself; and it is unmistakably the influence of that data (not quite, notice, objectively established *facts*) which certainly determines Hyacinth's fate. Therefore, the "experimental" aspect of this novel is perfectly apparent, and it generally follows the lead of the theory Zola developed in *Le Roman expérimental*.

I said at the outset of this chapter that while both *The Bostonians* and *The Princess Casamassima* deal with reform movements, the treatment in the latter is a much more serious affair. I meant that in *The Princess* the rumbling subterranean anarchist movement threatens revolution, threatens to affect drastically the whole structure of society, and is therefore treated with all the dark seriousness it warrants; whereas in *The Bostonians* the movement touches only fragments of the whole society and is therefore treated, not, certainly, without seriousness, but with lighter though sharp satire and even sympathetic wit. The subject of reform movements, in any case, is not typically Jamesian. Yet social reform—even revolution—was a common enough subject with Zola and the French Naturalists generally; and it is during this period alone—the period during which James was submitting to the Naturalist influence—that one finds extended treatment of the subject in his work. There are critics, however, who refuse to take this work into account, who maintain that James could not handle the common people and was not interested in their situation or their possible plight. When confronted with the rather large fact of *The Princess Casamassima*, then, those critics cry "artifice!" and cast doubt on the authenticity of the portrayal; they are particularly dubious of James's depiction of the faltering and inarticulate group at the "Sun and Moon," the human resources of the anarchist movement. How could James possibly have got it right (their question goes) since one can not observe that sort of thing from the window of the Athenaeum? Those critics are well answered in the brilliant essay on *The Princess* by Lionel Trilling. His convincing defense of James's potential revolutionaries explains that "The first great movement of English trade unionism had created an aristocracy of labor largely cut off from the mass of the workers [Paul is an example of that aristocracy] . . . ; the next great movement had not yet begun; the political expression of men such as met at the Sun and Moon was likely to be as fumbling as James presented it."[42] Mr. Trilling assures us further that Hyacinth's situation, his pledge to commit an assassination on demand of his superiors "is not the extreme fancy of a cloistered novelist, but a classic anarchist situation." The persuasive and carefully argued essay draws to this conclusion:

In short, when we consider the solid accuracy of James's political detail at every point, we find that we must give up the notion that James could move only in the thin air of moral abstraction. A writer has said of *The Princess Casamassima* that it is 'a capital example of James's impotence in matters sociological.' The very opposite is true. Quite apart from its moral and aesthetic authority, *The Princess Casamassima* is a brilliantly precise representation of social actuality.[43]

Even though one may be convinced of the authenticity of James's portrayal of the social situation, he may yet object to the novel's ultimate comment on the situation. The feeling may well be that James has failed to make any satisfactory contribution to the solution of the social problem he presents in the novel. Hyacinth sees clearly the monstrous sores and ulcers that plague the world of his brothers and sisters, yet he would defend the aristocratic institutions responsible for the social disease form the attack of the revolutionaries. He would defend those institutions for the sake of the beauty they have made possible—the monuments and treasures of art, the conquests of learning and taste, even the great palaces and properties. But the grievances of the people are real and Hyacinth recognizes them; therefore he can be condemned for his disaffectation from the anarchist movement. And since James does not "punish" Hyacinth in the novel, does not condemn him but even attempts to retain our sympathy for him to the end and certainly does not seem even to judge him, James himself may also be criticized for offering no solution to the problem and merely evading the social issues he has raised. Yet in spite of this, the novel does have its comment to make by offering a word of caution to the intelligent revolutionary mind. Hyacinth's disaffection results in part from his fear that revolution will mean vengeful retributive destruction accompanied by no positive and creative side to the anarchist policy. The novel asks us to consider whether, in satisfying the people's perfectly justified demand for bread, the revolution will be able to offer anything but bread alone. And James is thus anticipating some post-revolutionary critic of the affluent society who will point out that inside every bread-stuffed man there is an inner man who is starving. Malnutrition of the soul is the awful, de-humanizing disease that James and the contemporary social critic urgently warn us of.

The Princess Casamassima does perhaps fail to manage the problem in a satisfactory sociological and economical way. But surely one is wrong to demand such solutions from the novel—from any art form. Its success is hardly to be measured by such strictly utilitarian standards. The proper concern of the novel has always been other, and its achievement otherwise gauged. The Princess does enjoy some success in its proper pursuit: it speaks effectively to the question of personal revolution, of personal moral restoration. The story of Hyacinth Robinson is typically Jamesian in its personal comment. It is a dramatic expression of the Socratic idea of the paramount importance of self-knowledge. With this is firmly associated the Emersonian corollary of the necessity of self-trust. The Princess Casamassima traces Hyacinth's attempt at self-knowledge, as I have said, and emphasizes the importance of self-trust based on that knowledge. The dramatic tension in the novel, expressed by the conflicting affinities that Hyacinth feels—with the people and with the cultured way of life—is ultimately the result of the conflicting demands of Duty and Impulse. Hyacinth's Duty to support the anarchist movement, to hold himself ready to redeem his oath, is an increasing burden on his conscience; and as that burden increases it is accompanied by a slow but steady growth of clarification about himself—a gradual increase of awareness, of consciousness of his essential nature and its dearest needs. His tragedy is that he has committed himself before he has known himself; that impetuousness led him to his dilemma. He has tried to be what he feels he ought; he recognizes—too late—that he must be only what he is. The implicit exhortation for the reader is "Know thyself; trust thyself!" The novel's implicit argument is that one must do his best to discover his essential self and act in accordance with the demands of one's own true being; one is not to fret over determining a "right" line of action —the right line of action is that dictated by the impulse of one's being and will follow naturally. Let one be *conscious* of what he is: he will need no *conscience* to tell him what he ought to do. This self-trust, James believed, will lead to the best self-realization; and the *summum bonum* in James's ethical system was always the fullest possible development of the individual human being. And in the endeavor for individual development, the demands of the soul and the spirit take absolute precedence over the demands of the flesh and the world. Man owes his human identity to the divine spark within him that we call variously his soul or spirit; and be he ever so stout an animal, he is just so much the less human as his soul is starved. It is fear of the threat of spiritual starvation, which Hyacinth sees in the anarchist success, that prompts his disaffection. Man cannot live by bread alone, and only he lives whose soul is not dead. That, I think, is the comment on the human condition which one finds, at last, thickly wrapped in the solid envelope of the story of Hyacinth Robinson.

"My Last Long Novel"

James had called *The Bostonians* and *The Princess Casamassima* "my two best things."[1] They were intended to inaugurate his new period as a successful professional. They were fashioned to an appreciable extent in the mode of French literary Naturalism, which—especially under the pen of Emile Zola—was succeeding very well in the world of letters south of the Channel. James's expectations were high, yet these two novels of 1886 suffered a sorry fate. "They have reduced the desire, and the demand, for my productions to zero," he lamented to Howells at the beginning of 1888.[2]

It might have been expected, then, that James would seriously reconsider the line he had taken—the adaptation of Naturalist theory and practice—and try a new tack. He did not do so; at least not immediately. His next novel, *The Tragic Muse*, indicates the persistence of the Naturalist influence and it is another purely European story. Disappointment at the apparent failure of the two earlier novels did not move him out of the path he had begun to follow, although he did make some modifications in direction, as we shall see. The persistence in the chosen line may have been due simply to a kind of inertia, or, more accurately, evidence that James had not yet done with his fictional experiment—not, that is, to his own satisfaction. Certainly *The Tragic Muse* was associated in his mind with the two earlier novels, for its inception dates from June of 1884, as an entry in his Notebooks indicates.[3] But there is reason also to believe that the very failure of those two novels ("from which I expected so much and derived so little") may have been responsible for his persistence in the line he had taken. That is to say that *The Tragic Muse* may be seen as James's working out, artistically, the very problem which that dual failure presented to him so urgently—the "problem of art and the world," as he was to describe it in the preface to the novel. The subject of *The Tragic Muse* had, in any case, been simmering in his mind for some time before it was brought to a boil in 1888, when he began to set it out.

Two events of that year help to account for the modifications in James's chosen path. One is the publication of his essay "Guy de Maupassant" in the *Fortnightly Review* for March, 1888; the other is the invitation extended him by the actor Edward Compton, at the end of that year, to prepare *The American* for theatrical production. If the Naturalist influence of the earlier years of the decade is focused in the figure of Zola, that of the later years is focused in Maupassant. Now of course the forte of Maupassant was the short story rather than the novel; and it was precisely to that form that James began to devote his energies. His correspondence during the latter half of the eighties contains numerous references to his attempts at "short things." He had, to be sure, always written tales, yet the proportionate number of them during the late eighties is unusually high even in so prolific and various a writer as James. And in the essay on Maupassant, James clearly expresses his admiration for the achievement of the young master of the short story. That essay may safely be taken as the principal statement of James's esthetic position in the closing years of the decade. It is less theoretical than "The Art of Fiction," yet the theory behind it is intimately related to that of the earlier essay. In other words, "Guy de Maupassant" is a reaffirmation of James's faith in many of the ideas and accomplishments of French Naturalism.

The essay admires Maupassant's manner and rejoices at his achievement. The nature of James's critical approval indicates that he has retained his earlier esthetic position; one sentence in particular seems to sum up the reason for his approval. Of Maupassant's best performances James says "the whole thing is real, observed, noted, and represented, not an invention or a castle in the air."[4] The paramount importance of "the air of reality (solidity of specification)" is again recognized; the ability to observe acutely and to take note accurately is again cherished; the faithful rendering of noted impressions—without rearrangement—is once again acclaimed. Maupassant he recognizes as one of those blessed with artistic sensibility, and more, as one who makes excellent use of it: he is one of those upon whom nothing is lost. He praises the use Maupassant makes of his "exceptionally acute" sense of smell and particularly of his keen visual sense.

His eye *selects* unerringly, unscrupulously, almost impudently— catches the particular thing in which the character of the object or the scene resides, and, by expressing it with the artful brevity of a master, leaves a convincing, original picture.[5]

The key word there is obviously "selects"; and it indicates a slight shift in emphasis from "The Art of Fiction." James had admitted that art is certainly selective, but quickly added that it must take care to be inclusive. The new emphasis is more naturally Jamesian, I think, closer to his own habitual tendency; and we shall see that the new emphasis is carried into the later novel, where there is less enumeration of items and more the choice of the single telling detail. Obviously enough, then, another important term in the quotation above is "brevity." That is a quality which, as James himself was painfully aware, had never been a salient feature of his own fiction. But from the middle eighties there appears as a constant admonitory refrain in James's Notebooks the exhortation "A la Maupassant!"—"Oh, spirit of Maupassant, come to my aid!" he exclaims: "This may be a triumph of robust and vivid concision; . . ." And during the actual writing of *The Tragic Muse* James again spurs himself on with this reminder:

Variety and concision must be my formula for the rest of the story— rapidity and action. . . . Let me write it as if, at any stage, it were to be a short story. . . . A la Maupassant must be my constant motto.[6]

Concision, hardness, compactness—those were the features he admired in the young Frenchman's art. Maupassant achieved his effects with a striking economy, yet his stories were complete, hard bright little nuggets without a gap in their surface. In achieving that effect of compact firmness, of smooth completeness, he had manifestly realized the principle James set forth in "The Art of Fiction"—that a work of fiction is an organic whole, all one and continuous, with every part a deliberately functioning contributor to the total effect. Thus James is full of grateful praise for Maupassant's ability to make "every epithet a paying piece."[7] This is the manner of producing a work of art that will stand on its own feet, self-sufficient, self-expressive, and dramatically immediate; and Maupassant, James points out, has done just that. He singles out *Une Vie* for special praise as an example of a self-reliant piece of fiction, a story in which the form is self-sustaining; here the attendant explanatory hand of the parental author is unnecessary—the literary umbilical cord has been neatly cut.

In the Maupassant essay James also touches on the subject of freedom, which dominates "The Art of Fiction." He quotes with approval statements of Maupassant's to the effect that by the nature of things individuals differ and consequently so do their views of life; thus we must grant the writer his own views—grant him his own *donnée,* James had said—and judge him on what he makes of that. This principle is of course a reiteration of that implicit in Zola's definition of the novel as *un coin de la réalité vue à travers un tempérament;* and it carries with it the tacit plea for the artist—*Laissez-le écrire comme bon lui semble.*

James remains fully aware of the risk one runs in granting absolutely free rein to the novelist; and again his attitude is that we can perhaps distinguish between "good" and "bad" subjects—but not by facile conventional standards. He faces squarely the old moral question in this essay, as he had in "The Art of Fiction," and is even more scrupulous about the dotting of i's and the crossing of t's. He addresses directly the question of sex, of the portrayal of "the carnal side of man," and as we might expect his conclusion has little to do with conventional moral standards. It is on the basis of honesty and humanity—or fidelity to the truly human—that he rests his judgment of the matter. He treats with some deference Maupassant's shockingly frank (for the time) portrayal of man's sexual side, and cautiously offers the proposition that too extensive attention to "the empire of the sexual sense" tends to diminish the human aspect of man and heighten man's simian aspect. At least, James generously concludes, that is how we Anglo-Saxons see it—"as we Anglo-Saxons pretend we see, M. de Maupassant would possibly say."[8] He admits that man's carnal side may seem very characteristic—if you are preoccupied with it; yet he contends that the more you consider man's other side, the less characteristic does that whole business— "the business, as I may say, of the senses"—seem to be. James's argument, finally, is rather close to the Arnoldian dictum about seeing life steadily and seeing it whole: let the author beware of exaggerat-

ing this or that side of the human condition, but on the other hand
let him have the courage to portray what he honestly sees there. The
demand of courage he directs particularly to his English and American colleagues, who are liable to be misled by some moral convention
about what *ought* to be seen in man's state.

We have doubtless often enough the courage of our opinions . . . , but
we have not so constantly that of our perceptions. There is a whole
side of our perceptive apparatus that we in fact neglect, and there
are probably many among us who would erect this tendency into a
duty.[9]

This repeats exactly the note he had sounded in "The Art of Fiction."

The Tragic Muse reflects the persistence of the Naturalist influence
as well as the modifications in theory that I mention. It also reflects
another preoccupation of James's—his interest in the theater. The
invitation extended him in December, 1888, to dramatize his early
novel, *The American,* was an important event in his life. From the
beginning, James had been interested in the theater, and he had
responded some years earlier to the opportunity of dramatizing his
"Daisy Miller." It was never produced. Yet that disappointment did
not prevent his accepting Edward Compton's offer; in fact, James
seems naturally enough to have regarded it as a compensatory opportunity. Furthermore, writing for the theater was a means of reaching
a large group of the public immediately. It also meant large financial
returns—if one succeeded. That sort of opportunity was not to be
turned down by the earnest professional eager to make his mark—
and his little pile as well. At any rate, James was full of the thought
of the possibilities (and aware of the attendant difficulties) which
now hung before him as a result of the new dramatic venture. His
fiction of the period, and particularly *The Tragic Muse,* is likewise full
of the material of the theater. The very subject of the novel, as the
title announces it, is largely concerned with the dramatic art. But
more than that, the narrative manner in James's fiction tends at that
time to be more dramatic: generous sections of the stories read like
scenarios; there is much more use of dramatic entrances and exits, of
coups de théâtre; and there are several set *scènes à faire.* And even
beyond that we find a much higher incidence of theatrical metaphor
in the stories of the end of the eighties. One might almost say that
"the dramatic years" had their beginning in the fiction of this period.
In truth, *The Tragic Muse* has some aspects of a pivotal work; it points

ahead toward the dramatic experiment of the first half of the nineties while it unmistakably carries on with the naturalist experiment of the eighties.

The Tragic Muse, published in the *Atlantic Monthly* during 1889 and 1890, is one of James's largest novels. It is somewhat a combination of two stories—the "political case" and the "theatrical case," as James called them. The former of these concerns Nick Dormer, son of a political family, who successfully campaigns for a seat in the British House of Commons. He is urged on by his mother and by the memory of his father, Sir Nicholas, to whom he has given his pledge to carry on the political tradition of the family. He is encouraged and promised material support in this pursuit by the substantial Mr. Carteret, an old friend of his father; he is further encouraged by his rich and attractive cousin, the widow Julia Dallow. Continued political success will mean marriage with the politically ambitious and influential Julia, which in turn will mean a home for his mother and unmarriageable sister Grace—in one of Julia's houses; and consequent to that marriage, a generous settlement from the very rich and politically powerful Carteret. The difficulty in all this, which renders Nick's political victory rather Pyrrhic, is the fact that Nick Dormer is—as he says—"two men": one enjoys the flurry of campaigning and the flush of political victory, while the other yearns for the quiet privacy of the painter's studio. One man is the responsible public servant, the other the "irresponsible" private dévoté of art. While most of Nick's family and friends appeal to the public man in him, the private or inner man heeds the encouragement of Gabriel Nash, a friend of Nick's during his time at Oxford and apparently something of an aesthete, and the quieter support of his sister Biddy Dormer—a dabbler in sculpture. Quite obviously, the drama results from the conflict between the public political Nick and the private artistic Nick. The former enjoys the initial triumph, but soon the latter makes his demands felt: thus, his fiancee, Julia, breaks their engagement, and Nick resigns his seat as M. P. and turns to follow his penchant for painting. The conclusion of the novel brings him and Julia—and painting!—all together again. But the end is somewhat ambiguous: one seems to be left in doubt about the final victor.

The theatrical case deals with the career of Miriam Rooth, daughter of a woman with aristocratic pretensions and of an artistic Jewish *brocanteur*. She first appears, in her vulgarly genteel poverty, as a burning aspirant to the stage, and momentarily under the skeptical wing of Gabriel Nash. She is introduced to Peter Sherringham, brother of Julia Dallow, who is a rising young diplomat and an amateur of the theater. He in turn introduces Miriam to the semi-retired Mme Carré, one of the glories of the French stage, and becomes her sponsor. He also falls at least half-way in love with her. Although Miriam's beginnings are rough and rude, her success is rapid and she becomes the darling of the London theater—the English Rachel. At an early stage of her success Miriam sits for Nick Dormer for her portrait as The Tragic Muse. She finally refuses Sherringham's offer of marriage, for his conditions are that she leave the theater and confine herself to private life as a diplomat's wife. She marries Basil Dashwood, a fellow actor. Her career will present other difficulties to overcome, but her continued success seemed to be assured.

James was worried that in treating both "cases" his novel would fall into two halves, that the union of the political and the theatrical subjects would not be sufficiently complete. Two of the secondary characters, Gabriel Nash and Peter Sherringham, contribute to the cementing of the two subjects—Gabriel through his relations with both Nick and Miriam as a kind of inspiring representative of Art, and Peter through his romance first with Miriam and then with Nick's sister Biddy. But beyond that the two subjects are really united by their similarity of theme: the conflict between the demands of "art and the world" is the common theme, and its treatment in each case provides a comment on the other. *The Tragic Muse* resembles in this respect Shakespeare's *King Lear,* except that the plot involving Miriam bulks larger than does the Gloucester plot in the play. The novel achieves its unity of effect, all right, as I shall demonstrate in a monent.

The theme of the novel, James wrote in his preface, had been in his mind from far back; he confesses that he must, indeed, practically always have had it in mind.

To "do something about art"—art, that is, as a human complication and a social stumbling-block—must have been for me early a good deal of a nursed intention, the conflict between art and "the world" striking me thus betimes as one of the half-dozen great primary motives.[10]

The actual subject he had sketched in his notebooks in 1884, but what brought it to the front of his mind was the particular press of circumstances in the middle eighties—the rude shocks that met his determination to succeed as a professional artist. The conflict of art and the world was acutely present to him especially after the public reception of *The Bostonians* and *The Princess Casamassima.* And then, as he entertained the idea of writing for the stage once again, he must also have realized that he would be experiencing a more immediate and blatant confrontation of his art and the world: one was so much more exposed in the theater, where one's professional and artistic success or failure would be so awfully public and advertised. Furthermore, he suffered some doubt about his own motivation in accepting the challenge of the theater: was he risking prostitution— would he have to write solely to please "them"? Theatrical success meant large financial reward, and he wanted that as well; was his determination merely to secure the shekels? There was ample reason, indeed, why the theme that must always have been with him (as he said) should have demanded treatment just at that moment; and all the more so since he had decided that *The Tragic Muse* should be his last long novel—at least for the forseeable future. He wrote Stevenson in July, 1888, that he had just begun the novel and that when it was finished he proposed to do nothing but short stories "for a longish period."[11] Then, as the last installment appeared in *The Atlantic,* he wrote to his brother William, *"The Tragic Muse* is to be my last long novel. For the rest of my life I hope to do lots of short things with irresponsible spaces between."[12] His final performance in the large form, as he intended this novel to be, would naturally offer him the occasion (if he wished to avail himself of it) to make some final state-ment on the theme of art—at least insofar as the art of the novel is concerned—something in the nature of an *apologia pro vita sua* as novelist. And certain aspects of *The Tragic Muse* strongly suggest that James intended something of the sort by it.

Among the apparent literary resources behind *The Tragic Muse* we must note first of all *Miss Bretherton* by Mrs. Humphrey Ward. Mr. Oscar Cargill has listed several points of similarity between the two novels, which he suggests argue for James's indebtedness to Mrs. Ward's story.[13] James's real indebtedness here, however, was less to the novel itself than to Mrs. Ward's idea for her novel, which she mentioned to him some months before the novel was published—and obviously before he had read it. His *Notebooks* record (June 19th,

1884) her idea "for a story that might be made interesting—as a study of the histrionic character." But as the note continues, we see that James has already begun to develop the germinal idea according to his own bent; and we also find brief passing reference to other, supporting resources beside Mrs. Ward's interesting idea. "The girl I see to be very crude, etc. The thing a confirmation of Mrs. Kemble's theory that the dramatic gift is a thing by itself—implying of necessity no *general* superiority of mind. The strong nature, the personal quality, vanity, etc., of the girl: her artistic being, so vivid, yet so purely instinctive. Ignorant, illiterate. Rachel."[14] So far as Mrs. Ward's completed novel is concerned, James politely regretted the failure of realization of such a promising idea. Specifically, he objects to the happy ending of *Miss Bretherton*—not simply for itself alone, but for the unsatisfactory development that made that ending possible: the abdication of the artist (Isabel Bretherton) to merely *personal* demands.

I wish [he wrote to Mrs Ward] that your actress had been carried away from Kendal . . . by the current of her artistic life, the sudden growth of her power, and the excitement, the ferocity and egotism (those of the artist realizing success, I mean; I allude merely to the normal dose of those elements) . . . . Isabel, the Isabel you describe, lapses toward him as if she were a failure, whereas you make her out a great success. No![15]

James's letter (December 9, 1884) gives vigorous promise of what his depiction of the *nature d'actrice* will be in the character of Miriam Rooth of *The Tragic Muse.*

While his conception of Miriam may have derived something from Mrs. Ward's Isabel—or rather her idea of her—it also may have benefited from the Jewess in the Goncourts' *Manette Salomon* and from Edmond de Goncourt's *La Faustin.* Certainly James also had in mind (as the Notebook entry from which I quoted above indicates) the fabulous Elisa Félix, the natural Jewish genius who was known on the French stage as Mlle Rachel. James had never seen her, but he knew of her fame. On the other hand he was acquainted with several established actresses: he knew Fanny Kemble well and also Julia Bartet and the fascinating singer Pauline Viardot—close to the heart of Ivan Turgenev; and he had seen the great Sarah Bernhardt. Furthermore, he also knew the beautiful and controversial American actress Mary Anderson, who was the "original" of Mrs. Ward's Miss

Bretherton.[16] Finally (and this is not uncommon in James), another aspect of Miriam Rooth seems to be derived from a comparatively undeveloped character in his short story "A New England Winter" (coincidentally published the same year as James's germinal note for *The Tragic Muse*, 1884). That character is the attractive bait dangled before the hero, Florimond Daintry, to keep him from leaving Boston for Europe: she is "pretty, in a strange unusual way—black hair and blue eyes, a serpentine figure; old coins in her tresses; that sort of thing." There is an exotic, oriental quality about her, and with her coins and amulets and seamless garments she appears rather "like a Circassian or a Smyrniote."[17] The exotic, gypsy quality of Miriam Rooth, particularly in her first appearance in the novel, is distinctly foreshadowed in the girl from "A New England Winter," whose name, interestingly enough, is Rachel.

The career of Miriam Rooth as exemplary of the histrionic talent accounts for only one of the two main concerns of the novel. One of the characters who helps draw those two concerns together is the apparently perplexing Gabriel Nash. This character has fascinated the few critics who have looked at him at all carefully. He stands behind the hero Nick Dormer as his "evil genius"—"evil" in exactly the way a spirit from Blake's Hell would be—who urges him to chuck politics for art. Gabriel's relation to Miriam is somewhat similar: he first of all makes the connection for her with the theater, and attends irregularly on the stages of her success. He stands for Art, for the "irresponsible" artist-life; he is recognizably an aesthete—or something like it. His way of taking life James obviously derived from a friend of his older brother's, Herbert Pratt. A long passage in the *Notebooks* records a number of details about him, his exotic travels, his irresponsible passion for merely gathering impressions in picturesque lands—"simply for their own sake." Nash's first words in the novel announce him as a traveler in orient lands: "my feelings direct me ... Where there's anything to feel I try to be there!" The similarity between Nash and Pratt is striking. James wrote of Pratt, "I shall certainly put him into a novel. I shall even make the portrait close and he won't mind. ... A good deal might be done with Herbert Pratt."[18]

There is the notion, first offered very tentatively by the late R. P. Blackmur and developed extensively by Mr. Oscar Cargill, that Gabriel Nash is a fictional portrait of Oscar Wilde. There may be something in this: Wilde was the popular idea of the aesthete, he had an Oxford background, he wrote a novel. But the contention that Nash is a satirical portrait of Wilde rests on the flimsiest of arguments and a misreading of the character as presented in the novel. Much more solidly founded is Mr. Leon Edel's suggestion that James put a good deal of himself into the character of Gabriel Nash.[19] There is a most striking similarity between Nash's long castigation of the English stage, and James's attack in his article of June 1889, "After the Play," which must have been written at about the same time. Both attacks express the same attitude and even make use of the same phraseology.[20] But in addition to his ideas, Nash seems also to have been endowed with some of James's physical characteristics. He is initially described to us as a "young man . . . fair and fat and of the middle stature; he had a round face and a short beard and on his crown a mere reminiscence of hair . . ."; a depiction which aptly enough portrays Henry James as he was in the late eighties. And even Nash's peculiarity of speech—"a rare variety of English"—not quite foreign yet not quite native, may be taken as an adequate rendition of the deliberate and *soigné* utterance of James: it had "a conspicuous and aggressive perfection."(VII,22,23).

And there is James's short story of 1869, "Gabrielle de Bergerac." The heroine of this tale bears certain important marks of resemblance to Nash—in addition to the name, of course—and the tale itself embodies some of the themes and values which are central in *The Tragic Muse.* Gabrielle has some of those heavenly or divine qualities which James gives to Nash, in what seems to be a jocular way. She is frequently dressed in blue—Mary's color—and her lover calls her (quite naturally, for all that) his angel. She inspires her lover to draw her portrait, which he destroys; Nick's portrait of Nash fades away. The lover's name, incidentally, is Coquelin, the name of the French *comédien* whom James had known in boyhood and later admired for his dramatic excellence. The pair of lovers combines some of the elements that are found in Nash and Nick Dormer. When Gabrielle and Coquelin have their interesting discussion of eternal values, she quotes "Lovers die but love survives" and adds that "the loved object disappears"; he replies that his philosophy is "simply to make the most of life while it lasts. I'm very fond of life. . . . When once you love her she's absolute." Gabrielle's tentative decision to give up Coquelin and retire to a convent raises the question of the mistaken sense of duty—which is, according to Nash, precisely the problem Nick has to face. Gabrielle explains to her brother, "I chose between happiness and duty,—duty as you would have laid it down: I preferred duty." This very early tale concludes with an unusual happy ending: Gabrielle and Coquelin, preferring at last happiness, decide to marry. But a final note reminds us again of *The Tragic Muse*: "Coquelin was an excellent fellow . . . painted portraits and did literary work." The little tale managed to contribute its generous mite to the later novel.

Something from all these items was undoubtedly simmering genially in the cauldron which brewed *The Tragic Muse*. But as usual the principal stock was James's direct impression of life as noted in London and Paris combined with his dearest ideas on the life of art. He has "caught the very note and trick of life" and fixed it effectively in this large crowded novel. Mr. Leon Edel has expressed the opinion that James has nowhere better evoked the sense of London streets and Parisian boulevards or given us a more vivid feeling of strolling and loitering in those capitals.[21] That is certainly true enough: the sensitive reader feels that the atmosphere of those cities, their streets and houses and cafes and public buildings has been fully expressed in the novel. Yet James has achieved the effect by means somewhat different from what he employed in *The Princess Casamassima:* with a very few marked exceptions, there are no extensive passages of description. A myriad brief but telling strokes, scattered generously and judiciously, here serve the purpose of creating the accurate and compelling sense of place. The opening pages of the novel set the scene and introduce the Dormer family. The garden of the Palais de l'Industrie is quickly sketched—"the central court of the great glazed bazaar where among plants and parterres, gravelled walks and thin fountains, are ranged the figures and groups, the monuments and busts. . . ."[22] And as our eye is guided over the English family, members of the "tweed-and-waterproof" class of tourists, other details are dropped in unobtrusively to add their little weight to the general impression—the fresh diffused light of the Salon, the green bench on which they are seated, the endless picture-lined corridors through which they have trudged, etc. This technique is very like the brief and starkly economical descriptive method of Maupassant; and it is the method upon which James has principally relied in this novel, as we might have expected from his newly matured appreciation of the young Frenchman's art. A glimpse of the little restaurant, to which the Dormers soon repair for lunch, consists of "white-clothed tables, straw-covered chairs and long-aproned waiters"; one of the daughters munches "a morsel from a long glazed roll" while the waiter solicitously offers the *carte* and suggests "Poulet chasseur, filets mignons, sauce béarnaise." There is little more; but there, in a few carefully chosen details, is the sufficient impression of the Parisian restaurant. A bit later we find Nick Dormer and his cousin Julia Dallow seated at a sidewalk table where they have ordered a bock; the impression of the evening boulevards is conveyed with only a few deft touches.

The novel is generously sprinkled with other glimpses of Paris—the clean fresh Rue de Constantinople on a July morning, the forsaken Champs Elysees in August; but they group together and accumulate and weigh heavily, at the last, as an impressive representation of the French scene. The English scene is represented in the same manner, of course, with an absence of set descriptive pieces and instead a dependence on the cumulative effect of numerous sharply etched details.

But there are the exceptions, and two of these in particular demand special notice. One is the rather full presentation of the Théâtre Français in the Rue de Richelieu. Chapters XX and XXI are full of the *maison de Molière*, and the reader must turn over the more than two-score pages devoted to it in order to get the full impact. These chapters lead us on a scenic tour that starts in the auditorium of the theater and then follows its devious corridors right into the "holy of holies"—as it appears to Miriam—the dressing-room of a leading actress. We follow Miriam and Peter and the others

out of their *baignoire* into those corridors of tribulation where the bristling *ouvreuse*, like a pawnbroker driving a roaring trade, mounts guard upon piles of heterogeneous clothing, and, gaining the top of the fine staircase which forms the state entrance and connects the statued vestibule of the basement with the grand tier of boxes, opened an ambiguous door, composed of little mirrors, and found themselves in the society of the initiated. . . . They traversed a low curving lobby, hung with pictures and furnished with velvet-covered benches, . . . and arrived at an opening on the right from which by a short flight of steps there was descent to one of the wings of the stage.

Ultimately, Miriam is taken to the "wonderfully upholstered nook" which is the dressing-room of the actress Mademoiselle Voisin, and we are given a description of that. There is in James's description of the Théâtre Français something reminiscent of the prison scene at the opening of *The Princess Casamassima* and also, inevitably, of the

opening of Zola's *Nana,* which gives a detailed picture of the theater
—including a visit of the Prince d'Ecosse to Nana's dressing-room.
The impression of authenticity is strong; and we know that James was
able to draw on first-hand experience. Shortly before composing this
section of the novel he had visited the loge of Julia Bartet, who was
then appearing in *L'Ecole des Maris* at the Comédie Française.[23]

It is perfectly appropriate that James should have devoted the
amount of space he did to a detailed description of the Comédie. No
other edifice in Europe could better represent the art of the theater,
which is one of the two major concerns of *The Tragic Muse.* It is
further appropriate that our impression of the Comédie should be
given via the point of view of Miriam Rooth: not only will her hungry
and eager eye miss none of the salient and telling details, but her own
enthusiastic devouring of the scene will encourage a sympathetic
appreciation in the reader. The description is shot through with a
sustained metaphor which at once expresses Miriam's evaluation of
the experience and also tends to influence similarly the reader's
response to the scene. Peter Sherringham is likened to a "cicerone
showing a church," and indeed, that passage continues, there was in
the place "the tone of an institution, a temple"; the stillness there
conveys a sense of "the gravity of a college or a convent" which
becomes, as they press forward, "still more monastic." In the "holy
of holies," la Voisin's dressing-room, Miriam notices the small draped
doorway which leads to "the inner sanctuary." (This extended metaphor recurs in the novel and becomes an important means of expressing the meaning and significance of the story.)

To balance this portrayal of the Comédie Française as the principal
edifice in the *scène de la vie de théâtre* James has described the
dwelling of Mr. Charles Carteret, Beauclere, which dominates his
scène de la vie politique. It stands for the weight of political cause
in the novel. The solid rectiliniar regularity of Beauclere and its
interior appointments serves to express the demands of the duty of
the public servant, the rectitude of party fidelity, the conception of
patriotic service. It symbolizes an established view; it cannot be
avoided. A sample passage will recall the flavor of the whole ample
picture given us in chapter XVI.

Everything at Mr. Carteret's appeared to be on a larger scale than
anywhere else—the tea-cups, the knives and forks, the door-handles,
the chair-backs, the legs of mutton, the candles and the lumps of coal:

they represented and apparently exhausted the master's sense of
pleasing effect, for the house was not otherwise decorated. . . . Mr.
Carteret's interior expressed a whole view of life. . . . Nowhere were
the boiled eggs at breakfast so big or in such big receptacles; his own
shoes, arranged in his own room, looked to him vaster there than at
home. He went out into the garden and remembered what enormous
strawberries they should have for dinner. In the house there was a
great deal of Landseer, of oilcloth, of woodwork painted and
"grained."

In this extensive description of Beauclere, within and without, the
emphasis rests heavily upon things—their sufficient abundance, their
imposing solidity, their substantial presence. We are made to feel the
weight as well as to see the array. And at the same time the passage
manages to contribute to the characterization of Nick Dormer—as
the flavor of the description of the Comédie Française adds to the
characterization of Miriam. We do not need to be told how Nick's
experience of Mr. Carteret and his substantial establishment affects
the young M.P., how it adds to the wretched political burden he has
already assumed: we can see for ourselves. In such ways as this James
has made the novel self-expressive, self-explanatory, self-sufficient.

But it will be noted that in these passages, much more than in
comparable descriptive passages in *The Bostonians* and *The Princess
Casamassima*, the element of impressionism plays an influential role.
That modification in technique may also be associated with James's
new found admiration of Maupassant. It was Maupassant who expressed dissatisfaction with the generic terms of *realism* and *realist*:
his contention was, in effect, that the writer's affair was not the
reproduction of the real so much as the creation of the illusion of
reality. *Illusionisme*, he suggested, was a more accurate term than
réalisme. And James, indeed, had employed the phrase "illusion of
reality" in "The Art of Fiction" to explain the end toward which the
writer's efforts be directed. Already in *The Tragic Muse* we find
James beginning to move definitely away from the typically Zolaesque technique, which he finally came to feel resembled too much
the itemized catalogue. It was not only that the same task could be
accomplished by a few carefully selected details, but that one might
as successfully render a scene by resorting to means that were not in
the strictest sense realistic at all: in addition to certain factual details
that might be objectively verified he would employ the impressionistic, the subjective, the suggestive. Thus, for example, the vastness of

Nick's shoes when at Beauclere is by no means a verifiable fact—as
the passage implicitly admits—but Nick's impression of their increased substance adds to our sense of the whole effect of Beacuclere.
It helps to create the illusion that James wants to impose, the illusion
that we know Beauclere as it *really* is: for we share in an impression
of the place that approximates what we should actually experience
if we were present there.

The same modified technique is to be seen in James's description
of the characters. The novel presents a very crowded canvas. There
are several principal characters—Nick, Miriam, Peter, Julia; several
major characters—Gabriel Nash, Biddy, Lady Agnes, Mrs. Rooth;
and several important secondary characters—Charles Carteret, Mme
Carré, Basil Dashwood, Grace Dormer; and a number of the background crowd who emerge briefly but distinctly to play their little
roles—Chayter, Mrs. Gresham, Mlle Voisin. Even the least of these
is brought to life with a few deft verbal strokes, so that we have in
reading *The Tragic Muse* the sense of a full and bustling world.

At the very outset of the novel the Dormer family is briefly
sketched; in the third paragraph we learn that Nick is "a lean, strong,
clear-faced youth, with a straight nose and light brown hair, which
lay continuously and smoothly back from his forehead, so that to
smooth it from the brow to the neck but a single movement of the
hand was required." Other details are added throughout the novel;
yet it is a just criticism, I think, that we never see Nick as clearly as
we do the other leading characters: he is not realized in the physical
sense, not solidly specified. In spite of that, however, we feel that we
know him, he is real to us: continued intimate association with him
makes our acquaintance strong and sufficient. Miriam Rooth, on the
other hand, is fully represented. The development of her portrait also
progresses gradually as the novel proceeds; yet the additions to her
picture are bold, broad strokes in high color, and with each touch our
view of her is brighter and stronger. We are very much aware of her
pale face and low forehead, her thick black hair and dark flashing
eyes; her portrait alters but we never lose the impression of the
strangeness of her garb that Biddy first noticed—her light, thin,
scanty gown of "flowered figures and odd transparencies," beneath
which appeared her low shoes that "showed a great deal of stocking
and were ornamented with rosettes." She reminded Biddy of a
Gypsy—and she retains something of that characteristic to the end
of the book. Miriam's character is completed for us by her constantly

attendant mother. The Gypsy quality is augmented by the large loose shawl which Mrs. Rooth seems always to wear, and which constantly threatens to escape her shoulders (as Miss Birdseye's cap did her head); and her habitual gesture of recovering it lends to her attitude an air of ineffectual hovering which is a suitable accompaniment to the flustered hen-sureness of her attention to her daughter.

Unlike the principal characters of James's other two novels of the eighties, Nick and Miriam are not given a home setting which helps to fill out and complete their portrait. Nick is never "at home" at home; and it is precisely part of his burden that political responsibity will establish a proper home for his mother and sisters—something they have been deprived of by the system of primogeniture that the elder son, Percy, has cruelly taken advantage of. But the political background against which we see Nick for some time in the first half of the novel, and against which he rebels, is quite vividly realized by the indelible presence of Mr. Carteret and his substantial dwelling, Beauclere. Nick's own setting is of course his studio hideaway in Rosedale Road, an extension of his artistic side. Our sense of it is vague: we have seen its ample divan and appreciated its good north light, and we have noted the piles of canvasses and the litter of sketches, brushes, cloths, and palettes. It lacks the substantial presence of Beauclere. But the contrast between these two representative settings is admirably suited to express the corresponding contrast in Nick's soul: the political life is "real" and solid and substantial, it consists of things to be manipulated, it has fixed boundaries and regular trimmed paths and definite corridors of power; the artistic life, on the other hand, is vague and unsubstantial and "irresponsible"—its rules are not externally imposed but must come from within. We come to feel and know this contrast as Nick feels and knows it, partly as a result of James's presentation of the two contrasting settings.

Similarly, Miriam's "home" setting is passed over very lightly. We are given glimpses of her dwelling, for instance, in St. John's Wood: the room filled with cigarette smoke, a coffee-service on the piano, "importunate" photographs everywhere, "odd volumes from the circulating library . . . tumbled about with cups or glasses on them" and dominating all, like the attendant spirit of disorder, Mrs. Rooth lounging in an unbuttoned wrapper (at five in the afternoon) and toying with a large tinsel fan that looks like a theatrical prop.[24] But the setting which really explains Miriam, represents her initial aim and becomes her natural place, is quite simply the theater, and that is fully drawn in the novel—first in the ample description of the Théâtre Français, which we have seen, and later in somewhat briefer descriptions of Miriam's London theater. The contrast between the domestic mess and the theater's glory also reflects the contrasting sides of Miriam's character; her theatrical being is the important part of her life—substantial, real, large, and satisfying; the domestic side claims little of her attention, and thus need claim little of ours.

It is interesting to note at this point that the novel compares Nick and Miriam as two souls devoted to art: it records something of the struggles both undertake in pursuit of their artistic goals, and stresses the sacrifices both make for the sake of their art. Yet there is within this comparison a rather striking contrast. The scene or setting of Miriam's artistic pursuits is solid and palpable, ordered and definite, while the scene of Nick's artistic pursuits is unsubstantial and vaguely realized, cluttered and dim. The difference is further emphasized by the fact that Nick and Miriam share the same attitude of religious devotion to their respective arts; we noted the sustained "religious" metaphor used to describe the Théâtre Français as it appeared to Miriam; we find that Nick's dingy little hideaway in Rosedale Road is for him "his little temple with his altar and his divinity." I will comment more fully on this particular contrast later on; it must suffice for the moment to indicate that Miriam's art is by its very nature broadly *public*, Nick's predominantly *private*, and that popular judgment of Miriam's performance tends to be immediate, but of Nick's comparatively slow; and finally that financial reward for the former is commensurately quick and abundant, while for the latter it is belated and only hesitantly generous. Consequently this contrast proves to be a further and perhaps less obvious aspect of the contest between art and "the world."

The techniques of characterization in *The Tragic Muse* represent, then, a modification of those James employed in the two preceding novels. Passages of set description are much rarer and markedly briefer and more economical here than in *The Bostonians* and *The Princess Casamassima*. Another difference in *The Tragic Muse* is that the characters are allowed much fuller opportunity to express themselves dramatically in their own words. As this lets the characters speak for themselves, so it also is a means of letting the story speak for itself and so of relieving the author of the risky obligation of appearing in his own person to explain his creation. Furthermore, we find that in several instances the task of narration is taken over by the characters themselves. Narrative couched in the idiom of one of the characters is a device used freely in *The Bostonians* and *The Princess Casamassima* but less frequently in *The Tragic Muse*. Nevertheless, there are some good examples, such as the passage in Miriam's idiom after she has performed at Peter Sherringham's little gathering. A long paragraph interrupts her dialogue with Peter; it begins as narrative description—"she went on, communicative, persuasive, familiar, egotistical (as was necessary), and slightly common, or perhaps only natural";—but soon lapses into Miriam's idiom, at about this point:

She had seen very little acting—the theatre was always too expensive. If she could only go often—in Paris, for instance, every night for six months—to see the best, the worst, everything, she would make things out, she would observe and learn what to do, what not to do: it would be a kind of school. But she couldn't, without selling the clothes off her back. It was vile and disgusting to be poor; ... Wasn't it divine, the way the old woman had said those verses, those speeches of Célie? If she would only let her come and listen to her once in a while, like that, it was all she would ask. ... But she didn't think her even good enough to criticize; for that criticism, telling her her head was good. Of course her head was good; she didn't need to travel up to the *quartiers excentriques* to find that out. [etc.](VII,159-160).

The passage exhibits three features which always characterize this narrative technique—dramatic immediacy, reflexive characterization, and economy. Since the language is that of the character immediately in question (her peculiar idiom) the passage has the dramatic effect of direct quotation; and by the same token the tone of the passage, the highly personal subjective coloring lent by the terms and turns of phrase to the events narrated and the things described and evaluated, tends as much to illuminate the "speaker" herself as the subject of her discourse (which in this instance is, coincidentally, largely herself); consequently, the ends of straight narration, of descriptive characterization, and of drama are all simultaneously satisfied.

There is one additional example of a related device which employs peculiar idiom. The authentic flavor of the utterances of Mme Carré is achieved in part by the liberal sprinkling of French phrases in her discourse. Yet even more effective, because less obvious, is that practice which James had followed in representing the speech of the

Poupins and Herr Schinkel in *The Princess Casamassima*—the literal translation into English of typically French turns of phrase. Note, for example, Mme Carré's common use of the definite article where English regularly omits it: "The nerves, the nerves—they're half our affair." And then her frequent little urgent remark to Miriam, "Put yourself there" (which sounds stilted and un-English) is simply a literal rendering of the French "Mets-toi là." Items like these effectively augment the convincing portrayal of la Carré; they are authentic and realistic, and they function quite unobtrusively.

The dramatic quality of the novel is further enhanced by the high percentage of actual dialogue and by the fact that much of that dialogue—indeed most of it—is without narrative comment: the accompanying prose retails facts but little or no interpretation. Whole chapters of *The Tragic Muse* are comprised almost exclusively of dialogue: see for example Chapter XXIV. After a page and a half of stage setting the chapter is developed by means of dialogue between Nick and Gabriel punctuated by the occasional "said Nick" or traditional variations of that indentification. There are but two brief narrative intrusions—the first a mere stage direction, the second a comment on Nick's reaction to the scene. Another example of extended dialogue is the long interview between Nick and Mr. Carteret in chapter XXXII.

In some of the short stories written at the same time as *The Tragic Muse* we find further examples of James's dramatic dialogue. Much of "The Patagonia" (1888) is built up of large blocks of uncommented dialogue. The opening of "Mrs. Temperly" (1887) reads like a script and might serve without change for the stage—and it would compare favorably, in the matter of dramatic technique, with the best of Ibsen. The story opens on a conversation already in progress; identification of the speakers and the topic of their discourse comes only gradually, in bits and pieces, and it is the dialogue itself—not the author in interpretative narration—which conveys the information. The brief prose passages accompanying the dialogue are for the most part simply stage directions. This dramatic aspect of James's technique is realistic and also adheres to the principle of self-sufficiency in the work of art: it permits the author to keep himself hidden, off stage, and thus to avoid the distraction which his intrusive explanatory presence would provide.

With the greater amount of dialogue there is yet another dramatic or perhaps theatrical element in *The Tragic Muse* which appears only

infrequently in James's earlier work. We might call it the fictional
coup de théâtre. Consider, as an example of this feature, Julia Dallow's entrance into Nick's studio to find him alone there with Miriam;
or the two abrupt intrusions of Mrs. Rooth upon intimate scenes
between her daughter and Peter Sherringham; or perhaps best of all,
in that it strikes a double *coup,* the last scene in Nick's studio. Nick
and Biddy are somewhat pessimistically considering what chances
there are of getting a ticket for her to see Miriam's opening as Juliet:

> "Don't you think you could get another?" Biddy quavered.
> "They must be in tremendous demand. But who knows after all?"
> Nick added, at the same moment looking round. "Here's a chance—
> here's quite an extraordinary chance!"
> His servant had opened the door . . . "Miss Rooth!" the man an-
> nounced[!]; but he was caught up by a gentleman who came next and
> who explained, laughing and with a gesture gracefully corrective:
> "No, no—no longer Miss Rooth!"[!!](VIII,424-425).

And then, as though to underline the theatrical aspect of the scene,
James describes the entrance of the former Miss Rooth—now Mrs.
Basil Dashwood: "Miriam entered the place with her charming familiar grandeur—entered very much as she might have appeared, as she
appeared every night, early in her first act, at the back of the stage,
by the immemorial middle door. She might have exactly now have
been presenting herself to the house. . . ."(VIII,425).

Another such passage, worth particular mention though far too
long for adequate quotation, is chapter XXXVII: Miriam is given a
wonderfully dramatic *scène à faire* on the occasion of her being
visited by the four men in her life—Basil, Gabriel, Nick, and Peter
—all at once. All the varied facets of her character sparkle before us
as she turns them severally against the four present reflectors, drawing each of the men out or putting each in his place in her ordered
little universe. It is quite the kind of scene (on stage or off) that a
living English Rachel would be delighted to attempt. Miriam carries
it off admirably. And James's dramatic—as well as theatrical—talent
functions well in permitting the character to expose herself directly
and immediately.

The important presence of the four reflectors, as I call them—the
men who shed light on the brilliant Miriam in this long scene—
constitutes a slight variation of the technique of point of view which
James employs consistently throughout the novel. After the opening
sentences of the initial chapter, virtually all of the novel—narration,

description, dialogue—is presented from the point of view of one or other of the characters; and that is true of even the most obviously *dramatic* passages. James very seldom depends upon his own authority as the author; almost always authority is attributed to one of the characters. In the opening paragraph of the novel, indeed, where James is obliged to introduce the Dormer family and set them on stage in front of us before he can justifiably employ them as focusing agents, he is careful to posit an imaginary viewer, an hypothetical authority:

The spirit of observation is naturally high at the Salon, quickened by a thousand artful or artless appeals, but no particular tension of the visual sense would have been required to embrace the character of the four persons in question . . . and even the most superficial observer would have perceived them to be striking products of an insular neighbourhood, representatives of that tweed-and-waterproof class with which, on the recurrent occasions when the English turn out for a holiday—Christmas and Easter, Whitsuntide and the autumn— Paris besprinkles itself at a night's notice.

Thus James successfully creates the illusion that the scene is presented not from the author's omniscient angle of vision, but refracted through an observer present at the scene; and the sense of the manipulative touch of the omnipotent story-teller is kept to a minimum. Virtually always thereafter a focusing character is present to assume authority.

A further importance of this device is its function in the description of setting and of character. We have seen that while James's description in *The Tragic Muse* is still detailed and factually accurate —realistic—it tends nevertheless to be more selective, closer to the style of Maupassant than to that of Zola; furthermore, we noted that it now is more markedly impressionistic than it had been in the earlier novels and stories of the eighties. James's refinement in the technique consists in his coupling of selective and impressionistic description with use of the focusing character: the impression given is that of the character whose point of view is used. Not only does this descriptive method aim at conveying the atmosphere and sense of the object as well as its appearance and thus achieve a fuller realization of its actual essence, it serves also (as we have seen above) to contribute to the development of the character who is giving us his impression—what I have called reflexive characterization. The story is carrying on its own development dramatically, as we might say—and apparently quite independently of its author. That, at least, is the illusion sought.

James's constant interest in experimenting with narrative technique and with various solutions to the formal problems presented by his art is amply attested to by the short fiction he wrote during the eighties as well as by the novels themselves. In particular, the problem of narrative authority, which we have just been looking at, figured largely in his experiments; and many of the short stories of this period employ the first person narrator in a somewhat novel manner. The novelty lies in the creation of a narrator whose authority is unreliable. A good example of the dubitable authority is offered by "The Solution," a story which James began immediately after *The Tragic Muse* was off his hands. The kernel of the story is this: a naive young American undersecretary with the diplomatic staff in Rome is the victim of a little joke; he is persuaded by his European friends that his behavior (quite innocent enough, in fact) with a young lady has so seriously compromised her that he is virtually obliged to marry her. The story of the joke on Henry Wilmerding is narrated by one of the young jokers, and much of our information results from the discussion of the joke between the narrator and the woman with whom he is in love, the widowed Mrs. Rushbrooke. When he realizes how successful he has been and that poor Henry seems indeed about to do "the honorable thing," the narrator is overcome by the pangs of conscience. Mrs. Rushbrooke quiets him and assures him that everything will turn out all right. And so it does.

The story has some memorable passages of impressionistic description—given, of course, as the impressions of the narrator. For example, Wilmerding's "chief " is presented as "the drollest possible type. . . . He was a product of the Carolinas and always wore a dress-coat and a faded superannuated neckcloth; his hat and boots were also of a fashion of his own. He talked very slowly, as if he were delivering a public address. . . . He used to remind me of the busts of some of the old dry-faced powerful Roman lawgivers and administrators. He spoke no language but that of his native State, but that mattered little, as we all learned it and practised it for our amusement." These few lines give an indication of the evocative power of James's impressionistic description, and the last sentence illustrates something of its effectiveness as reflexive characterization: the narrator gives himself away just a little. He is more revealing of himself (unintentionally, of course) in his impression of Henry: "Wilmerding was a gentleman and he was not a fool, but he was not in the least a man of the world.... He was full of natural delicacy ... his ancestors had been Quakers, and ... there was something rather dovelike in his nature, suggestive of drab tints and the smell of lavender." The revelation, subtle as it is, appears in the condescending and (as it turns out) imperceptive note in the concluding clause. The truth is, of course, that the reader is scarcely sensible to the "giving away" I mention as he follows the development of the joke on the gullible Henry. But when the plot is completed, all these touches come crowding back on us like latent echoes. Henry Wilmerding settles graciously any compromise he has been vaguely guilty of with Veronica and then marries the charming Mrs. Rushbrooke—rather to the consternation of the narrator! The joke of the story finally turns on the narrator himself, who had laughed at the peculiarities of the minister, had regarded so condescendingly the drab and lavender Henry, had considered Mrs. Rushbrooke ("If the 'Bohemian' had been invented in those days she might possibly have been one. . . . She was in short the woman a fellow loves.") as his companion and confidant, and himself, clearly, as a dashing and devilish wag—but with a conscience! And we had been taken in, somewhat: as the story progressed, however, we had grown a bit suspicious of the narrator, especially in his relations with Mrs. Rushbrooke, who (it was becoming increasingly clear) was far less interested in the fellow than he thought she was. To some considerable extent, it is the narrator himself who is the "hero" of the story, which turns out to be the story of how he was the dupe of his own duping.

This is not simply the Jamesian version of the typical O'Henry story: the conclusion comes not as a completely surprising turn of events, for we grow suspicious of the narrator's impressions and particularly of his interpretations as our familiarity with him increases. To some extent, then, our pleasure in the story results from watching the narrator expose himself to us little by little. This method of story telling James resumed on several occasions during the next decade and a half, as he seems to have recognized in it certain peculiar virtues: not only does it contribute to the dramatic quality, the self-sufficiency, of his fiction, it also invites and encourages intimate participation in the story itself as the reader discovers he must be alert to the decreasing reliability of the authority whom he is traditionally accustomed to trust.

In the dramatic little story "The Patagonia" there is a situation which makes an oblique comment on the technique illustrated by "The Solution." Mrs. Nettlepoint and her attractive and somewhat caddish son Jasper have agreed to chaperone a young lady crossing the Atlantic to be married in Europe to a man she has not seen for some years. The narrator is also making the crossing, of course, on *The Patagonia*. Since Mrs. Nettlepoint is not a good sailor and thus will keep to her cabin, the narrator promises to keep her informed of what goes on during the voyage—an intriguing occupation, since Jasper will largely replace his mother as caretaker of the affianced. The narrator assures Mrs. Nettlepoint, "You'll participate at second hand. You'll see through my eyes, hang upon my lips, take sides, feel passions, all sorts of sympathies and indignation." He seems, in fact, to be announcing himself as an excellent narrator, something like the acceptable authority in fiction—the useful "focusing character" we have looked at in James's novels and tales. And Mrs. Nettlepoint certainly hangs on his lips, but refuses simply to see through his eyes; she recognizes that he is not quite reliable, and confronts him with the just accusation, "You don't observe—you know—you imagine." The truth is that the narrator both observes *and* imagines. What matters, however, is that Mrs. Nettlepoint does not just accept passively the visions and versions offered her as though her friend the narrator were a pair of spectacles: she carefully distinguishes between fact and impression and attempts to evaluate for herself the impressions her narrator conveys to her. She takes in his observations but takes in the observer as well, and in so doing is much more actively involved in—and of necessity much more attentive to—the affairs related for her entertainment and instruction. Her rewards will be commensurate with her active investment. Mrs. Nettlepoint is obviously the equivalent of James's ideal reader.

The technical success of "The Solution" is not breathtaking, but it is worth notice as an early stage of the development of a narrative technique that was to reach its culmination in the novel which James considered to be "quite the best, 'all round,' of my productions"— *The Ambassadors*. The role of the dubitable or unreliable authority is extremely important in "The Turn of the Screw" (1898), in *The Sacred Fount* (1901), and in "The Beast in the Jungle" (1903) as well; and variations of the technique can be seen in the novel *What Maisie Knew* (1897) and in the novelette *In the Cage* (1898). The beginnings of this development in narrative technique are visible, as I say, in the novels of the eighties and especially in *The Tragic Muse*.

Some of James's short pieces published during the later eighties demonstrate his continued interest in Zola's theory of experimental fiction. One example is "The Modern Warning," published as "Two Countries" in *Harper's* for June, 1888. It concerns the difficulties that arise from the conflict between an anti-American Englishman and an Anglophobe American; the conflict centers in the American Agatha Grice, who marries the Englishman (Sir Rufus Chasemore) against the wishes of her Anglophobe brother (Macarthy Grice). Agatha's difficulty in accepting Sir Rufus is accounted for by her American heredity: "I suppose [she tells Sir Rufus] that those hostilities of race —transmitted and hereditary, as it were—are the greatest of all." Those feelings of hostility in the Grice blood are quieted in Agatha by her love of Sir Rufus; yet they are actively roused by her husband's preparation of his bitterly denunciatory study of the United States (*The Modern Warning*—i.e. to the English against the American "invasion"). Having read the proofs of his attack, Agatha explains why her hereditary nationalism must rise in opposition (and notice that, American as the Grices are, they remain conscious of their Irish inheritance and also of their commoner side as opposed to Sir Rufus' aristocratic):

she reminded her husband that she had Irish blood, the blood of the people, in her veins, and that he must take that into account. . . . She was far from being a fanatic on this subject, as he knew; but when America was made out to be an object of holy horror to virtuous England she could not but remember that millions of her Celtic cousins had found refuge there from the blessed English dispensations and be struck with his recklessness challenging comparisons which were better left to sleep.

Agatha finds herself caught, like Hyacinth Robinson, between two loves: she is victimized by her conflicting loyalties to husband and to brother, who represent opposing factions. For her as for Hyacinth there is no solution in life. It is not quite a simple matter of her being "determined" irrevocably by the native force of heredity brought into conflict with that of environment: again like Hyacinth, Agatha suffers as a result of her *consciousness* of her heredity and its relation to her environmental situation. In either case, however, her dilemma would apparently permit of no resolving choice.

The Tragic Muse is a full-scale example, the third of this period, of the Jamesian "experimental novel." It is concerned, indeed, with a double experiment. We have Nick Dormer, bred up in a richly political atmosphere and with traditionally political antecedents, introduced to environmental influences which push him in two opposed directions—into the House of Commons and into the artist's studio. We also have Miriam Rooth, the progeny of an artistic Jew and of a daughter of the house of Neville-Nugent, determined by heredity to the life of art, but with a tinge of the commercial and mercenary always present.

The political strain in Nick Dormer's blood is made abundantly clear, and the presence of his father, the earlier Nicholas, is only less pervasive in this novel than that of Mrs. Newsome in *The Ambassadors*. Like Hyacinth Robinson, Nick is acutely conscious of his ancestry and the force with which it weighs upon him. He enumerates to his old friend Gabriel Nash the items that comprise that force: "every thing, every one that belongs to me, that touches me near or far; my family, my blood, my heredity, my traditions, my promises, my circumstances, my prejudices; my little past—such as it is; my great future—such as it has been supposed it may be." (VII,180-181) And later in the novel he reiterates to Julia Dallow the "tremendous force" of his "hereditary talent" for politics: "Innumerable vows and pledges repose upon my head. I'm inextricably committed and dedicated. I was brought up in the temple like the infant Samuel; my father was a high-priest and I am a child of the Lord." (VIII,75-76) This is the force, of heredity and of part of his environment, which Nick feels is propelling him relentlessly into the House of Commons.

But there is a strong suggestion that he has, like Hyacinth Robinson, a mixed heredity. Two statements by Lady Agnes (VIII,183-184, 186) are revealing. In upbraiding Nick for neglecting his political duty she refers to an inveterate (and "irresponsible") interest in painting: "he had had from his earliest childhood the nastiest hankerings after a vulgar little daubing trash-talking life." Yet when his sister Grace deplores his taking up painting—because he will never do things people will like—Lady Agnes is quick to affirm that "as it happened, her children did have a good deal of artistic taste: Grace was the only one who was totally deficient in it. Biddy was very clever." We might put no particular credence in this defensive statement of Lady Agnes' except for her happy reference to Biddy: Biddy does confirm the suggestion, with her dabbling at sculpture, that the artistic flair has been inherited from some antecedent black sheep.

This apparent mixture of influences accounts for Nick's confusion, his perplexity in the face of the antagonistic attractions in the environment warring for his soul. He tries to explain the difficulty to his mother, that he is two men, "two quite distinct human beings, who have scarcely a point in common." Julia Dallow comes to recognize the duality which Nick describes, charging him (in unintentional irony) with really being everything he pretends not to be. Finally Nick laments to Gabriel, "I don't know *what* I am—heaven help me!"(VII,244, 181)

The hereditary strains are realized for Nick in the contacts he makes in his customary milieu. First, his immediate family, excluding Biddy, clearly "stand for" the political strain; likewise the solid presence of Mr. Carteret at Beauclere, who never fails to remind Nick of his political heredity—that he is his father's son; and then the figure of Julia Dallow, who virtually symbolizes the attraction of the political life for Nick—"you're the incarnation of politics" Nick pointedly tells her.[25] But on the other hand his environment presents him with the inspirational Gabriel Nash (firmly on the side of Art and in favor of Nick's chucking politics for painting), and with the compassionate Biddy. Nash assures Nick that he has artistic ability and ought to pursue his artistic penchant. And then, of course, Nick's interest in Miriam Rooth—the tragic muse and a kind of goddess of art—brings him again into close connection with another realization of that side of his heredity.

Miriam Rooth's case is almost as fully treated as Nick's: her heredity is frequently emphasized. Biddy's comment on Miriam's papa is: "A Jewish stockbroker, a dealer in curiosities: what an odd person to marry—for a person who was well born!" The "well born" person, Mrs. Rooth, claims to be a Neville-Nugent of Castle Nugent; and Gabriel Nash assures us:

That's the high lineage of [Miriam's] mama. I seem to have heard it mentioned that Rudolf Roth was very versatile and, like most of his species, not unacquainted with the practice of music. He had been employed to teach the harmonium to Miss Neville-Nugent and she had profited by his lessons. If his daughter's like him—and she's not like her mother—he was darkly and dangerously handsome. So I venture rapidly to reconstruct the situation.(VII,62, 63).

Nash's rapid reconstruction points out that Miriam also had a mixed hereditary complement, and incidentally that the paternal contribution to her strain was itself mixed. (And notice also, by the way, that Miriam's case exemplifies the theory of hereditary "crossing"—whereby the son inherits the mother's characteristics and the daughter the father's—which Zola accepted from Lucas' *Traité de l'hérédité naturelle.*) Peter Sherringham's observations on Miriam's progenitors increase the novel's emphasis on these determining forces. He thinks it odd that the histrionic Miriam should have sprung from Mrs. Rooth's loins, "till he reflected that the evolution was after all natural: the figurative impluse in the mother had become conscious, and therefore higher, through finding an aim, which was beauty, in the daughter." He agrees with both Gabriel and Nick, however, that Miriam most favors her father: "the Hebraic Mr. Rooth, with his love of old pots and Christian altar-cloths, had supplied in the girl's composition the aesthetic element, the sense of colour and form."(VII,220).

Miriam's genetic background is, then, quite fully enough presented, so that we can hardly ignore its apparent bearing on her actions in the novel, its determining role in the "experiment." What is odd, however, is that at first glance it would seem that Miriam's environmental experience consists chiefly of the realization of the artistic strain in her character. She certainly has not a completely smooth row to hoe, but the chief obstacle she has to overcome seems to be the roughness of her own genius—not some opposed influence pulling her away from artistic pursuits. While Nash professes skepticism about Miriam's ability and even her potentiality, he nevertheless introduces her to Mme. Carré. La Carré is also at first quite dubious about Miriam's promise, yet she too is largely instrumental in propelling the girl toward her goal. And finally the interest of Sherringham in things theatrical and his personal attention to Miriam —including some substantial material favors—are likewise apparently the means of adding impetus to her drive to become the English Rachel.

But Peter Sherringham's role is somewhat complex: his assistance to Miriam depends on selfish motives—he is interested in the woman rather than in the actress—and therefore comes really to represent an antagonistic force in Miriam's environment. Mrs. Rooth regards him as an admirable match for Miriam, a match that would mean her leaving the stage, as Peter ultimately demands in asking for Miriam's love. There is the strong suggestion that she is seriously attracted to

Peter and even that, could she have been entirely sure of his intention, she might have accepted his offer of marriage. In response to her mother's confident assertion that Peter has already proposed a dozen times—

"Proposed what to me?" Miriam rang out. "I've told you *that* neither a dozen times nor once, because I've never understood. He has made wonderful speeches, but has never been serious."

". . . He's in love with me, *je le veux bien;* he's so poisoned—Mr. Dormer vividly puts it—as to require a strong antidote; but he has never spoken to me as if he really expected me to listen to him, and he's the more of a gentleman from that fact. He knows we haven't a square foot of common ground—that a grasshopper can't set up a house with a fish. So he has taken care to say to me only more than he can possibly mean. That makes it stand just for nothing."-(VIII,315).

Miriam's situation, then, has been as difficult as Nick's, and the appearance of smooth progress to her goal has been illusory. Her struggle is quite descernible, after all, in such touches as her brushing away her tears as she informs her mother of Peter's imminent departure. But her acceptance of that departure amounts, finally, to her recognizing the right road for her. The place of marriage in her life dedicated to art is sardonically sketched out by Nash: "She ought to marry the prompter or the box keeper." He continues his portrait of her proper husband—imagines him writing her advertisements, adding up her profits, carrying her shawl, and spending his days in her rouge-pot. She marries Basil Dashwood. In accepting (or taking) him Miriam is simply (given her temper, her hereditary complement) allowing her dominant passion to be directed into its proper channels —the theater.

Nick Dormer has also been involved perceptibly in Miriam's problem, and his own in a way parallels hers: the Nick-Julia connection strongly resembles the Miriam-Peter. Like Miriam, Nick has been driven by a dominant passion—the passion for doing his duty. And Nick's passion is guided, like Verena Tarrant's, by forces of his environment into channels which, according to values expressed by the novel, are the wrong ones. His dilemma results from his failure to recognize the true path of duty; and there is a strong suggestion that Nick is all the while really aware of his error and is engaged in an attempt at self-deception. The motif of sporting imagery frequently associated with Nick's political activity serves to imply that that activity was a caprice on his part, a game undertaken for the fun of it. ("He had risen to the fray as he had risen to matches at school," etc.)[26] Two voices, however, admonish him that he has not really been playing the game, "one of them fitfully audible in the depths of his own spirit and the other . . . [that of] Gabriel Nash." Yet he persists in the imitation, feeling that he must do his duty as it is clearly understood by his mother and sister, by Julia Dallow, by Mr. Carteret, and by the spirit of his father. His successful pursuit of his duty culminates, symbolically as well as realistically, in his engagement to Julia—the incarnation of politics.

No sooner has he succeeded in this one pursuit than he feels, like Hyacinth Robinson after a similar success, an acute distaste for "the beastly cause." And he blurts out in awful honesty to Julia that he has imperiled his immortal soul, that he has been hypocritical, dishonest with himself as well as with others. For the moment, however, he seems willing to stand by his wretched success. But his situation is immediately complicated again (and again we are reminded of *The Princess Casamassima*) by his subsequent success in the other cause, his almost abandoned art. Nash's visit to his studio convinces Nick that his painting is successful: Nick "found himself imputing value to his visitor—attributing to him . . . the dignity of judgment, the authority of knowledge. Nash was an ambiguous character but an excellent touchstone." This occurrence opens his eyes, he now sees his proper road and, like Verena Tarrant, is ready to follow the true dictates of his nature—or at least to let himself be propelled in that direction, for he is still somewhat confused about his duty (and he *must* attend to his duty—for that is his dominant passion). Nash sets him straight on that, too; and by stealing his thunder.

"Don't you recognize in any degree the grand idea of duty?"
"If I don't grasp it with a certain firmness I'm a deadly failure, for I was quite brought up on it," Nick said.
"Then you're indeed the wretchedest failure I know. Life *is* ugly after all."
"But what do you call right? What's your cannon of certainty there?"
"The conscience that's in us—that charming conversible infinite thing, the intensest thing we know. . . . One must do one's best to find out the right, and your criminality appears to be that you've not taken the commonest trouble."(VIII,24, 25).

Fortunately, Julia herself cancels the vow Nick has made to her, so that he can be saved from Hyacinth Robinson's fate and can follow straight to his goal—beset with doubts and confronted with obstacles, to be sure, but essentially unwavering. Both Nick and Miriam, then, were determined to meet the ends they do: in both cases they followed an hereditary impulse. The environmental representatives of their mixed hereditary strains so contrived, in the ensuing struggle of the elements, to make clear to Nick and Miriam the right direction of their most profound passion and their best self-realization.

The experiment of *The Tragic Muse* winds up with Peter Sherringham marrying, to everyone's relief, Biddy Dormer. Miriam's marriage to Dashwood is really little more than a symbolic expression of her being wedded to the theater: so far as the satisfaction of her essential passion is concerned, nothing is altered. And Nick Dormer's finally returning to Julia to paint her portrait indicates to the careful reader that, in spite of Nash's dire prophecy, Nick has remained faithful to his true path of duty—to remain the celibate artist. The complex experiment is done, and the conclusion to be drawn therefrom is a familiar Jamesian lesson: it is the lesson of the master.

It hardly needs to be pointed out that, as was true of Verena Tarrant in *The Bostonians* and of Hyacinth Robinson in *The Princess Casamassima*, Nick and Miriam are by no means merely passive objects swept on by the hereditary and environmental forces in their respective situations: again it is the character's *consciousness* of the forces within and around that determines his lot. Discovery of the significance of the dominant passion—for love, say, in Verena and for doing one's duty, in Nick—and the ability to choose the best avenue for the satisfaction of that passion, those are of principal importance in these novels. But James has emphasized the influential roles of heredity and environment in *The Tragic Muse* as in the two earlier novels: they determine what his hero's *consciousness* can do and they set the limits within which the character's choice is free to work.

The central theme of *The Tragic Muse,* as James outlined it in his preface to the novel, was in his eyes extremely important and one that had been in his mind "from far back." But the particular combination of circumstances which faced him in the closing years of the decade of the eighties must have seemed to make that theme immediately relevant and intimately personal to him. It is not really difficult to see in *The Tragic Muse* James's working out the general problem of "art and the world" as it applied most specifically to him at that moment. That problem involved the apparent failure of the two novels which preceded *The Tragic Muse,* but more urgently the proposed venture into the theater—a not completely disinterested wooing of the not entirely chaste theatrical muse. It would seem that the relation of Nick to Miriam in the novel is a metaphoric equivalent of James's personal situation vis-à-vis Compton's offer of a career as dramaturge. James had always considered writing for the theater to be "the most cherished of all [his] projects"; but now, in the eighties, that project had a mercenary edge to it—he was interested in the quick and abundant returns possible to the successful playwright. He had decided to devote the time usually spent on the novel to "pot-boiling" for the stage. Here would be a solution to his financial problems;[27] here also would be the opportunity to reach a large audience professionally. James must, however, have suffered something like a twinge of conscience in contemplating this venture with its faint aroma of prostitution. (It will not do, of course, to attempt to brush aside this consideration by claiming that James the professional always wrote for money: he did, but not as his principal aim.)[28] This troublesome aspect of his situation is clearly represented in the relation of Nick to Miriam as a model for his canvas: she functions to some extent as Nick's muse, but he is troubled by an ambiguous quality in her—the mixture of the aesthetic and the mercenary.

Nick is pleased to paint Miriam as "The Tragic Muse" but does not complete a second painting of her. Indeed he is never unequivocally at ease with her as a model, and the bothersome quality is expressed in terms of her racial characteristics: as he works at her portrait Nick is "troubled about his sitter's nose, which was somehow Jewish without the convex arch." (VIII,49). He is impressed by her resemblance to her father, the Jewish stockbroker, and entertains the notion that her mother is probably Jewish too:

He found himself seeing the immemorial Jewess in her hold up a candle in a crammed back shop. . . . it had never occurred to him before that she was a grand-daughter of Israel save on the general theory, so stoutly held by several clever people, that few of us are not under suspicion. The late Rudolf Roth had at least been, and his daughter was visibly her father's child; so that, flanked by such a pair, good Semitic presumptions sufficiently crowned the mother. (VIII,305).

It is Miriam's Jewishness that bothers Nick as he paints her, a quality associated in his mind with her father, himself an odd mixture of the aesthetic and the commercial. These are the salient terms of the metaphor (as I would call it) which James employs to help express Nick's doubts about his own artistic pursuits, and which reflects James's own doubts about his projected pursuits in the theater.

Now this is certainly not to suggest that Miriam is herself mercenary, an artist devoted to the commercial reward. It is just that something of that quality expresses itself to Nick. Indeed it is a fear—the commercial threat—which Miriam herself has good reason to entertain: she laments freely in the novel those popular successes which threaten to prevent her from trying her talents in a variety of roles and so coming to master her demanding art. So much the better for the metaphoric aspect of the novel as it was developed under James's pen: Miriam does represent the dramatic art with all its annoyance of glaring publicity, its need to satisfy the many-headed monster, its susceptibility to the influence of the shekel. And as Nick, the private artist who struggles throughout the novel to learn to be true to himself, contemplates this ambiguous representative figure, he cannot but be troubled.

If Nick has some misgivings about this muse, he needs some more satisfactory source of inspiration to rely on—some ultimate authority for his activity about which he finally need have no doubts. That authority would be some divine representative of the pure spirit of art who would inspire him not to specific acts of creation but, more generally, to lead the artist's life and do the artist's work in whatever form came to hand. For Nick that divine authority appears in the form of the appropriately named Gabriel Nash. Indeed it is Gabriel's annunciation that first made him aware of the artistic burden he bore. Gabriel is a fascinating character in the novel: he is unusual, capricious, marvellous. After encouraging Nick to forsake all for art he returns to chastise Nick mildly for pursuing his painting so industriously. He seems suspicious of any *doing* at all: what one *does* is of little moment, but what one is matters supremely. Nash's point seems to be simply that *being* is the important consideration, for what one does will follow from that safely; whereas attention to what one *does* can lead to dishonesty, hypocrisy—one can *do* without being. And in being an artist (whatever one does) one *participates* in the eternal Being of Art. Nash is himself apparently the manifestation of that timeless essence: "I will never grow old," he tells Nick, "for I shall

only *be,* more and more . . . I daresay I'm indestructible, immortal."
It is significant that this exchange (jocular in tone but surely of
profound seriousness for James and reader alike), on the occasion of
Nick's painting Gabriel's portrait, is introduced by a description of
the subject's discomfiture at being fixed on canvas: "it was new to
him to be himself interpreted. . . . From being outside the universe
he was suddenly brought into it, and . . . reduced to [the position] of
humble ingredient and contributor." The chapter concludes with
other significant allusions to Nash's relation to temporality—"punctuality was not important for a man who felt that he had the command
of all time," and "Nick now recalled with a certain fanciful awe the
special accent with which [Nash] had ranked himself among imper-
ishable things."(VIII,410-412). After sitting to Nick for his portrait
Nash disappears from his life; and similarly the portrait itself gradually fades away to nothing but a blur resembling the roughest preliminary sketch. Nick explains this phenomenon to Biddy by saying that
"Nash has melted back into the elements—he's part of the great air
of the world."(VIII,419).

It is apparent that Gabriel Nash serves as the temporal manifestation of the eternal essence in which Nick as artist participates. James
has used him as the symbol of the undying spirit of art. And we can
see that in this metaphoric expression James embodied his own problem and its potential solution at the moment when he was bidding
farewell to the novel and hail to the theater. It expresses his fear that
he might suffer seriously as an artist by his theatrical "pot-boiling"
but also his trust that an exalted and ultimate inspiration would see
him through—would enable him to continue to *be* the faithful artist
regardless of the kind of thing he might undertake to *do.*

Some doubt about Nick's success at the end of the novel remains,
and that dubiousness casts a grim light on my rather sanguine reading
of *The Tragic Muse* as an expression of hope. Gabriel Nash's dire
prophecy that Nick would succumb to Julia's attraction at last seems
near to being fulfilled:

She'll get you down to one of the country houses, and it will all go
off charmingly—with sketching in the morning, on days you can't
hunt, and anything you like in the afternoon, and fifteen courses in
the evening. . . . You'll go about with her and do all her friends, all
the bishops and ambassadors, and you'll eat your cake and have it,
and everyone, beginning with your wife, will forget there's anything
queer about you, and everything will be for the best in the best of

worlds. . . . That's the sort of thing women do for a man—the sort of thing they invent when they're exceptionally good and clever. (VIII,406-407).

For Nick does accept Julia's invitation to go down for Christmas and while there sketches "the whole company"; worse yet, he finally does a rather successful portrait of Julia. But at this point we may recognize an ambiguous note in Gabriel's utterance: like all prophecies, it has its ambiguity, is both a warning and a forecast, and contains both an indication of the means to success as well as the caution against failure.

The key indication is the painting of the portrait. The novel developes a minor motif which might be called "the law of the portrait": to put it simply, this law is that the effect of painting someone's portrait is to assure his disappearance from the artist's life. Nick paints Miriam; she marries another and removes herself from his orbit. He later paints Nash, who also disappears from his life. Nick indeed seems subconsciously aware of this mysterious law: upon his original engagement to Julia he refuses her request to sit to him for her portrait, and with the startling and apparently inexplicable "Never, never, never!" Miriam's refusal to sit again to Nick makes explicit reference to the law:

". . . You'll find other models. Paint Gabriel Nash."
"Gabriel Nash—as a substitute for you?"
"It will be a good way to get rid of him. Paint Mrs. Dallow too," Miriam went on . . . , "paint Mrs. Dallow if you wish to eradicate the last possibility of a throb."
"The last possibility? Do you mean in her or in me?"
"Oh in you. I don't know anything about 'her.' "
"But that wouldn't be the effect," he argued with the same supervening candour. "I believe that if she were to sit to me the usual law would be reversed."
"The usual law?"
"Which you cited a while since and of which I recognised the general truth. In the case you speak of," he said, "I should probably make a shocking picture."
"And fall in love with her again? Then for God's sake risk the daub." Miriam laughed out as she floated away to her victoria. (VIII,398-399).

The penultimate paragraph of the novel refers, not to "a shocking picture," but rather to "the noble portrait of a lady" which attracted general attention at a recent exhibition. We may safely assume, surely, that the usual law was not reversed after all, and that Nick Dormer remains the devoted, irresponsible, and unworldly artist, celebrating the cult of Gabriel Nash—the great religion of Art.

The Tragic Muse occupies a position of peculiar importance in the Jamesian canon: it offers the fullest fictional development of certain recurrent themes pertaining to the life of art and the artist, and it permits the clearest understanding of the close relationship between James's stories of artists and his stories of man in general. The aesthetic attitude expressed in the novel by Gabriel Nash is rehearsed in numerous short stories, the majority of which were written and published during the last decade and a half of the nineteenth century. And many of these tales are concerned with the opposition between artistic *being* and *doing* as Gabriel Nash expressed it in *The Tragic Muse*. Typically, the faithfully dedicated artist recognizes his need of patient leisure and "irresponsible spaces" for contemplation and careful *couvage* in order for his artist conception to develop and flower; but he is faced always with the importunate demands of the world that he look to his obligation of doing his duty, of producing something "to show." And if he does produce—publish books, paint pictures, carve statues which society can handle and heft, visit and view—then he will have succeeded in the impercipient eyes of the world. Yet in doing his "duty" as the world expects, he runs the grave risk of misdirecting his energies and being unfaithful to his art; he risks rendering all to Caesar.

This theme appears as early as "The Madonna of the Future" (1873) and in several of the stories of the nineties. It is effectively expressed in "The Next Time" (1895), where the hero Ralph Limbert is in the strange position of being incapable of producing a pot-boiler with vulgar appeal: he cannot "make a sow's ear out of a silk purse"[29]—he *cannot do* what he *is not.* He remains a failure in the eyes of the world while his sister-in-law, Jane Highmore (who never spoke "of the literary motive as if it were distinguishable from the pecuniary") succeeds wonderfully. James's opinion of that success emerges sharply in such passages as this:

Between our hostess [Mrs. Highmore] and Ray Limbert flourished the happiest relation, the only cloud on which was that her husband eyed him rather askance. When he was called clever this personage wanted to know what he had to "show"; it was certain that he showed nothing that could compare with Jane Highmore. Mr. Highmore took his stand on accomplished work and, turning up his coattails, warmed his rear with a good conscience at the neat bookcase in which the generations of triplets were chronologically arranged.

Now Mr. Highmore obviously has a good deal in common with Mrs. Coventry of "The Madonna of the Future," who was anxious for the painter Theobald's *show* to begin: for both, what matters is what shows; they care nothing for one's attempt to *be* the faithful artist. They are thus related to George Gravener and Miss Anvoy of "The Coxon Fund" (1894) as regards their attitude to the artist Frank Saltram: "But what is there, after all, at his age, to show?" The same idea echoes in the words of Mrs. Warren Hope of "The Abasement of the Northmores" (1900), who wonders about her husband's career —"what was there, at fifty-seven, as the vulgar said, to 'show' for it all but his wasted genius, his ruined health and his paltry pension?" To these can be added Morgan Mallow, the successful mediocrity of "The Tree of Knowledge" (1900), as he faces his son, returned from an "irresponsible" artistic sojourn in Paris:

[Morgan] had come down on him for having, after so long, nothing to show, and hoped that on his next return this deficiency would be repaired. *The* thing, the Master complacently set forth was—for any artist, however inferior to himself—at least to "do" something. "What can you do? That's all I ask." *He* had certainly done enough, and there was no mistake about what he had to show. Lance had tears in his eyes. . . . It wasn't so easy to continue humbugging—as from son to parent—after feeling one's self despised for not grovelling in mediocrity.

James attempts to enlist out sympathetic response to the faithful artists by means of religious imagery associated with them and their activity—frequently it is a sort of angelic motif. Theobald of "The Madonna of the Future" is spoken of by his model, Serafina, in this way: "I'm sure *nostro signore* has the heart of an angel and the face of a saint." The work of Ralph Limbert persists, in spite of his efforts at vulgarization, in "addressing itself to the angels." In "The Death of the Lion" (1894), Miss Fanny Hurter, who is one of the very few capable of properly appreciating the work of Neil Paraday, has "the face of an angel"; and the narrator of the story, another of the appreciative few, expresses his awakening dedication to Paraday's

162f HENRY JAMES

And this all finds a strong parallel in *The Tragic Muse*, where the
attitude of Miriam and Nick to their art and their place of artistic
activity is frequently expressed with the aid of religious imagery, and
where the significantly named Gabriel Nash plays an important role.[30] Not only does he impress on Nick the importance of *being* the
artist and of trusting his essential artist-self and its promptings—"that
charming conversible infinite thing, the intensest thing we know"—
he also scorns the world's insistence on doing something to show:
"having something to show's such a poor business. It's a kind of
confession of failure."

This attitude of James's is reminiscent of Emerson's comment that
" 'Tis not important how the hero does this or this, but what he is.
What he is will appear in every gesture and syllable."[31] But the idea
was apparently given James by his father; the autobiographical *Notes
of a Son and Brother* records this reminiscence of his father's advice:
"What we were to do ... was just to *be* something, something uncon-
nected with specific doing, something free and uncommitted, something finer in short than being *that*, whatever it was, might consist
of."[32]

A representative passage from the writings of James's father will
also indicate the connection between the artist and the ordinary man
in James's fiction, for the connection made by father and son is
essentially the same. In *Moralism and Christianity* Henry James, Sr.
wrote:

But now observe that when I speak of the aesthetic man or Artist, I
do not mean the man of any specific function, as the poet, painter,
or musician. I mean the man of whatsoever function, who in fulfillment of it obeys his own inspiration or taste, uncontrolled either by
his physical necessities or his social obligation. He alone is the Artist,
whatever be his manifest vocation, whose action obeys his own internal taste or attraction, uncontrolled by necessity or duty. The action
may perfectly consist both with necessity and duty ... but these must
not be its animating principles, or he sinks at once from the Artist into
the artisan.[33]

And we recall again Nash's urging Nick simply to *be*, to recognize his *duty to himself.*

This antinomy of being and doing in the stories of artists, and especially in *The Tragic Muse*, is closely related to the central oppositions in James's other fiction, most obviously in the international stories—where the opposition is between "America" and "Europe." The dilemma of the innocent American is that he is confronted, in Europe, by a world which relies on what shows—correct manners and conventional behavior. The particular evil of that world and its code of manners is that it permits the grossest hypocrisy: what one smoothly does is no necessary reflection of what one really is. The naive American has no artifice to enable him to appear other than he really is—which was, we recall, the ironic dilemma of Ralph Limbert in "The Next Time." One horrible alternative open to the American is to adopt the manners he sees, with no assurance that they will faithfully represent *him.* In that case he will cease to be what he spontaneously *is* and try to do things according to the way of the world. The classical example of that choice is Gilbert Osmond of *The Portrait of a Lady*, the polished veneer on a personal void, who blandly confesses "I'm not conventional: I'm convention itself." The painful solution is to come to terms with that world without losing fidelity to one's self, to accept only those features of conventional behavior which honestly represent what one is—and to avoid being "ground in the very mill of the conventional."

James's stories of artists simply examine the same problem in those particular terms most appropriate to the life of the artist. In attempting to achieve a workable compromise with "the world," the artist must still remain faithful to his essential nature as artist—"the intensest thing we know." Clearly this is the problem which both Nick Dormer and Miriam Rooth share: their problem is one, although their artistic mediums are apparently quite opposed. And each must cherish his "silk purse." So the "theatrical case" and the "political case" of *The Tragic Muse*, as James calls them, are really closely united in their treatment of the problem of the conflict of "art and the world"; and can be seen, finally, to be typically Jamesian in their profoundest concerns.

CHAPTER VI

From "my own old pen"—
"the best, 'all round,'
of my productions."

As Henry James completed *The Tragic Muse*, he turned with high expectations and firm determination to writing for the theater. He promised himself that he would allow five years to see whether he could succeed at his new venture. The story of James's theatrical experiment, 1890-1895, has been told by Mr. Leon Edel in his introduction to *The Complete Plays of Henry James* (1949). The highlights of that story are these: during 1890 James completed his dramatised version of *The American* for Edward Compton's company. It ran successfully in the provinces and enjoyed a modest run in London of some seventy performances in the late fall of 1891. James then completed four comedies without having any of them produced—although Augustin Daly seemed on the verge of doing one. Then, in 1893, he entertained an invitation from George Alexander to write a play suitable for him and his company. James worked diligently through 1894 at *Guy Domville*, trying to make it the kind of thing that would succeed with the English theater-goers. He persevered at his task—and at the bolstering of his optimism—but as his familiarity with the demands of actors, managers, producers, and the public increased, his cynicism grew apace. More and more it seemed to James that being a professional dramaturge was "a most unholy trade." As the time for the opening of *Guy Domville* approached, he wrote in exasperation to his friend Henrietta Reubell that while he might have been meant for the drama, "God knows!—but I certainly wasn't meant for the theatre."[1] The distinction is an important one!

Opening night for *Guy Domville* was January 5, 1895. The play was sumptuously staged and the characters ornately costumed, but it ended in what James considered a fiasco. The truth is that it met with a mixed response: some drama critics, notable George Bernard Shaw, were most favorably impressed. But the immediate vocal reaction from a rather rough gallery was decidedly unfavorable, and when James appeared before the curtain at the end of the play he noticed only the hooting and catcalls. He felt certain that his theatrical experiment was a distinct failure and he determined to wash his hands of it all. His own account of that sad Saturday, written five days after the event, is calmer and more philosophical than his initial reaction: it puts the blame for the row where it belonged, but it also inculpates by extension the theater crowd as a whole.

The only thing they understand or want here, is *one kind* of play— the play of the same kind as the unutterable kind they already know. With anything a little more delicate they are like a set of savages with a gold watch. Yet God knows I had *tried* to be simple, straightforward and British, and to dot my i's as big as with targets. . . . But the theater is verily a black abyss—and one feels strained with vulgarity rien que d'y avoir passé. Thank heaven there is another art.[2]

He had tried and failed, like his own Ralph Limbert in "The Next Time," to make a sow's ear out of a silk purse. He was determined to have no more of it.

Before the month was out James had recorded in his Notebooks his decision to return to that other art he gratefully mentioned: "I take up my *own* old pen again—the pen of all my old unforgettable efforts and sacred struggles. To myself—today—I need say no more. Large and full and high the future still opens. It is now indeed that I may do the work of my life. And I will."[3] And so, to be sure, he did.

When James wrote of returning to his own old pen it may well have been with a sense of the bitterness of defeat and of the comfort to be found in the old familiar ways. But there is no evidence that that return was simply a falling back to what he had been and done. All the signs agree in suggesting that it was once again a fresh start— although in the familiar and congenial medium of the novel. He was adhering to the old but perpetually valid principle of "The Art of Fiction"—"Art lives upon . . . experiment, upon curiosity, upon variety of attempt, upon the exchange of views and the comparison of standpoints. . . ." For the work to which his own old pen was put proved to be work of further experiment, artistic adventures, technical progress. The question is whether these new ventures are at all indebted to the attempts hazarded and the lessons learned during the Naturalist experiment of the eighties, and whether they realize any benefit at all from his foray into the "most unholy trade" in the early nineties.

James's critical position in the Major Phase is expressed in his prefaces, written for the collected edition of his work in the first decade of this country (the New York edition), in his late volume *Notes on Novelists* (1914), and in several essays on individual novelists published during this last period. He still looks to the great master Balzac, to Zola, to Flaubert and Maupassant, as to admirable models in the realm of prose fiction, and he continues to stress the importance of realistic rendering in the novel and short story. In an essay published late in 1899, "The Present Literary Situation in France," he pays frank tribute to Zola's literary method: "I mention it, indeed, mainly to pay it publicly my respects. For it has been in its way an intellectual lesson ... it has shown, at least, admirably what a method can do."[4] Then, in his last book of essays, *Notes on Novelists,* James again voices his admiration for the "totally represented world" of Zola's fiction: "I doubt if there has ever been . . . any thing more founded and established, more provided for all round, more organized and carried on."[5] Even more striking than those notices, of course, is the revealing essay "The Lesson of Balzac," James's principal lecture for his American tour of 1904-1905, published in 1905. It is a generous avowal of admiration for "the packed and constituted, the palpable, provable world" of the *Comédie Humaine;* and a completely ingenuous expression of grateful indebtedness to the writer James regarded as both "the greatest master" and "the father of us all."

I speak of him, and can only speak, as a man of his own craft, an emulous fellow-worker, who has learned from him more of the lessons of the engaging mystery of fiction than from anyone else, and who is conscious of so large a debt to repay that it has had positively to be discharged in installments; as if one could never have at once all the required cash in hand.[6]

Such remarks clearly manifest the persistence of that critical predilection, expressed in "The Art of Fiction," that "the air of reality (solidity of specification) seems to me to be the supreme virtue of a novel—the merit on which all its other merits . . . helplessly and submissively depend." Yet even as he praises the solidity of specification in those works he had admired from far back, he now adds a rather stern qualification. It is a sharp word of warning against an abundance of factual material, of caution against the threat of overpowering factual data. In his 1903 essay on Zola, for instance, James admits that "his documents . . . yield him extraordinary appearances of life."[7] The term "appearances" underlines the faintness of this praise. Two years later the praise is even fainter, as James explains that Zola's performance amounts to "an extraordinary show of representation imitated"; although he justly allows that in his best work (*l'Assommoir,* say) that imitation "breaks through into something we take for reality."[8] But for the most part Zola is a prime example of the artist who has been victimized by exhaustive documentation, who has become the slave of his notes. Even Balzac "sees and presents too many facts."[9] This is the more lamentable, James points out, inasmuch as "the most wonderful adventures of an artist's spirit are those, immensely quickening for his 'authority,' that are not yet reducible to his notes."[10]

This new word of caution in James's critical comments is augmented by certain revealing metaphors which underline the distinction he wishes to make. In "The New Novel" (1914), he speaks of the importance of "hugging the shore of the real . . . and of pushing inland, as far as a keel might float."[11] At first glance the metaphor seems merely to emphasize the importance of realistic representation; but a second look reveals significant implications not to be neglected. The figure implies that it is not at all the "shore of the real" that keeps the artistic boat afloat (that not being the nature of shores!), and that, pressed too far inland, the boat will founder, will be wrecked and left high and dry on the land of the real. The note of warning sounds subtly but clearly.

A second metaphor frequently recurs in the critical writing of James's last period, and further develops the implications already noted. It compares the artistic imagination to a simmering brew in a crucible: the data picked up from observation in life's garden are the ingredients in the brew. The point of the metaphor is to stress the importance of artistic "rendering" of the raw material thus gathered so as to produce the finished "dish"—the work of art. The observed data (to put it prosaically), presented as items in a catalogue, will not suffice: something must be done to make of them a vital creation. That

necessary artistic action James calls "the mystic process of the crucible, the transformation of the material under aesthetic heat."[12] In his
preface to volume XV of the New York edition he gives full development to this useful metaphor:

We can surely account for nothing in the novelist's work that hasn't
passed through the crucible of his imagination, hasn't, in that perpetually simmering cauldron his intellectual *pot-au-feu*, been reduced to savoury fusion. We here figure the morsel, of course, not as
boiled to nothing, but as exposed, in return for the taste it gives out,
to a new and richer saturation.... [But] if it persists as the impression
not artistically dealt with, it shames the honour offered it and can
only be spoken of as having ceased to be a thing of fact and yet not
become a thing of truth.[13]

The emphasis now falls much more heavily on the importance of
rendering, artistic doing—in a word, on technique. While he continues to insist on realistic representation, the word of caution is always
inescapable: the data must be there, accurate but carefully selected
and not in over-abundance. In "The New Novel" he explains—

Nothing is further from our thought than to undervalue saturation
and possession, the fact of the particular experience, the state and
degree of acquaintance incurred, however such a consciousness may
have been determined; for these things represent on the part of the
novelist, as on the part of any painter of things seen, felt or imagined,
just one half of his authority—the other half being represented of
course by the application he is inspired to make of them.[14]

What James envisages is an artistic brew that shall be, not thick, but
rich—not so much palpable as palatable.
    It is not only that a plethora of fact may overwhelm the artist,
dictate to him and so prevent the truly artistic rendering of his
material—so as to extract is best savour, its significance. An attendant
danger that looms as large is probably, at last, the most serious of all
—and this strikes at the very heart of realism. One of his pointed
criticisms of Zola's heavily factual creation was its one-sidedness: in
one essay he complains that Zola gives us "an immense deal of life,"
but yet "comparatively little consciousness."[15] A later essay adds the
explanation that Zola "had to leave out the life of the soul, practically,
and confine himself to the life of the instinct, of the more immediate
passions, such as can be easily and promptly caught in the fact."[16]

The point here is that to omit consciousness and the life of the soul is to be imcomplete in one's rendering of reality. Furthermore, James was to feel increasingly that the most revealing, the most significant aspects of reality were precisely those which Zola's teeming representations were liable to omit—the aspects of psychological reality. Flaubert's escape of Zola's dilemma is instructive: *Madame Bovary* illustrates the kind of realism James now most admires. "Emma interests us by the nature of her consciousness and the play of her mind, thanks to the reality and beauty with which those sources are invested."[17] A younger exemplar of the approved realistic approach, Paul Bourget, also comes in for significant praise: "M. Bourget literally *inhabits* the consciousness. . . . His relation to it is not that of a visitor for a purpose or of a collector with a note-book; it is that of a resident . . . the consciousness inhabited by M. Bourget *is* luxuriously appointed."[18]

The development illustrated by these critical observations is paralleled in James's own fiction. The new work from his "old pen" manifests continued interest in experimenting with narrative technique, principally in the matter of point-of-view. But these experiments are by no means an entirely new departure: they are quite definitely an extension and elaboration of the narrative technique employed in the major fiction of the eighties—and of the peculiar attempt noted in "The Solution." The principal characters of James's "experimental novels" (Verena Tarrant, Hyacinth Robinson, Nick Dormer), determined though they apparently were by the force of heredity and environment as possible (indeed probable) influences; and that consciousness in each case was largely responsible for determining the fate they met. In each of those "experimental" stories of the eighties the *peripeteia* is (with classical correctness) closely accompanied by the *anagnorisis*. The increasing interest in consciousness is reflected in the technical experiment of *What Maisie Knew* (1897)—one of James's first major works following his experience in the theater. That novel employs consistently a single central observer, little Maisie of the title; and the peculiar interest of the rather sordid philanderers' quadrille which the novel rehearses derives principally from its being focused in Maisie's more or less innocent eye. *The Awkward Age* (1899) turns that focusing technique inside-out: at the center is the heart of the drama itself, rather than a focusing character, and that central situation is developed by a series of observers who variously illuminate its different facets.[19]

It was the attempt of *What Maisie Knew* that proved to hold the greatest fascination for James and to be the more fruitful experiment. *In the Cage* and *The Turn of the Screw* (1898) and *The Sacred Fount* (1901) not only follow and develop the technique of *Maisie*, they resume the earlier attempt of the short story "The Solution."[20] In each of these stories the action is focused by a single observer; one point of view dominates and controls. This technique continued to exhibit its recognized virtues: it contributes to the unity of the story by means of its single angle of vision; it supports the story's self-sufficiency by providing what seems to be an authority other than that of the managing, omniscient author; and it aids the story's independence as a means of self-expression—in functioning as reflexive characterization.

In addition to those familiar virtues, there is another feature of this developing technique of narrative point of view that was most important in James's career. The principal focusing characters in the stories mentioned are all unreliable authorities of dubious credibility who do not always see clearly, who leap to conclusions on the basis of insufficient evidence or evidence more or less grossly misunderstood. As we saw to be the case with "The Solution," so with the later stories the reader tends to be taken in by the unreliable authority—at least for a time; gradually he comes to recognize the dubiousness of that authority, he realizes that he is not to be trusted, that he has to be watched. Indeed, the reader finds that he is watching the dubious authority every bit as much as he is the drama being narrated. Eventually, the principal interest comes to be not *what* the authority is reporting, but the reporting itself. It is not what is seen that matters, but the character's way of seeing. He becomes the hero of the story of which he believes himself to be merely the reporter: the drama becomes the drama of his consciousness. And the culmination of this development in narrative technique is to be found in *The Ambassadors*. James apparently came to recognize with increasing clarity what exciting possibilities lay in this manner of narration; and the realization of those possibilities was the work of his Major Phase and one of his most important contributions to the development of modern fiction.

That recognition owed something, however, to James's initially disheartening experience with the theater. There is ample evidence in the pages of his Notebook which follow his departure from the theater to indicate that that five-year sojourn brought abundant recompense for its traumatic shock. He discovered, as he put it, "the divine principle of the Scenario." And the long passages of planning the novelette *The Spoils of Poynton* are interrupted on several occasions by parenthetical reminders of what he has gained from his sortie into the "most unholy trade." The notes for February 14th, 1895, contain this interjection:

Compensations and solutions seem to stand there with open arms for me—and something of the "meaning" to come to me of past bitterness, of recent bitterness that otherwise has seemed a mere sickening, unflavoured draught. Has a *part* of all this wasted passion and squandered time (of the last 5 years) been simply the precious lesson ... *of the singular value for a narrative plan too* of the (I don't know *what* adequately to call it) divine principle of the Scenario? ... this exquisite truth that what I call the divine principle in question is a key that, working in the same *general* way fits the complicated chambers of *both* the dramatic and the narrative lock. ...

And for August 11th, 1895, he wrote this:

When I ask myself what there may have been to show for my long tribulation, my wasted years and patiences and pangs, of theatrical experiment, the answer, as I have already noted here, comes up as just possible *this*: what I have gathered from it will perhaps have been exactly some such mastery of fundamental statement—of the art and secret of it, of expression, of the sacred mystery of structure. Oh yes—the weary, woeful time has done something for me, has had in the depths of all its wasted piety and passion, an intense little lesson and direction. What that resultant is I must now actively show.[21]

Throughout these pages and on to the end of the Notebooks we find James penning as a constant theme of exhortation to himself the advice "Dramatize, dramatize!"And to accompany the evidence of the Notebooks we have, of course, that of the fiction itself. Critics have noticed that the post-theatrical fiction seems to have a different quality, that the later stories are predominantly "scenic" rather than "pictorial," as James "has succeeded in marrying the intensity and directness of the drama to the breadth of vision and depth of implication of the novel."[22] This heightened dramatic quality would have particularly appealed to James not only for its own sake—as making a more immediate and direct appeal to the reader, and hence being more life-like and realistic—but also from a more strictly technical point of view, as being the most effective means of overcoming the nuisance of the illusion-destroying intruder, the omniscient and omnipotent author. The technique of dramatizing fictional narrative—toward which he had been working, consciously or not, for some years—was in a way the natural culmination of the variety of attempt which the Naturalists had been concerned with in their aim at achieving the air of reality in their stories.

And the dramatizing technique suited itself admirably to the other line of technical development in which James had been involved—the expression of psychological realism. The character whose point of view frames the story and who is initially, it seems, merely a part of the technique, gradually becomes the very hero whose peculiar psychology is expressed dramatically: the story he tells (or "views") is the dramatic externalization of his psyche, his own soul. The story is, then, the dramatization of his consciousness. That is the situation in *The Turn of the Screw, In the Cage, The Sacred Fount,* "The Beast in the Jungle," etc. *The Ambassadors* is the culmination of this development, and it exhibits the fruits of James's dual experiment of the eighties and nineties—the Naturalist and the theatrical.

The difficulty in handling an unreliable observer, whose unreliable point of view is increasingly the main concern of the story, is the danger that the ironist always faces: the irony may go undetected. Hence the problem which critics of *The Turn of the Screw* wrestled with for years, and which made intelligent criticism of *The Sacred Fount* apparently impossible until the last decade. Critical readers tended to take the Governess and the narrator of *Fount* at their word, and to try on that basis to figure out "what was going on" in the stories. Sanity returned when attention was directed to the peculiar observer and his way of observing. What is obviously required in this type of story, especially by an author who is committed to silenced omniscience, is some means of control to make the dramatic irony perceptible, to give expression to the values in question, to guide reader response. The only satisfactory way of meeting the requirement is through the means of artistic form. To those means James was of course ready and able to turn.

James's criticism during this period reflects his increased interest in the value of artistic form. And once again he looks to the example of the eldest grandson of Balzac. In his essay of 1902 he observes that *Madame Bovary* has a perfection "that makes it stand almost alone"; and that perfection results from its excellence of form:

The form is in *itself* as interesting, as active, as much of the essence of the subject as the idea, and yet so close is its fit and so inseparable its life that we catch it at no moment on any errand of its own. That is to *be* interesting—all round; that is to be genuine and whole. The work is a classic because the thing, such as it is, is ideally *done*, and because it shows that in such doing eternal beauty may dwell.[23]

Such perceptive criticism would have delighted Flaubert, for James there puts his finger on the realization of one of Flaubert's dearest aims—the fusion of form and content. That aim is given its most striking expression in a letter of Flaubert's to Louise Colet written while he was deep in the creation of *Madame Bovary*—

What seems to me beautiful, what I should like to write, is a book about nothing, a book dependent on nothing external, which would be held together by the strength of its style ... ; a book which would have almost no subject, or at least in which the subject would be almost invisible, if such a thing is possible. The finest works are those that contain the least matter; the closer expression comes to coinciding and merging with it, the finer the result. I believe that the future of Art lies in this direction. ...

It is for this reason that there are no noble subjects or ignoble subjects; from the standpoint of pure Art one might almost establish the axiom that there is no such thing as subject, style in itself being an absolute manner of seeing things.[24]

James's comment on the form of *Bovary* also illuminates his own achievement in the works of his Major Phase, and especially in *The Ambassadors*.

In the preface to the New York edition of that novel James spoke of it as "frankly, quite the best, 'all round,' of my productions." His reason for so judging it is evidently that it most satisfactorily fused form and content: the manner is superlatively suited and wedded to and indeed fused with its matter. He must have seen that it was as true of *The Ambassadors* as of *Madame Bovary* that the form "is in *itself* as interesting, as active, as much of the essence of the subject as the idea."

The idea of *The Ambassadors* James got, of course, from the advice of William Dean Howells to young Jonathan Sturges in Paris: Live all you can! It's a mistake not to, etc. From this germ he developed the whole situation of Strether on his embassy in Paris. The advice to Live! Strether gives to the young Bilham. It is important to notice, however, that the novel offers a neat definition of Strether's advice:

Bilham remembers it incorrectly as "*See* all you can, [etc.]" Bilham's "mistake" not only goes uncorrected, but is supported by the whole weight of the novel, which develops that innocently made equation to its fullest extent. To live is to see. Strether's task in the novel is to see what really is the situation he has been sent to Paris to look at— the association of Chad and Marie de Vionnet. To put it quite simply, seeing that situation is Strether's life: he had "missed too much. . . . Would there yet perhaps be time for reparation? . . . The answer to which is that he now at all events *sees*; so that the business of my tale and the march of my action, not to say the precious moral of everything, is just my demonstration of this process of vision."[25]

To turn from the theme of the novel, which is rather an important one in James's fiction, to the question of his demonstration of this process of vision is to confront the interesting technical aspect of *The Ambassadors*. The most obvious feature of the narrative technique in this novel is its consistent use of Strether's point of view. Strether is the single authority: virtually the whole story depends on Strether's angle of vision. In a very real sense it is, so far as technique at least is concerned, Strether's novel. The story of Chad and Marie de Vionnet has an interest of its own, to be sure, but the particular interest of the novel is ultimately in Strether's way of viewing it. Although the novel relies on Strether as its single focusing agent and authority, it does permit the reader a kind of bi-focal view: he "hears" the conversation Strether hears and sees the facts which Strether sees, yet he cannot accept Strether's interpretations—his way of looking at things (as we say). So the reader finds himself watching Strether more and more, to see what he will make of things; and in all those matters for which Strether is the sole authority the reader becomes increasingly suspicious. In Strether's role as observer, it is his observation which matters most. The reader soon enough (say in the first quarter of the novel) realizes that Strether is another of those unreliable authorities who derive ultimately from the narrator of "The Solution." Quite clearly, then, the story is the story of Strether; it is concerned with the clearing of his vision, the growth of his understanding, the maturing of his attitude. In a word, it is the story of his psychological development. That development is presented dramatically; it is acted out, not *told*, in Strether's response to and participation in the central situation involving Chad and Marie. Strether's "telling"—his technical function in the novel as focusing agent and narrative authority— is in fact the *expression* of his perplexity over the situation he is observing, of his gradually clearing view of it all. And the very problems which so perplex him are in their turn acted out by Chad and Marie and the Pococks, et al.: what they do—or rather the significance of what they do—is precisely the content of his perplexity. The action of the novel—viewed in the traditional way—is the externalization, the dramatic expression of the problems bothering Strether's psyche, for it is *his* vision that colors the scene and which finally reflects upon and brilliantly illuminates him. In this James has followed Flaubert's exhortation (which he undoubtedly heard expressed many times), *Soyons exposants et non discutants.* *The Ambassadors* is a novel of psychological realism in the dramatic mode.

It is further that kind of supreme artistic achievement in which the form is superlatively appropriate to its content: technique and substance, manner and matter are fused—not just admirably suited to each other, but fused. We are constantly sensible of the importance of Strether's seeing things properly; our involvement in that important concern covers both technique and theme. The form of *The Ambassadors* is quite "as much of the essence of the subject as the idea."

Specific items in the technical form of the novel—which also merge with its substance and texture—are noteworthy as examples of James's ability to control his subject and his reader's response. That control is of course particularly important in a novel of this sort, which seems to depend on an untrustworthy or at least dubious authority: the danger in this is, as I said, that the dramatic irony will go undetected—the whole point will then be missed. Two items of special interest will serve to exemplify the control I mention. They are a pair of extended metaphors, innocent enough and merely "apt" at first glance, which express the fact that Lambert Strether does not (*will* not) see things as they really are. To make them the more easily recognizable, they may be given their common expression: one is the cliché simile "pretty as a picture" and the other the metaphor "all the world's a stage."

They are both introduced early in the novel, at the outset of Book Second, and in near juxtaposition. Strether's relation with Maria Gostrey has just begun to blossom, and the two of them have dined together preparatory to going to the theater:

Miss Gostrey had dined with him at his hotel, face to face over a small table on which the lighted candles had rose-coloured shades; and the rose-coloured shades and the small table and the soft fragrance of the lady—had anything to his mere sense ever been so soft?—were so many touches in he scarce knew what high picture.(N.Y. ed., XXI, 50).

It is singularly appropriate that with this first announcement of the "picture" metaphor there should be the accompaniment of rose-colored light. One of the principal problems with the vision of this unreliable but good-willed innocent is precisely that it is rose-colored: he tends to see life in romantic Paris through rose-colored glasses. But that is not all. When he and Maria then go to the theater Strether is dazzled by the spectacle—the spectacle, that is, of the audience quite as much as that of the stage: indeed, Strether is unable to distinguish between the two!

It was an evening, it was a world of types, and this was a connexion above all in which the figures and faces in the stalls were interchangeable with those on the stage.
He felt as if the play itself had penetrated him with the naked elbow of his neighbour, a great stripped handsome red-haired lady who conversed with a gentleman on her other side in stray dissyllables which had for his ear, in the oddest way in the world, so much sound that he wondered they hadn't more sense; and he recognized by the same law, beyond the footlights, what he was pleased to take for the very flush of English life. He had distracted drops in which he couldn't have said if it were actors or auditors who were most true, and the upshot of which, each time, was the consciousness of new contacts.(XXI,53).

The paragraph concludes with reference to the play they are witnessing in such a way as to lend further emphasis to the point at issue. There is a bad woman in a yellow frock who is making a pleasant, weak, good-looking young man in perpetual evening dress do dreadful things. Strether finds himself anxious about the young man, and his thoughts immediately turn to Chad—"Would Chad also be in perpetual evening dress? He somehow rather hoped it."(XXI,54).

The metaphors persist throughout the novel and accumulate in their subtle but inescapable expressiveness. And what they express is the distressing fact that Strether will not see life for what it really is, will see it—prompted with all the good will in the world—as a picture or as a play upon a stage. He will, to be sure, see things always light on that original dinner with Maria Gostrey.

As the novel proceeds, of course, Strether's vision adjusts itself little by little; and before the novel's end it receives a rude shock that leads to the correction of that vision. Strether's scene of recognition occurs in the well known episode in Book Eleventh is which it is made unmistakably clear to him that Chad and Marie de Vionnet have indeed been "intimate," have been lovers in the profoundest sense. What makes that scene particularly interesting and impressive for the reader is the effective use made in its development of the two metaphors in question. (Incidentally, a third metaphor which has recurred throughout the novel makes its significant appearance in this scene of recognition as well: Strether has had, during much of the action of the novel, the jolly sense that he and Chad and Marie have been all in the same boat—as this third metaphor has frequently expressed it.) Strether has come to feel that his career in Europe is now virtually over: a second wave of ambassadors from Woollett has displaced him. He gives himself over to the pleasure of a visit to one of the banlieux of Paris; the rural setting delights him for, of course, it is as pretty as a picture—indeed, as a particular picture (a Lambinet) he remembers seeing back home in Boston: "that French ruralism, with its cool special green, into which he had looked only through the little oblong window of the picture." He loves this scene —"it was France, it was Lambinet"—and he continues *in the picture* all afternoon:

He really continued in the picture—that being for himself his situation—all the rest of this rambling day . . . and had meanwhile not overstepped the oblong gilt frame. . . . He had walked many miles and didn't know he was tired; but he still knew he was amused, and even that, though he had been alone all day, he had never yet so struck himself as engaged with others and in midstream of his drama. . . .

For this had been all day at bottom the spell of the picture—that it was essentially more than anything else a scene and a stage, that the very air of the play was in the rustle of the willows and the tone of the sky.(XXII, 251-253).

The combined force of the coinciding metaphors here is to set up Strether (and the reader) for the blow which is immediately to fall. For into that lovely picture, onto that charming stage, come Chad and Marie de Vionnet—their very presence attesting to the intimacy of the relation and drawing the inescapable "smudge of mortality" across the canvas of life as Strether has persisted in viewing it. The shock of recognition is accompanied by the emphatic expression of the sense that Strether is by no means *in the same boat* as his youthful vicars: "What he saw was exactly the right thing—a boat advancing round the bend and containing a man who held the paddles and a lady, at the stern, with a pink parasol." Of course the pair in the boat are Chad and Marie, and of course Strether does not "see" at once the significance of the situation; but eventually he must. He comes to see it in awful clarity. His first reaction is to revert momentarily to the vision of Woollett—that Chad and Marie are of course as evil as the people back home had imagined, that the two are involved in the "typical tale of Paris." But his balance returns. He finally sees the truth: that Marie is the lady he had always supposed—but that she is human; and that Chad is improved almost as much as he had supposed—though not quite enough to prevent him from forsaking Marie. He has been through his ordeal of consciousness[26] and has seen all that he could—which in the novel's terms is to say that he has lived indeed.

The Ambassadors is not quite the novel without a subject, which Flaubert claimed he wanted to write, for its subject is patently present and one which James cherished—the importance of clear consciousness, spontaneous and free from the restraints of prejudice, convention, bias, the letter of the law, from all that an externally imposed Duty dehumanizingly demands. But its subject is so perfectly inseparable from its manner—from such features as the extended metaphors discussed above and the accompanying motifs and symbology—that the one is inconceivable without the other: the medium is the message (to borrow Mr. Marshall McLuhan's timely dictum). It is easy to understand why James would have regarded this novel as his best.

I have chosen to dwell thus, briefly, on *The Ambassadors* because it best represents the culmination of James's development into the Major Phase from his principal preoccupations of the last two decades of the nineteenth century. It is quite apparent that the influences which encouraged his main interests in the art of fiction —particularly, here, the influences to which he submitted during his Naturalist experiment—continued to contribute even to his last and greatest work. In that last work James has to a considerable extent fulfilled the promise of development which Naturalism held, even in the eyes of its own adherents. The direction which Naturalism was to take was indicated by certain critical observations of Edmond de Goncourt and Maupassant (in addition to those of Flaubert like that quoted above from his letter to Louise Colet). It was to leave its current preoccupation with the *menu peuple* and turn to those of finer sensibilities and more complex psyches; its realism was to become psychological realism; its concern to get free of the appearance of the manipulating author was to lead to the poetic creations of the modern art novel. As early as 1879, Edmond de Goncourt was expressing dissatisfaction with the current train of Naturalist writing and envisaging the development that must occur: his preface to *Les Frères Zemganno* forecasts that "the cruel analysis which my friend M. Zola, and perhaps I myself, brought to the painting of the lowest of society will be taken up by a writer of talent and employed in the reproduction of men and women of the world in their settings of education and distinction."

We began with the mob, because men and women of the people, closer to nature and the savage state, are simple and uncomplicated creatures, while Parisians of society, the excessively civilised, whose distinct originality is made up of nuances, half-tones, all those elusive nothings which are the equivalent of the dainty and neutral nothings which characterize the distinguished woman's dress require years for one to penetrate, to understand, so that one really *grasps* them,—and the novelist of the greatest genius, you can be sure, will never figure out these types of the salon, with the friendly chit-chat that serves him for exposition in this world.

This project of the novel which was to take place in the great world, the most quintessential world whose delicate and fleeting elements we gathered slowly and minutely, ... the success of realism lies there and there alone, and no longer in the literary rabble, exhausted at the present moment by its predecessors.[27]

What the Goncourts aimed at was "le roman réaliste de l'élégance." And while Maupassant could not accept the similar advice of Taine—that he extend the range of his observation to include the cultivated upper class, the higher bourgeoisie of culture and fine sensibilities—his own developing interest nevertheless led him in essentially the same direction as that indicated by the Goncourt preface: it led him to a realism interested in perception, sensibility, consciousness, in a word to the psychological. His preface to *Pierre et Jean,* "Le Roman," and indeed the novel itself attest (along with such pieces as "Le Horla") to Maupassant's growing preoccupation with the psychologically real. The career of another disciple of Taine, Paul Bourget, also manifests the development of the Naturalist tendency into the realm of the psychological. The relation of this view is expressed in one of Ezra Pound's provocative essays.

Indeed, but for these almost autobiographical details pointing to his growth out of Balzac, all James would seem but a corollary to one passage in a Goncourt preface ... the preface to *Les Frères Zemganno* in 1879. . . .

If ever one man's career was foreshadowed in a few sentences of another, Henry James' is to be found in this paragraph.[28]

Pound was right. But there is more to say: James's literary career, from 1864 to his death in 1916, embraced and illustrated the various fashions of prose fiction for that half-century—and beyond. It began by reflecting certain features of Hawthornesque romance; rather soon after that it gave evidence of the rising current of "realism," and then (as this study has maintained) of the impact of Naturalist theory and practice. In its last phase James's career leaps beyond much of the work of his contemporaries to indicate the direction is which the modern novel of this century was to develop—following the lead then just discernible in Flaubert's *Madame Bovary.* The work of the Major Phase, and especially *The Ambassadors,* provides the bridge to the stream-of-consciousness and internal monologue and other techniques which characterize the fiction of Virginia Woolf, Marcel Proust, James Joyce, and of his compatriot William Faulkner. To read the fiction of James is to follow a short course in the history of the novel for almost a century. Throughout his development James's constant concern was to discover the most effective means of creating on the printed page a convincing illusion of the reality of life. It is perhaps in terms of that aim that we must understand his claim that Balzac was his "greatest master." It remains true, nevertheless, that James learned much of profit from the master's younger assistants, the grandsons of Balzac.

NOTES—INTRODUCTION

[1]Henry James, "Ivan Turgenieff," *Partial Portraits* (London and New York: Macmillan, 1888), p. 300: "In the young French school he [Turgenev] was much interested; I mean, in the new votaries of realism, the grandsons of Balzac." The essay was first published in the *Atlantic Monthly*, LIII (January 1884), 42-55.

NOTES—CHAPTER I

[1]Henry James, "A Small Boy and Others," *Henry James: Autobiography*, ed. F. W. Dupee (New York, 1956), p. 33.

[2]Quoted in Leon Edel, *Henry James: The Untried Years* (New York, 1953), p. 118.

[3]See F. O. Matthiessen, *The James Family* (New York, 1947), p. 71.

[4]Quoted in Edel, *Untried Years*, p. 308.

[5]"Notes of a Son and Brother," *Autobiography*, p. 544.

[6]Sainte-Beuve's terms—"D'affranchir l'humanité des illusions, des vagues disputes, des solutions vaines, des idoles et des puissances trompeuses," quoted in Pierre Martino, *Le Naturalisme français*, 4 ème éd. (Paris, 1945), p. 5.

[7]See Guy Robert, "Trois textes inédits d'Emile Zola," *Revue des Sciences humaines*, no. 51 (1948), pp. 181-207; and F. W. J. Hemmings, *Emile Zola* (Oxford, 1951). p. 20.

[8]"Introduction," *Histoire de la littérature anglaise*, 4ème éd. (Paris, 1877), I, ix-x; my translation.

[9]*Ibid.*, I, xxxii; my translation.

[10]"Taine's Italy," *Nation*, VI (7 May 1868), 374.

[11]*The Achievement of T. S. Eliot* (New York, 1958), p. 9.

[12]*Hawthorne* (New York, 1880), p. 4.

[13]See Sir William Osler, *An Alabama Student* (New York, 1908), pp. 57-58.

[14]See expecially the essay of 1915, "Mr. and Mrs. Fields," republished in *The American Essays of Henry James*, ed. Edel (New York), pp. 269-270.

[15]*Oliver Wendell Holmes*, American Writers Series, p. 256.

[16]*Untried Years*, p. 269.

181

[17] *The Letters of Henry James,* ed. Percy Lubbock, 2 vols. (New York, 1920), II, 221; reprinted in *American Essays,* p. 157.

[18] *American Essays,* p. 146; originally in *Harper's Weekly* for June 19, 1886.

[19] *Le Roman naturaliste* (Paris, 1893), p. 222; my translation.

[20] See William J. Hyde, "George Eliot and the Climate of Realism," *PMLA,* LXXII (March, 1957), 147-164, and especially 148-151.

[21] "Honore de Balzac," *The Two Young Brides,* trans. Lady Mary Loyd (New York), p. v.

[22] *The Future of the Novel,* ed. Edel (New York, 1956), pp. 102, 104.

[23] "Avant-Propos," *Oeuvres Complètes* (Paris, 1946), I, i-ii; my translation.

[24] *Ibid.,* I, i.

[25] See the excellent explication of Balzac's technique in *Le Père Goriot* given by Erich Auerbach, *Mimesis,* trans. Willard Trask (Doubleday Anchor Books), pp. 413ff.

[26] Letter to Louise Colet, January 16, 1852, *The Selected Letters of Gustave Flaubert,* ed. Francis Steegmuller (Vintage Books, 1957), p. 126.

[27] *"Germinie Lacerteux,* Preface à la première édition," *Préfaces et manifestes littéraires* (Paris, 1888), pp. 19-20; my translation.

[28] Matthew Josephson also notes the similarity between Emma's case and Germinie's: "The whole thesis of *Bovary* was here, dominant, as it was forever afterward in the realistic masterpieces: a given personality, conceived as a unit in a mass, pitted against its environment, the milieu into which it was born." See his *Zola and His Time* (New York, 1928), p. 92.

[29] *"Germinie Lacerteux,"* Mes Haines, Oeuvres, XXX, 56-57; my translation.

[30] Hemmings, *Zola,* pp. 119-120. See Martino's semantic discussion "Le Mot naturalisme," *Naturalisme français,* pp. 1-6.

[31] Hemmings observes that "One of the few authorities cited by Taine in his *Introduction à l'histoire de la littérature anglaise* ... was Prosper Lucas; and it may have been Taine's footnote which led Zola to consult Lucas' *Traité de l'hérédité naturelle,* unless Michelet's mention of the same work in *L'Amour* had already encouraged him to do this." (*Zola,* p. 39.) Of Lucas' work Josephson says (in his *Zola,* p. 152): "it has adopted more or less the idea of Darwin that there were determinable laws of transmission, and that the whole animal

organism on an infinitely small scale was formed in the cells of the embryon. . . . Then Lucas, further, favored especially the theory of atavism . . . and Zola accepted it from him. Also the theory that characteristics of mother and father were 'crossed,' the son resembling the mother, and vice versa."

[32] At the outset of the essay Zola asserts, "Je n'aurai à faire ici qu'un travail d'adaptation, car la méthode expérimentale a été établie avec une force et une clarté merveilleuse par Claude Bernard, dans son *Introduction à l'étude de la médecine expérimentale.*" (*Le Roman expérimental, Oeuvres,* XXXV, 11.)

[33] *Roman exp.,* XXXV, 24-26; my translation.

[34] *Roman exp.,* XXXV, 36; my translation.

[35] "De la moralité dans la littérature," *Oeuvres,* XXVI, 316; my translation.

[36] "De la moralité," XXVI, 295; my translation.

[37] See *Roman exp.,* XXXV, 166: "Le romancier [naturaliste] invente bien encore; il invente un plan, un drame; seulement c'est un bout de drame, la première histoire venue, et que la vie quotidienne lui fournit toujours. Puis, dans l'économie de l'oeuvre, cela n'a plus qu'une importance très mince. Les faits ne sont là que comme les développements logiques des personnages. La grande affair est de mettre debout des créatures vivantes, jouant devant les lecteurs la comédie humaine avec le plus de nature possible."

[38] Quoted from the Manuscript Plans for *La Fortune des Rougon* in the Bibliothèque Nationale in Paris, in Josephson, *Zola,* pp. 141-142.

[39] *Zola,* trans, Mary B. and Frederick C. Green (New York, 1933), p. 106.

[40] *Naturalisme français,* p. 158.

[41] See my essay, "James's Debt to Alphonse Daudet: The Appeal of Poetic Naturalism," in the forthcoming volume, *The Constant Recognition: Studies in Anglo-French Literary Relations,* ed. Frederick J. Hoffman.

[42] See Daniel Lerner, "The Influence of Turgenev on Henry James," *Slavonic Yearbook,* XX (1941), 28-54.

[43] See Andre Maurois, *Tourgéniev* (Paris, 1931), p. 207.

[44] "Le Roman" [1887 preface], *Pierre et Jean, Oeuvres Complètes* (Paris, 1909), p. ix.

[45] "Le Roman," p. xv; my translation.

NOTES—CHAPTER II

[1]"Miss Prescott's 'Azarian,' " *Notes and Reviews*, ed. Pierre de Chaignon la Rose (Cambridge, Mass., 1921), p. 26; originally published in the *North American Review*, C (January, 1865), 268-277.

[2]"The Limitations of Dickens," *Views and Reviews*, ed. LeRoy Phillips (Boston, 1908), p. 154; originally published in the *Nation*, I (21 December, 1865), 786-787.

[3]*French Poets and Novelists*, ed. Edel (New York, 1964), p. 221.

[4]"Turgénieff," *French Poets and Novelists*, p. 231.

[5]*French Poets and Novelists*, p. 196.

[6]*French Poets and Novelists*, p. 201.

[7]*Letters*, ed. Lubbock, I, 49; and Virginia Harlow, *Thomas Sergeant Perry: A Biography* (Durham, N.C., 1950), p. 292.

[8]*Letters*, ed. Lubbock, I, 48-49, 51.

[9]*Letters*, ed. Lubbock, I, 51.

[10]*Hawthorne*, pp. 110, 132, 26.

[11]"Alphonse Daudet," *Partial Portrait* (London and New York, 1888), p. 217.

[12]"Parisian Festivity," *New York Tribune*, 13 May 1876, 1-2.

[13]*Portraits of Places* (Boston, 1885), p. 87.

[14]"Il n'y a que Zola!" From a letter of November 2, 1879, quoted in Harlow, p. 304.

[15]*The Future of the Novel*, ed. Edel, p. 96.

[16]See above, p. 33.

[17]Harlow, *Perry*, p. 309.

[18]See my forthcoming essay, "Henry James's Debt to Alphonse Daudet."

[19]"Three French Books," *Galaxy*, XX (August 1875), 278.

[20]"Alphonse Daudet," *Les Romanciers Naturalistes* (Paris, 1910), p. 259.

[21]"Alphonse Daudet," *Literary Reviews and Essays*, ed. Mordell (New York, 1957), p. 184.

[22]"Daudet," *Partial Portraits*, p. 197.

[23]*Letters*, ed. Lubbock, I, 104-105.

NOTES—CHAPTER III

[1]*The Notebooks of Henry James*, ed. Matthiessen and Murdoch (New York, 1955), p. 47.

[2]*Letters,* ed. Lubbock, I, 31.

[3]*Hawthorne,* pp. 42-43.

[4]*Letters,* ed. Lubbock, I, 72-73.

[5]Gosse, *Questions at Issue* (London, 1893), p. 139; and Frierson, *L'Influence du naturalisme français sur les romanciers anglais de 1885 à 1900* (Paris, 1925), pp. 194-195.

[6]"Indeed you can hardly see anything else in 'The Romance of Certain Old Clothes,'" wrote F. O. Matthiessen, *American Renaissance* (New York, 1941), p. 293.

[7]A letter of March, 1878, to his mother indicates that James was busy at *The Portrait* by the middle of 1877: he refers to "The story ... of which I wrote you last summer that it would be to the *American* 'as wine unto water.'" See the *Selected Letters of Henry James,* ed. Edel (New York, 1955), pp. 52-53.

[8]See his *Notebooks,* p. 35.

[9]*Notebooks,* pp. 23-24.

[10]*Notebooks,* p. 40.

[11]*Notebooks,* pp. 44, 45.

[12]*Letters,* ed. Lubbock, I, 102.

[13]"The Art of Fiction," *The Future of the Novel,* ed. Edel (New York, 1956), p. 9.

[14]"Art of Fiction," p. 25.

[15]"Art of Fiction," p. 14.

[16]In "The Author of 'Beltraffio'" James touches on exactly this question when he makes the writer, Mark Ambient, complain "I've always arranged things too much . . . smoothed them down and rounded them off and tucked them in—done everything to them that life doesn't do."

[17]"Art of Fiction," p. 15.

[18]Harlow, *Perry,* p. 316.

[19]Quoted in *Notebooks,* p. 47.

[20]*The Bostonians,* Modern Library Edition, p. 137.

[21]*Notebooks,* p. 47.

[22]In considering a possible title for the novel, he writes (*Notebooks,* p. 67): "everything that is just descriptive won't do— *The Newness— The Reformers—The Precursors—The Revealer*—etc.—all very bad, and with the additional fault that people will say they are taken from Daudet's *Évangéliste.*"

[23]See Matthiessen and Murdock, eds. *Notebooks,* p. 48; Marius Bewley, *The Complex Fate* (London, 1952), pp. 14-28; Oscar Cargill,

The Novels of Henry James (New York, 1961), pp. 124-126, 128-129.

[24]See *The Blithedale Romance,* chap. xiv, *The Complete Novels and Selected Tales of Nathaniel Hawthorne,* Modern Library, p. 511.

[25]*Bostonians,* p. 339; cf. pp. 275, 378.

[26]*L'Evangéliste* (Paris, 1883), p. 52.

[27]*Partial Portraits,* pp. 198-199.

[28]*L'Evangéliste,* p. 153.

[29]*L'Evangéliste,* p. 159.

[30]*Bostonians,* pp. 4-5.

[31]*Bostonians,* pp. 10-11.

[32]*Bostonians,* p. 19.

[33]*Bostonians,* p. 339.

[34]*Bostonians,* p. 16.

[35]*Bostonians,* p. 16.

[36]*Bostonians,* p. 178.

[37]*Bostonians,* p. 59.

[38]*Bostonians,* pp. 58-59.

[39]*Bostonians,* p. 113.

[40]*Bostonians,* p. 116.

[41]*Bostonians,* p. 70.

[42]*Bostonians,* p. 80.

[43]*Bostonians,* pp. 26-27.

[44]*Bostonians,* p. 29.

[45]*Bostonians,* pp. 334-335.

[46]*Bostonians,* pp. 368-369.

[47]*Bostonians,* p. 327; my italics.

[48]*Bostonians,* pp. 43-44.

[49]William C. Frierson, *The English Novel in Transition, 1886-1940* (Norman, Oklahoma, 1942), p. 111.

[50]*Notebooks,* p. 49.

[51]"Lady Barberina," *The Complete Tales,* ed. Edel (Philadelphia and New York, 1963), V, 249.

[52]"Lady Barberina," p. 224.

[53]"Lady Barberina," p. 262.

[54]"Lady Barberina," p. 296; my italics.

[55]*Bostonians,* p. 33

[56]*Bostonians,* p. 78; cf. p. 111.

[57]*Bostonians,* p. 78.

[58]*Bostonians,* p. 110.

[59] *Bostonians,* p. 117.

[60] *Bostonians,* p. 253.

[61] *Bostonians,* p. 301.

[62] *Bostonians,* pp. 84-85.

[63] *Bostonians,* p. 74.

[64] *Bostonians,* pp. 158-159.

[65] *Bostonians,* pp. 396-397.

[66] *Bostonians,* pp. 27, 35.

[67] *Bostonians,* p. 222.

[68] A letter from James to his brother William on February 14, 1885, shortly after the first installment of *The Bostonians* had appeared in the *Century Magazine,* is of peculiar interest: "I am quite appalled by your note of the 2nd, in which you assault me on the subject of my having painted a 'portrait from life' of Miss [Eliza] Peabody! I was in some measure prepared for it by Lowell's (as I found the other day) taking for granted that she had been my model, and an allusion to the same effect in a note from Aunt Kate.... I absolutely had no shadow of such an intention."

His subsequent defense against the accusation (including mention of Miss Peabody's spectacles, which "were always in the wrong place"!) is wonderfully revealing: "If I have made my old woman *live* it is my misfortune, and the thing is doubtless a rendering, a vivid rendering, of my idea. If it is at the same time a rendering of Miss P. I am absolutely irresponsible—and extremely sorry for the accident." He admits he thinks Miss Birdseye "the best figure in the book," and quite reasonably allows, at last, that "You may think that I protest too much." See *Letters,* ed. Lubbock, I, 115-117.

[69] The horror of the intrepid newspapers and their "reporters" had long been a sore point with James. One of his avowed aims in *The Bostonians* was to scourge that realm of society. See his *Notebooks,* p. 47: "There must, indispensably, be a newspaper man—the man whose ideal is the energetic reporter. I should like to *bafouer* the vulgarity and hideousness of this—the impudent invasion of privacy —the extinction of all conception of privacy, etc." Much of that sentiment is echoed in his sympathetic letters to Edmund Gosse, in the autumn of 1886, on the occasion of an attack on him in the *Pall Mall Gazette.* The letter of October 26 reads: "the public *d'élite* feels the greatest sympathy for you as having been made to an almost unprecedented degree the subject of a peculiarly atrocious & vulgar

form of modern torture—the assault of the newspaper—which all civilized & decent people are equally interested in resisting the blackguardism of." (In the 1st volume, 1882-1887, of the James-Gosse correspondence in the Bretherton Library of the University of Leeds. I am grateful to the Keeper of the Bretherton Collection for his permission to quote this correspondence.)

Another horrible example of the newspaper's invasion of privacy came to James through an experience which touched his friend Mrs. Katherine de Kay Bronson. He refers to the episode in his *Notebooks* (November 17th, 1887), pp. 82ff., as "the queer incident of Miss Mc C's writing to the New York *World* that inconceivable letter about the Venetian society whose hospitality she had been enjoying—and the strange *typicality* of the whole thing." James's letters to Mrs. Bronson on the affair sound a familiar note. On January 21, 1887, he wrote: "there is, I believe, no limit to what we are capable of in that particular line—I mean that of having no sense, where our ... newspapers are concerned, of certain discretions & perversions. I have known dreadful things of this kind before...." In a letter of January 26, 1887, he comes down on the guilty Miss Mc C.: "She is Americanissima—in the sense of being launched as a young person before the Lord, & no wonder the poor dear old Venetian mind can't understand such incongruities. I should like to write a story about the business, as a pendant to *Daisy Miller,* but I won't, to disperse [?] the complication." (These letters of James's to Mrs. Bronson and to her daughter Edith, Contessa Rucellai, are in the archives of the Palazzo Rucellai in Florence. I am grateful to Marchesa Nannina Fossi-Rucellai, Count Bernardo Rucellai, and Count Gian-Giulio Rucellai for permission to quote from them.)

Of course James did write a story "about the business" in *The Reverberator* (1888), a delightful companion piece to *The Bostonians,* which also manages to "*bafouer* the vulgarity and hideousness of this."

[70]*Bostonians,* p. 343.

[71]*Bostonians,* p. 244.

[72]*Bostonians,* p. 328.

[73]For a fuller treatment of this subject, see my essay "Henry James's Antinomies," *University of Toronto Quarterly,* XXXI (January, 1962), 125-135.

[74]*Bostonians,* p. 159.

[75]*Bostonians,* p. 268.

NOTES—CHAPTER IV

[1]See Nellie Van de Grift Sanchez, *The Life of Mrs. Robert Louis Stevenson* (New York, 1921), p. 121: "One of the interesting people she met while in England was Prince Kropotkin, the noted Russian revolutionist ... at the urgent request of Henry James she consented to meet him." Leon Edel's opinion is, however, that James likely knew Kroptkin only "after he had written *The Princess*": see *Henry James, The Middle Years* (London, 1963), p. 123.

[2]"The Princess Casamassima," *The Liberal Imagination* (New York, 1951), p. 72.

[3]Preface to *Roderick Hudson, The Art of the Novel*, ed. Blackmur (New York, 1953), p. 19.

[4]*The Princess Casamassima, The Novels and Tales* (New York Edition, c 1908, 1936), V, 46-47.

[5]Harlow, *Perry*, p. 319.

[6]*Princess*, V, 81-82.

[7]*Princess*, V, 343.

[8]*Princess*, V, 344.

[9]*Princess*, VI, 175-176.

[10]It is tempting to illustrate the contrast and indicate the fulness of James's depiction of the English scene by quoting at some length from the description of Medley. The bulk of Book Third is devoted to a description of Medley, the house and its luxurious interior and its generous grounds. The place and the gracious way of life are well developed to appeal to that side of Hyacinth which has no sympathy with a revolution aimed at the destruction of such beauty.

[11]*Princess*, V, 79-80

[12]*Princess*, V, 57ff.

[13]*Princess*, V, 78.

[14]Letter of October 28, 1885, in Janet Adam Smith, *Henry James and Robert Louis Stevenson: A Record of Friendship and Criticism* (London, 1948), p. 106.

[15]*Princess*, V, 61.

[16]*Princess*, V, 61-62.

[17]This is reflected in Hyacinth's later recognition: "She was bold and generous and incalculable, and if she was coarse she was neither false nor cruel. She laughed with the laugh of the people and if you hit her hard enough would cry with their tears." *Princess*, V, 163.

[18]*Princess*, V, 207.

[19] *Princess,* V, 285.
[20] *Liberal Imagination,* p. 60.
[21] *Notebooks,* p. 69.
[22] *Princess,* V, 50.
[23] *Princess,* V, 293-294.
[24] *Princess,* V, 137-139.
[25] Preface to *The Princess Casamassima, Art of the Novel,* p. 61.
[26] *Princess,* V, 174-175, 177.
[27] *Princess,* VI, 31.
[28] *Princess,* VI, 65-66.
[29] *Princess,* VI, 72-73.
[30] *Princess,* VI, 144.
[31] *Princess,* VI, 243, 244.
[32] *Princess,* VI, 264-265.
[33] *Princess,* V, 131.
[34] *Princess,* VI, 328-329.
[35] *Princess,* VI, 333.
[36] *Princess,* V, 157.
[37] *Princess,* V, 223.
[38] *Princess,* VI, 6.
[39] *Princess,* V, 86.
[40] *Princess,* V, 208.
[41] *Art of the Novel,* p. 62.
[42] *Liberal Imagination,* p. 71.
[43] *Liberal Imagination,* p. 74.

NOTES—CHAPTER V

[1] Harlow, *Perry,* p. 316
[2] *Letters,* ed. Lubbock, I, 135.
[3] *Notebooks,* pp. 63-64.
[4] *Partial Portraits,* p. 266.
[5] *Partial Portraits,* p. 252.
[6] *Notebooks,* p. 92.
[7] *Partial Portraits,* p. 263.
[8] *Partial Portraits,* p. 254.
[9] *Partial Portratis,* p. 249.
[10] *The Art of the Novel,* p. 79.

[11] *Letters,* ed. Lubbock, I, 138.

[12] *Letters,* ed. Lubbock, I, 163.

[13] *The Novels of Henry James* (New York, 1961), pp. 183-186.

[14] *Notebooks,* pp. 63-64.

[15] Quoted in Mrs. Humphrey Ward, *A Writer's Recollections,* 2 vols. (New York and London, 1918), II, p. 19.

[16] See Mrs. Ward's *Recollections,* II, 15-16: "*Miss Bretherton* was suggested to me by the brilliant success in 1833 of Mary Anderson, and by the controversy with regard to her acting—as distinct from her delightful beauty and her attractive personality—which arose between the fastidious few and the enchanted many . . . the situation in the novel was developed out of the current dramatic debate."

[17] "A New England Winter," *Novels and Stories of Henry James,* ed. Percy Lubbock, 35 vols. (London, 1921-23), XXV, pp. 84, 86.

[18] *Notebooks,* p. 31. James quotes Pratt: "I know such a sunny corner, under the south wall of old Toledo. There's a wild fig tree growing there; I have lain on the grass, with my guitar." In the novel Nash tells Nick: "Last year I heard of such a delightful little spot, a place where a wild fig-tree grows in the south wall, the outer side, of an old Spanish city. I was told it was a deliciously brown corner—the sun making it warm in winter. As soon as I could I went there. . . . I lay on the first green grass—I liked it." (N.Y. ed., VII, 177).

[19] See Edel, "Henry James: the Dramatic Years," *The Complete Plays of Henry James* (Philadelphia and New York, 1949), p. 40.

[20] See "After the Play," *The Scenic Art,* ed. Allan Wade (New Brunswick, N.J., 1948), pp. 232, 239: "[The theatre crowd] is huge and good-natured and common. It likes big, unmistakable, knockdown effects. . . . It's in a tremendous hurry, squeezed together, with a sort of generalized gape, and the last thing it expects of you is that you will spin things fine. . . . the sincere spirits of the stage . . . are conscious of all the other things—formidable things—that rise against them. . . . the grossness and brutality of London, with its scramble, its pressure, its bustle of engagements, of preoccupations, its long distances, its late hours, its nightly dinners, its innumerable demands on the attention, its general congregation of influences fatal to the isolation, to the punctuality, to the security, of the dear old play house spell."

And compare Nash's words in chapter IV of *The Tragic Muse* on the same subject: "It will be better known yet, won't it? When the essentially brutal nature of the modern audience is still more perceived, when it has been properly analysed: the *omnium gatherum* of the population of a big commercial city at the hour of the day when its taste is at its lowest, flocking out of hideous hotels and restaurants, gorged with food, stultified with buying and selling and with all the other sordid preoccupations of the age, squeezed together, in a sweltering mass, disappointed in their seats, timing the author, timing the actor, wishing to get their money back on the spot—all before eleven o'clock. Fancy putting the exquisite before such a tribunal as that! . . . What can you do with a character, with an idea, with a feeling, between dinner and the suburban trains?"(VII, 66-67).

[21]Introduction, *The Tragic Muse*, Torchbooks ed., p. viii.

[22]*The Tragic Muse, Novels and Tales* (New York edition), VII, 3.

[23]See *Notebooks* (February 2, 1889), p. 92: "Sherringham's visit to the Comedie Française with Miriam—my impression of Bartet, in her *loge*, the other day in Paris."

[24]*Tragic Muse*, VIII, 206; Mrs. Rooth's setting, not Miriam's.

[25]*Tragic Muse*, VIII, 75. Cf. Nick's earlier thoughts of Julia (VII, 263-264): "Mrs. Dallow . . . had suddenly become a still larger fact in his consciousness than his having turned actively political. She was indeed his being so. . . . She had made the business infinitely prettier, . . . converting it into a kind of heroic 'function,' the form of sport most dangerous."

[26]*Tragic Muse*, VII, 261: "his boyishness could still take a pleasure in an inconsiderate show of agility. . . . he could do these things because it was amusing and slightly dangerous, like playing football or ascending an Alp, pastimes for which nature had conferred on him an aptitude not so very different from a due volubility on platforms." Cf. VII, 263: "he appreciated the coincidence of the hit and the hurrah, the hurrah and the hit"; cf. VIII, 75, etc.

[27]See *The Selected Letters of Henry James*, ed. Edel (New York, 1955), p. 111: "[Mr. Edel writes] There is no doubt that he was impressed by the substantial royalties derived by playwrights from a successful box-office. Dependent as he still was then upon his literary earnings, he had also experienced some anxiety over the continued limited sale of his books and his increasing difficulties in placing his longer works in the magazines. It seemed to him that an immediate solution was to confine himself to the writing of short stories—*a la Maupassant*, he wrote in his notebooks—and to devote

the time he would have normally given his longer fictions to 'pot-boiling' for the theatre. His was a calculated siege of the theatre. He promised himself that he would persist even if at first he encountered defeat."

[28]It may be objected that this is an erroneous interpretation of James's situation; as who should say: "as a professional writer he always wrote for money." But to reason, as some have, in this manner is to share in the confusion of Mrs. Jane Highmore ("The Next Time"), who never spoke of the literary motive as if it were distinguishable from the pecuniary. James clearly felt that there was a distinction to be made between the two motives.

[29]Cf. *Notebooks*, pp. 181, 200; and Edel, *Selected Letters*, p. 112. James originally used the term to refer to his own failure in the theater, in a letter to his brother William of January 9, 1895, after the failure of "Guy Domville" (see *Letters*, ed. Lubbock, I, 229).

[30]I have given more detailed treatment to these ideas in three essays, "James's *The Tragic Muse: Ave Atque Vale*," *PMLA*, LXXIII (June 1958), 270-274, "Mr. James's Aesthetic Mr. Nash—Again," *Nineteenth-Century Fiction*, XIII (March 1959), 341-349, and "Henry James's Antinomies," *University of Toronto Quarterly*, XXXI (January 1962), 125-135. It will be readily seen that the attitude of Gabriel Nash bears some resemblance to that expressed in the works of Walter Pater, and especially in the conclusion to his *Renaissance* and in *Marius the Epicurean*. The similarity between James and Pater (noted by Stuart P. Sherman, F. O. Matthiessen, and Giorgio Melchiori) has been responsible, I suppose, for more recent attempts to identify Nash with Oscar Wilde, apostle of Pater. But a careful examination of "The Author of 'Beltraffio' " as well as of *The Tragic Muse* indicates that James is not aiming finally at the position of the aesthetes, at formulating a prescription for the 'art of life.' Even less is he attempting to satirize them in the person of Gabriel Nash. It is apparent that at the outset of the novel Nick Dormer is embarrassed about his association with Nash (and, indeed, his attraction to him), and therefore tries to avoid introducing him to his sister Biddy. The reason for this is obviously that Nick is full of his sense of "duty"— to the political career his family and friends have planned for him. It is equally obvious that the triumph of "art" in the novel is due to a great extent to the influence of Nash on Nick. No, James is concerned rather with the problem of how to live the artist's life in a world fundamentally inimical (as he felt) to such an existence. James's

position is close to that of Croce as expressed in his *Aesthetics,* and even closer to that adopted by the Bloomsbury Group under the influence of the ideas of G. E. Moore as expressed in *Principia Ethica.* (But cf. note 33, below.)

[31]"Society and Solitude," *The Complete Works,* ed. Edward Waldo Emerson (Boston and New York, 1883-1893), VII, 184.

[32]*Autobiography,* ed. Dupee, p. 268.

[33]Quoted in Frederick H. Young, *The Philosophy of Henry James, Sr.* (New York, 1951), p. 185.

NOTES—CHAPTER VI

[1]*Letters,* ed. Lubbock, I, 226.

[2]Letter of January 10, 1895, to Henrietta Reubell, *Selected Letters,* ed. Edel, pp. 124-125.

[3]*Notebooks,* p. 179.

[4]*North American Review,* CLXIX (October, 1899), 499.

[5]"Emile Zola," *Notes on Novelists* (London, 1914), p. 44.

[6]"The Lesson of Balzac," *The Future of the Novel,* p. 104.

[7]"Zola," *Notes on Novelists,* p. 28.

[8]"Lesson of Balzac," p. 114.

[9]"Lesson of Balzac," p. 108.

[10]"Lesson of Balzac," p. 114.

[11]*Notes on Novelists,* p. 256.

[12]"Lesson of Balzac," p. 114.

[13]*Art of the Novel,* pp. 230-231. The development of this idea clearly anticipates Mark Schorer's distinction between "content or experience" and "achieved content or art" in his brilliant essay "Technique as Discovery."

[14]*Notes on Novelists,* p. 258, A similar apportioning of emphasis is seen in Flaubert's letter of July 1862, to Mme Roger des Genettes: "Despite its occasional good bits this book [*Les Misérables*] is decidedly childish. Observation is a secondary quality in literature, but a contemporary of Balzac and Dickens has no right to depict society so falsely." See *The Selected Letters of Gustave Flaubert,* ed. Steegmuller (New York, 1957), p. 203.

[15]"The Present Literary Situation in France," p. 499.

[16]"Lesson of Balzac," p. 113.

[17]"Flaubert," *Notes on Novelists,* p. 63.

[18]"Literary Situation in France," p. 499.

[19]James's preface recalls his project for the novel as including the sketch of "a circle consisting of a number of small rounds disposed at equal distance about a central object. The central object was my situation, my subject in itself, to which the thing would owe its title, and the small rounds represented so many distinct lamps, as I liked to call them, the function of each of which would be to light with all due intensity one of its aspects." See *Art of the Novel*, p. 110.

[20]See above, Chap. V, pp. 146-148.

[21]*Notebooks*, pp. 188, 208.

[22]Elizabeth Livermore Forbes, "Dramatic Lustrum: A Study of the Effect of James's Theatrical Experience on His Later Novels," *New England Quarterly*, XI (March, 1938), 113; cf. Henry Popkin, "The Two Theatres of Henry James," *New England Quarterly*, XXIV (March, 1951), 60-83.

[23]*Notes on Novelists*, p. 63.

[24] *Selected Letters of Flaubert*, p. 126. Again, cf. Schorer's "Technique as Discovery."

[25]*Art of the Novel*, p. 308.

[26]I use the term as intended by Dorothea Krook in her indispensable study, *The Ordeal of Consciousness in Henry James*.

[27]*Preface et manifestes littéraires* (Paris, 1888), pp. 55, 56, 57; my translation.

[28]"Henry James," *Make It New* (New Haven, 1935), pp. 269-270.

Index

197

DATE DUE

JUN 0 1 2012			